BURDENS OF BELONGING

I0082961

Burdens of Belonging

Race in an Unequal Nation

Jessica Vasquez-Tokos

NEW YORK UNIVERSITY PRESS

New York

NEW YORK UNIVERSITY PRESS
New York
www.nyupress.org

© 2025 by New York University
All rights reserved

Please contact the Library of Congress for Cataloging-in-Publication data.

ISBN: 9781479822317 (hardback)
ISBN: 9781479822324 (paperback)
ISBN: 9781479822348 (library ebook)
ISBN: 9781479822379 (consumer ebook)

New York University Press books are printed on acid-free paper, and their binding materials are chosen for strength and durability. We strive to use environmentally responsible suppliers and materials to the greatest extent possible in publishing our books.

Manufactured in the United States of America

10 9 8 7 6 5 4 3 2 1

Also available as an ebook

CONTENTS

PREFACE

On January 6, 2021, the US Congress met to count and confirm the electoral college votes that would declare Joe Biden and Kamala Harris as the newly elected President and Vice President of the United States. That morning, at 10:15 am Pacific Time, I began my large-enrollment Sociology of Race and Ethnicity class by conducting a visual analysis of a painting depicting the scene at the signing of the Constitution of the United States. The painting, created by Howard Chandler Christy in 1940, shows George Washington of Virginia presiding over the Federal Convention of 1787 as delegates sign the US Constitution at Independence Hall in Philadelphia, Pennsylvania. Benjamin Franklin and Thomas Jefferson are notable leaders pictured among the delegates. The four-month-long Constitutional Convention was convened to decide how the United States was going to be governed; the resulting US Constitution laid the framework for the national government.

During class (we were meeting virtually because of the COVID-19 pandemic), students and I decoded the imagery of the painting portraying the leadership of the nascent country. Students volunteered several observations: All the decision-makers were White, no people of color were in the room; only men were pictured, no women; the fashion was uniformly fancy, frilled, and well-heeled, suggesting wealth; the room boasted high ceilings, curtains tied back from large windows, a chandelier, and the thirteen-colonies flag adorned the wall. The homogeneity of upper-class White men and their interests became encoded in the governing documents of the United States because they were the decision-makers and signatories; other voices and perspectives were omitted, judged to be governable rather than governors. White supremacy, patriarchy, and class divisions depicted in the painting illustrate the seeds of inequality that were planted in early days of the country. Generations later, the nation and its inhabitants contend with those continued inequalities.

Assigned reading for class that day highlighted systemic racism embedded in the founding of the country. For example, none of the fifty-five delegates "advocated that the abolition of slavery and freedom for all Americans should be an integral part of the new Constitution."[1] We had also read from W.E.B. Du Bois's *The Souls of Black Folk*. Students offered numerous favorite lines from the reading, all of which turn on structural reasons for racial inequality and the difficulties of living under the weight of oppression. Du Bois writes of Black people in the United States, "He simply wishes to make it possible for a man to be both a Negro and an American, without being cursed and spit upon by his fellows, without having the doors of Opportunity closed roughly in his face."[2] This "simple wish" is to dissolve structural racism ("doors of opportunity") as well as disappear social interactions loaded with racism ("cursed and spit upon").

After drawing links from the establishment of the country—imprinted with White supremacy, patriarchy, and class division—I informed students that the 20 by 30 foot oil painting hangs in the Capitol building today. By the time class ended that day, the siege of the Capitol building in Washington, DC by pro-Trump supporters had launched. There is a through line connecting who is literally "at the table" at the signing of the US Constitution—and whose interests are therefore represented and whose are excluded—and the insurrection at the Capitol building that had commenced during our class session. Despite having officially lost the 2020 election to Joe Biden by more than seven million votes,[3] Donald Trump whipped up his supporters with rhetoric of White entitlement and false victory, inciting them to make unlawful and violent claims to take over the nation. In the aftermath, observers noted wildly disparate police responses to Black Lives Matter protesters in summer 2020 following the death of George Floyd, when police in full riot gear lined the steps of the Lincoln Memorial in Washington, DC, and the underprepared and minimal security presence at the Capitol building on the much-anticipated day of counting the electoral votes in January 2021.[4] Allegations of White privilege resounded on social media and popular news sources, Black people decrying that had *they* sieged the Capitol building, they would have been met with lethal force. The symbolism of the signing of the US Constitution in 1787 by White men of the bourgeoisie juxtaposed with a mass of White insurrectionists storming the Capitol building shines a light on the White privilege seared into the nation. This vignette draws a straight line from the signing of a founding national document in 1787 that was being discussed in a University of Oregon class to the siege of the Capitol building that was co-occurring. This coincidence is not really a coincidence—it reveals that social power, social value, privilege, representation, and safety are distributed differentially by race. The problem of enduring racial inequality motivates this book.

Burdens of Belonging is rooted in the premise that not everyone feels equally valued in the United States, and that race is a dividing line of perceived worth. As political scientists Natalie Masuoka and Jane Junn write, "belonging exists on a continuum that reflects the racial hierarchy."[5] Belonging is a feeling and more—it concerns membership in a community. Society adjudicates membership through policies and institutions, enabling or constraining belonging through facilitating or curtailing access to group membership, influence or efficacy, fulfillment of needs, and shared emotional connection.[6] Reasons why belonging is shaded by racial status—and the varied consequences this has—are empirical questions that *Burdens of Belonging* takes on. My intellectual journey thus far has included investigating how racial identity is transmitted or transformed over multiple generations in a family (my first book *Mexican Americans across Generations*) as well as how race and racism influence marriage desires and decisions (my second book *Marriage Vows and Racial Choices*). I turn now to the question of how race affects a person's relationship to the nation—and how this perceived relationship rebounds in people's lived experience, bodies, behaviors, emotions, and goals.

Introduction

Burdens of Belonging

The definition of "Americanness" (sadly) remains *color* for many people.
—Toni Morrison

Belonging in the nation is conditioned by race. Equality may be an aspiration of the United States, but it is not yet the reigning reality. A sense of belonging in a national environment that is shaded by racial status is a signpost of stratification. Racial stratification in belonging does not lie inert "out there" in reports but deeply affects people's lives. People of color[1] experience the trends of racial inequality that flash across the television screen as headline news. Police brutality spawned the Black Lives Matter movement. Mass incarceration of Black and Brown bodies makes carceral punishment an anticipated life stage, the United States topping the global charts for imprisonment.[2] Murder of Indigenous women is a leading cause of death.[3] Colonization of Indigenous peoples and lands persists. Latin American families are separated at geopolitical borders. Unaccompanied minors remain alone in squalid, overcrowded immigration detention facilities. Muslim bans. COVID-19 death rates disproportionately killed Black, Brown, and Indigenous people. Anti-Asian xenophobia and hate crimes were enflamed by the pandemic. The Confederate battle flag, long a symbol of White insurrection, was brought inside the US Capitol building during the siege in 2021 before President Biden was sworn into office. In some places, voting protections are being rolled back when more people of color are registering and turning out to vote. A moral panic simmers over what children are being taught about race in schools. In addition to national happenings, regional dynamics also matter. The state of Oregon was founded in the hope of being a "White utopia"; state authorities and legislation forcibly

1

removed Native Americans, excluded African Americans, and marginal-ized other groups of color. Oregon now has a population that is 85.9% White (73.5% non-Hispanic White) . . . for historical reasons and with contemporary consequences.[4] Racism has been foundational to both the nation and the state of Oregon since their founding and it remains so. This is why we should care.

Exclusion and marginality for people of color in the United States have a long backstory. In 1903, African American scholar W.E.B. Du Bois, in *The Souls of Black Folk*, posed a question he felt "the other [White] world" asked of him: "How does it feel to be a problem?"[5] Du Bois asked this as an African American, with the weight of the African slave trade, racial capitalism, and Jim Crow segregation shaping his ex-perience as a Black man in the United States. Du Bois was referring to his own experience as an African American man at the turn of the twen-tieth century. This book makes an empirical and theoretical intervention in gauging this sentiment's applicability to additional groups of color in the twenty-first century. Much scholarship hinging on Du Bois centers on the Black/White divide, omitting Asian Americans, Pacific Islanders, Latinos, and Native Americans, the "overreliance on a Black-White heu-ristic . . . flatten[ing] the experience of non-Black, non-White people."[6] What mileage do we get from borrowing Du Bois's terminology and asking about its contemporary relevance? By asking the question ("How does it feel to be a problem?") of members of various racial groups, I aim to relationally examine racial realities in everyday life in a predomi-nately White locale in the United States. The overarching question for this book, based on interviewees living in Oregon, is: How does racial status affect sense of belonging in the United States?

This book draws from seventy interviews with people of varying ra-cial backgrounds conducted in Oregon and focuses on how racial status stratifies people's sense of belonging in the nation and their experiences therein. Broadly, it finds that people are met daily with racialized mes-sages about their belonging or non-belonging. Despite a common as-sumption that education is a great equalizer, my interviewees regularly recounted early educational experiences that centered White students and othered students of color. These lessons are important because schools are "mirrors of our society."[7] One interviewee, Angela Lawrence, an African American woman in her forties, illustrates how racial lessons happening in schools have staying power. Expressed to me with gravity, Angela indicts the lessons she learned about race in school that frame Black people as stuck at the bottom of a racial order and without ingenuity:

> [The history of Black people in the United States] is not really taught because the only thing that we really learned is that . . . we were slaves. . . . There's this person called Martin Luther King, Jr. and then there's this lady called Rosa Parks. And then we *may*, if we're lucky, learn about . . . the Underground Railroad. And there was this president named Barack Obama—we *may* touch on that because he was the first Black president.
>
> . . . When we talked about slavery, of course, everyone turned to me in the class in elementary school . . . because I'm the only Black person. . . . And they just look at you . . . like, "Oh, that is so sad." So now you're this sad, pitiful, "I'm so sorry you picked cotton" person in class. There are no empowering stories about W.E.B. Du Bois or Langston Hughes or the person who [invented] the stoplight [Garrett Morgan]. . . . There's *none of that.*

Angela recalls being a stand-in for historical material, her presence in a late twentieth-century classroom equated with slavery because of stilted knowledge production that obscures Black people's contributions. Social identity theory suggests that "the identity that others assign to us can be a powerful force in shaping our own self-concepts,"[8] meaning that students of color being taught one-sided lessons reinforcing oppression risk internalizing that learning.

When White-centric institutions, culture, and teaching eclipse Black people's agency, Blackness becomes associated with slavery rather than survival, resilience, or celebration.[9] Angela critiques formal education that locks away a Black history of authority and resistance:

> If we knew who we really were—if we knew that we were kings and queens—that would not be good [for the power structure], right? Because if you really know who you are and if you rise up . . . we are . . . powerful. . . . So it's like: You're a slave. That's what we're taught. The civil rights movement: We're getting sprayed with hoses and dogs [were unleashed]. . . . That's another image that we get to see about ourselves. . . .

> This is not encouraging for our young people or for our adults, or young
> people who become adults.

Educational curricula and media imagery that vacates Black empowerment perpetuates the "controlling image"[10] of Black people as
dominated. People cannot emulate role models that are stripped away.
Erasure is not limited to the obfuscation of Black "kings and queens."
Angela is in solidarity with Native Americans: "If you look at our history
books . . . looking for us [African Americans] and Native Americans
[sigh] . . . it just hurts my heart because they're not even thought of. . . .
It's like they're just extinct, right? . . . It's pretty scary." Angela gestures
toward key themes in this book: Belonging in the United States is colored by racial and colonial status, and the emotions, perspectives, and
actions that ensue are significant.

According to the US Census 2020, the United States is predominately non-Hispanic White (60.1%), followed by Hispanic/Latino
(18.5%), Black/African American (13.4%), Asian (5.9%), "two or more
race" (2.8%), American Indian and Alaska Native (1.3%) and Native
Hawaiian/Pacific Islander (0.2%).[11] Despite striking demographic
changes such as an increase in the foreign-born population and
growth in communities of color,[12] a White cultural core inheres in
and is perpetuated by many institutions. Take media, for example.
In 2013, when people of color comprised 37.4% of the US population,
"actors of color played 6.5 percent of lead roles in broadcast television
shows and 16.7% percent of lead roles in films."[13] Newsrooms—where
information is curated, produced, and disseminated—are strikingly
White. The employees of newsrooms are less demographically diverse
than US workers overall, three-quarters (76%) of newsroom employees being non-Hispanic White.[14] Newsroom employees are also more
likely to be men (61%), compared to 53% of workers in all other indus-
tries.[15] A danger crops up when perspectives showcased in national
media are White and male but presented as universal. While this dis-
parity has given rise to alternative news sources, viewers must seek
out such alternatives. Breaking in to the media establishment proves
difficult even for well renowned actors of color. Latino actor John Leguizamo reports that producers have told him "you're so talented, but
too bad you're Latin—otherwise you'd be so much further along," and

"people don't want to see Latino people."[16] This all leads to a multifaceted question: How does racial status affect sense of belonging in the nation and experiences therein?

Burdens of Belonging documents wide-ranging historical and contemporary ways racial and colonial status structures lives and futures. In addition to demonstrating the contemporary relevance of Du Bois's question about "feeling like a problem" over hundred years later, a contribution of *Burdens of Belonging* is the teasing out of multiple domains in which people of color are treated as a social problem (irrespective of the "type" of problem). Groups categorized as "problems" do not pre-exist racial domination and settler colonialism. Instead, the state and historical racial and global relations actively construct people of color as problems, with varying intonations that may be group-specific. Illustrating the depth and breadth of settler colonialism and systemic racism that engineer problem status, this book shows how the intertwined themes of "feeling like a problem," racial status, and belonging permeate social life. The omnipresence and entanglement of these themes signal that race structures social life continually.

Exploring Du Bois's question in a different time, place, and racial landscape than when he penned it, this book balances the weight of history and structure with the creativity of individual-level agency. It contends that marginality is a condition of belonging for many people of color. But where there is oppression there is resistance,[17] and this book links oppression to counternarratives, action, and goals, which honors agency and the power to make change. The through-line arguments of this book are that people of color are actively constructed as problems and this creates burdens for people of color whose belonging in the United States feels marginal or conditional and whose lives are indelibly marked by racial inequality at every turn.

Race and Nation-Making

Race is a fundamental element of social structure.[18] Race, racism, and settler colonialism all matter in nation-making and meaning-making for groups within the nation. My perspective on race embraces, but does not subordinate as secondary, settler colonialism that also structures US society. A form of social organization based on dominance, "settler

colonialism involves control over people and territory . . . [wherein] settlers create their own state on top of or in place of Indigenous nations."[19]
Attending to a noted gap in sociological scholarship on race that has
yet to engage settler colonialism,[20] this book testifies to the interde-
pendence of racism and settler colonialism. Sociology's prior disregard
for settler colonialism contributes to Indigenous invisibility and means
that effort must be put forth "to rectify our disciplinary contributions to
colonial unknowing."[21] To correct for this error that precipitated "colonial unknowing," I attend to the interlacing of racial domination and
settler colonialism and aim to overcome epistemological narrowness.
Rather than engage in the question of sequencing race and colonialism
(which came first?), it is the "interpenetration" of race and colonialism
that merits examination, both race scholarship and postcolonial inquiry
benefiting from consideration of "how they are perhaps *forged through
each other*."[22] Positioned this way, debate around origin points of race
and colonialism falls away in favor of exploring their historical and contemporary interrelationship and stressing the enduring importance of
both phenomena.

Groups are not "naturally" problems; they are constructed as such.
Racial and settler colonial ideologies and practices are put to work to
classify communities of color as problems, entrench color lines, and
establish Whiteness as the standard, baseline, and "not-a-problem."
US history has meted out inclusion, exclusion, and belonging differentially. The US Naturalization Act of 1790 established a racial prerequisite for granting naturalization privileges to foreign-born applicants.
At the turn of the nineteenth century, the US Supreme Court adjudicated which plaintiffs were deemed "White" and thus eligible for US
citizenship. During this time, social Darwinist notions of biological and
cultural superiority/inferiority were so prominent that the Naturalization Act of 1790 upholding Whiteness as a condition for naturalization
passed Congress with no debate.[23] A racial requirement for citizenship
figures Americanness as White and, accordingly, imagines non-White
groups as foreigners.[24] Immigration and citizenship laws have thus been
wielded as a "technology of racialization," positioning "European and
non-European immigrant groups on different trajectories with different
prospects for full membership in the United States."[25] Even as the 1952
McCarran-Walter Act abolished all racial requirements to citizenship,

and the Immigration Act of 1965 allowed for an inflow of migrants from Latin America and Asia, visions of the United States as an Anglo-Saxon society "at its core"[26] envision people of color as "disuniting"[27] the nation rather than being integral members of it.

Legal and socially recognizable Whiteness has reigned supreme as the litmus test for "Americanness."[28] Legal machinations aimed to dominate people of color have included theft of Native land and imposition of private ownership over community and communal knowledge,[29] slavery and Jim Crow segregation, and immigration restrictions such as the Chinese Exclusion Act of 1882 which halted immigration from China due to "yellow peril" racism.[30] Since their absorption into the United States in 1848, Mexican Americans have held second-class citizenship. The federal government desired land, not people, as stated by Senator Cass (1782–1866) of Michigan: "We do not want the people of Mexico, either as citizens or subjects. All we want is a portion of territory, which they nominally hold."[31] Popularly seen as "off-white" (socially constructed as non-White and racially inferior),[32] Latinos have been considered "perpetually inferior."[33]

Buoyed by racism and settler colonialism, Whiteness is the gold standard for inclusion and privilege within the nation. With Whiteness the default cultural norm,[34] American identity enshrines "exclusionist norms" such as Whiteness and English language use as prerequisites.[35] Overall, there is support for racial and ethnic diversity in the United States, with most believing diversity has a positive impact on the country's culture.[36] Yet, the unwritten requirements to be American are not yet dramatically changing. Convictions around what American identity entails vary: In tension with requirements that one must be a "white, English-speaking Protestant of northern European ancestry"[37] to be a "true American" is the survey finding that Black and Latino respondents believe that balancing assimilation with cultural diversity is possible.[38] Further, evidence suggests that national and ethnic identities are "highly compatible and complementary"—not mutually exclusive—at least among Mexican Americans living in Mexican-dense areas.[39] Nevertheless, with the "norm of Americanness" being Whiteness, the racialization of people of color as non-White makes for an imperfect correspondence between racial group identity and American identity.[40] *Burdens of Belonging* traces how settler colonial and racist history reaches into the present to affect lived experience. Even given the gravity of history, people are not silent observers of their worlds and fates; they are active participants.

This book is concerned with national belonging and yet, because people live in local spaces, it attends to how race and space inform each other. As scholar George Lipsitz puts it, "The lived experience of race has a spatial dimension, and the lived experience of space has a racial dimension."[41] Space includes physical space as well as meanings and ideologies that order relationships among people and social structures.[42] Space is not neutral but imbued with racial significance. The spatial and the social are not separate realms but "continually interact with and influence one another."[43] Interconnections between race, space, and power materialize in housing segregation, intergeneration wealth, environmental racism, incarceration rates, and health and education disparities. In the context of a largely White space, how the spatial and the social are mutually constitutive and how "spatial racism" (racism embedded into space) plays out come into view.[44] Racialized space, including and beyond racialized organizations,[45] is key to the reproduction of inequality because it entrenches racist ideas and maintains the dominant group's power and privilege.[46] "Spatial identity" also intersects with "racial identity" in the process of "homemaking."[47] Theorized as an immigrant integration process, "homemaking" attends to how racial identities and place identities are intertwined.[48] Homemaking provides insight into how we might think about internal migration—relocating from one place to another within the nation—and the possibility of making home within the national imaginary and in a local space.

Whiteness as a precondition for holistic belonging raises the question: Who is considered White or non-White? This question has given rise to much literature that debates the degree to which segments of racial minority populations (such as the lighter-skinned and higher-class) will become "honorary White" and be awarded the benefits and bona fides of Whiteness.[49] This "crossing," "blurring," or dissolution of group boundaries is not likely to occur evenly,[50] highlighting in-group heterogeneity.[51] Notably, the political-legal sphere etches lines of inclusion and exclusion, such as laws enacting "legal violence" upon non-White racial groups.[52] With White supremacy underpinning the nation, "racialized notions of belonging" reign.[53]

Attending to multiple axes of privilege and oppression, intersectionality is an analytic tool that facilitates understanding of combinations of social divisions such as race, gender, class, sexuality, and citizenship. As a mode of "critical inquiry," intersectionality can lead to comprehending the linkage between social structure and individual lives and foster action (or "praxis").[54] These critical inquiry and praxis dimensions of intersectionality are useful to tee-up *Burdens of Belonging* because they suggest that people gain knowledge as they reflect on how their lives are situated along axes of advantage and disadvantage and they also propose that this awareness does not stand idle but motivates feelings and actions.

The heart of this book lies in the exploration of respondents' experiences, opinions, and goals as they live in the United States, a racially stratified society. Hewing to a race-as-relational approach, this study does not simply compare groups (and assume that boundaries are stable) but examines how groups are positioned vis-à-vis other groups and interrogates the social forces that influence groups' status locations.[55] Employing a relational race perspective demands that Whiteness be included, not as a center but as an element to be examined and even de-centered in analysis. I hold to the perspective that "to ignore white ethnicity is to redouble its hegemony by naturalizing it."[56] *Burdens of Belonging* does not take position in a racial hierarchy for granted but interrogates it, asking: What racialized historical processes led to group status valuation? Global racial capitalism, settler colonialism, imperialism, and domestic systemic racism are all guiding forces that construct groups as problems or, in the case of Whiteness, concoct a highly valued status.

Sidestepping the usual technique of setting outcome measures to mark racial group status or progress, this book instead inquires: What do people who reside in the nation (respondents deliberately varied by race) have to say about whether or how race inflects access to, and experiences within, the national "imagined community"?[57] By exposing stratified, differential subjectivities among groups who comprise the nation, this research adds knowledge about racial groups' relative sense of fit and the ensuing consequences. *Burdens of Belonging* explores how race and colonization pattern the experiences, opinions, feelings, and goals of people from different backgrounds with respect to belonging in the nation.

A brief note on terminology and capitalization. When referring to individual respondents, I use their racial/ethnic label of choice. I also use the pronouns they prefer (he, she, or they). I have chosen to capitalize all racial group categories (unless quoting verbatim a scholar who does not). Some group labels, such as Asian American and Latino, derive from geographies that are typically capitalized. Capitalizing Black and Indigenous emphasizes specific racial histories of slavery and dispossession and their aftermath. W.E.B. Du Bois himself, as co-founder of the National Association for the Advancement of Colored People (NAACP), launched a campaign to demand that media outlets capitalize the word "negro" (the official terminology of the time), finding "the use of a small letter for the name of twelve million Americans and two hundred million human beings a personal insult."[58] Shared experience of discrimination, justice, and respect are all rolled into the political choice to capitalize. As articulated by journalism professor Lori Tharps: "Black with a capital B refers to people of the African diaspora. Lowercase black is simply a color."[59] In 2020, the National Association of Black Journalists formally adopted the policy of capitalizing Black, White, and Brown when referring to racial groups.[60] I use the term Latino or Latina rather than Latinx (unless Latinx is a respondent's preferred label) because, as of 2020, the vast majority of Latinos had not heard of the term and only 3% used it.[61]

Capitalizing all racial categories highlights that they are all social constructions. I capitalize White to call it out and reject the reification of Whiteness as a norm which more easily continues with the less detectable lower-case "w." Using a small "w" would be grammatical complicity with invisibilizing a location of structural power that shores up colorblindness. By contrast, capitalizing the "W" in White draws the eye to the racial descriptor just like other racial categories and begs readers to reckon with it. This move intends to push White readers to recognize that they, too, have a racial identity and are located in a system of power. Visually drawing the eye to Whiteness combats White privilege that manifests as "unraced individuality."[62] Historian Nell Irvin Painter's thoughts are instructive here:

> White Americans have had the choice of being something vague, something unraced and separate from race. A capitalized "White" challenges that freedom, by unmasking "Whiteness" as an American racial identity as historically important as "Blackness"—which it certainly is.[63]

First-letter capitalization makes race obvious for all: It dignifies racial groups as nouns and strips Whiteness of an assumption of absence or neutrality.

Racialized Feelings

Du Bois's question ("How does it feel to be a problem?") may be rhetorical, but this book converts it into an empirical research question. *Burdens of Belonging* interrogates the overarching question: How does racial background, in the context of a racially hierarchized society, influence sense of belonging in the nation? Individuals strive for a positive self-concept.[64] Belonging, or positively identifying with a group, is core to social identity. Based on both formal (legal) and informal grounds, belonging is consequential for social identity and how people operate in society. Felt at an emotional level, belonging concerns emotional attachment, a sense of "at home" and feeling "safe."[65] It is important to underscore that belonging "is a socially mediated matter shaped by wider policy discourses and institutional practices."[66] Belonging is not simply a result of individual will but is conditioned by how a society is organized and how it operates.

By linking racial and colonial status to sense of belonging and extending to feelings, experiences, and behaviors, *Burdens of Belonging* connects race and coloniality to feelings and then to consequences. Native Americans hold a unique position as being classified *politically* due to tribal status as well as *racially* because of how tribes and tribal members are subjected to racialized US laws and practices.[67] My usage of "race" with respect to Native Americans is intended to recognize the racial logics that drive their dispossession.[68] By addressing both the symbolic and material aspects of how race colors national membership, this book exposes racialized constraints and shows racism to be an "extra burden" that exacts psychological, emotional, and physical costs.[69] Yet it also uncovers how people leverage agency despite oppression. This book discusses power inequalities and zeroes in on racial dividing lines between core and peripheral members of society.

Du Bois's question asks directly about *feelings* ("How does it *feel*. . . ."). As an *end* in themselves and as a *conduit*, feelings have consequences. Feelings can motivate action. Consider the fallout from the US Supreme Court case of Bhagat Singh Thind (1923) wherein the Court denied the naturalization appeal of Asian American Hindu Thind on the ground that he was not "Caucasian" as "popularly understood."[70] With scientific evidence insufficient to prove Whiteness—a precondition for US citizenship at the time—the Supreme Court instead elevated "common knowledge" to determine Whiteness. Using the "understanding of the common man" principle, the federal government denaturalized Asian Indians, stripping them of citizenship, without regard for family, occupational status, or length of residence in the United States.[71] Dejection can spell suicide, as in the case of Vaishno Das Bagai who had fled British tyranny in India to become a successful art dealer with a family in the United States. He committed suicide as a protest against the US government's revocation of his American citizenship (which he had legally earned prior to the verdict).

Emotions play a role in racism and settler colonialism as well as in rebuttals to these forces.[72] Legal scholar Janine Young Kim emphasizes "racial emotions" as relating to social membership and hierarchy, noting that some emotions are so closely tied to racial experiences that they "typify an emotional dimension to the construct of race."[73] Sociologist of race scholar Eduardo Bonilla-Silva uses the term "racialized emotions," writing, "we *all* feel race because the category is produced not just 'objectively' but subjectively. Much like class and gender, race cannot come to life without being infused with emotions, thus, racialized actors feel the emotional weight of their categorical location."[74] Even as race is a social construction, it is real in its consequences, and this includes our emotional worlds. In alignment with how this book discusses racial stress, work with Karuk Tribal members finds that "emotional distress serves as a signal function confirming structures of power in relation to identity, social interactions, and ongoing colonialism."[75] Emotions and emotional subjectivity signal power differentials, reference one's location in a racial order, stir and reflect embodied consequences of inequality, and motivate behavior.

Sociology concerns itself with an "agency" (people's capacity to exert free will) versus "structure" (organization of society) debate. In my view, this debate unfairly dichotomizes processes that are imbricated with one another. José Itzigsohn and Karida Brown offer a beautiful description of the *relationship* between agency and structure:

The contemporary Du Boisian sociology we propose does not see those constraining structures as external to social action. They are, in fact, the *crystallization* of historical social action. Racism and colonialism are historical social formations and the product of the agency of individuals and groups. However, once institutionalized, they impinge on the lives of people as external forces. Yet those external forces are potentially subject to modification or even disruption and transformation through social action.[76]

Pictured this way, societal structure is the distillation of earlier discriminatory acts and policies. Societal organization encapsulates what economic sociologists Melvin Oliver and Thomas Shapiro call the "sedimentation of racial inequality," the additive role of history that has worked to keep Black people at the bottom of racial and economic hierarchies.[77] The racialized burden of history that is installed in social structure is ominous, yet the possibility of social change through individual and collective action is a ray of hope.

As a "knowledge project,"[78] where lived experience and ideas advanced by communities matter, this book turns up the volume on marginalized voices and identifies how race and coloniality organize burdens of belonging and embodied life experience for people of color. *Burdens of Belonging* reveals how racial and colonial status shapes differently racialized people's sense of belonging, their bodies and minds, and their pursuits. This book historicizes how racial inequality, in multiple manifestations, has been hurried along by the ideologies, policies, and practices of systemic racism and settler colonialism that underpin White supremacy. Not only does race structure the external world, but race also structures one's "inside world," crystallizing how people assess their relationship to US society, make sense of their experience, and formulate goals. With racialized feelings as an access point, we can discern how people comprehend and respond to their position in the racial hierarchy. Feelings are action-stimulating, undergirding cognitive, verbal, and behavioral actions.[79] This book takes seriously how racial status shapes experience, influences relationship to the nation, and has cascading effects that indelibly mark bodies, minds, and aspirations.

Why Study Oregon?

In contradistinction to much literature on "the nation" that concerns gateway communities, Oregon is not a top-twenty immigrant destination state.[80] Oregon is noteworthy for being on the Western "frontier" and as a bastion of Whiteness (a portrayal that erases Natives), its slow but sure demographic change, and its middle-rung racial and ethnic diversity index score. In Census 2020, Oregon's racial and ethnic diversity index was 46.1%,[81] this number indicating the probability that two people chosen at random would be from different racial and ethnic groups. This mid-range status in a predominately White state that is nonetheless home to some people of color is a fruitful locale in which to consider questions of inclusion and exclusion, privilege and oppression. Established in hopes of being a "White utopia," all residents irrespective of racial status must grapple with both Oregon's "White space"[82] and its demographic shift.

Oregon is a majority-White state, with 73.5% of the population claiming to be non-Hispanic White, as compared to 58.9% of the nation identifying as non-Hispanic White.[83] Oregon persists in being majority-White, even as shifts are occurring. In 1972, Oregon's White population (including Hispanics) comprised 97% of the state population, which reduced moderately to 86.4% in 2020.[84] Between 1990 and 2020, the Hispanic population grew from 4.0% to 13.7%, the Asian/ Pacific Islander population rose from 2.4% to 5.2%, the Black share increased negligibly from 1.6% to 2.0%, and Native Americans dropped from 1.3% to 1.1%.[85] Oregon is one of the twenty-one least diverse states in the country.[86] In 2018, Oregon's population was 4.2 million and sported a growth rate of eleventh in the nation, with most population growth (1.0 percent annual average) due to net in-migration.[87] Hispanics are the largest minority group and growing more rapidly than other groups. Oregon's population has increased at a faster pace than the nation as a whole: Since 1900, Oregon's population increased tenfold whereas the US population grew fourfold.[88] It is in this context of demographic shifting—White decrease in population and increases for groups of color—that this study takes place. It is here that we can see racial politics of belonging play out. For details on the study design, see the appendix, which details my methodology.[89]

With population increasing mainly as a result of in-migration, Oregon's population is diversifying in terms of race and ethnicity—yet it is one of the least diverse states in the country.[90] Changes in racial/ethnic demographic makeup occurring in historically "White space" mean that people of color are making inroads into White spaces. These shifts have repercussions for both White people who may fear status loss and people of color who may feel outnumbered and marginalized as they attempt to belong. Opinion polls indicate that from 2016 to 2020 there is greater receptivity to Black Americans, Latinos, and Asian Americans becoming a majority of the population in the next thirty years, yet White respondents were less likely to say this impending demographic change was good for the country (and more likely to say it was bad) in comparison to Black, Hispanic, and Asian American respondents.[91] Racialized space has strong implications for the politics of belonging. As a predominately White space, Oregon is an intriguing field site for it may serve as a harbinger for similarly situated states undergoing comparable slow but steady demographic change.[92]

A brief review of racial policy and relations in Oregon helps contextualize present-day race and racism in the state. The Oregon Territory achieved statehood in 1859, forty-seven years after the first recorded direct contact between the native Kalapuyan people and White settlers.[93] In 1812, French Canadian fur traders first arrived to the Willamette Valley, home of the Kalapuya, and initiated a permanent non-Native presence in the region.[94] During the eighteenth and early nineteenth centuries, Natives and Euro-American fur traders had extensive commercial interaction and frequently intermarried, resulting in multiethnic families and peaceable inter-group relations.[95] This accord broke down with an influx of in-migration of White settlers to the region after the Oregon Treaty of 1846 set the boundary between the United States and Canada. Federal treaty negotiators threatened Native genocide to compel acquiescence, one federal agent threatening that Yakama leaders (in territory now known as Washington) would "walk in blood knee deep" if they did not sign the expropriative treaty.[96] White colonial migration and settlement that overtook Indigenous land set in motion conflictual race relations and marked the ascendancy of White people in Oregon.[97]

The year 1850 ushered in the Donation Land Act (in place until 1855) which restricted land ownership in Oregon to White settlers and "American half breed Indians."[98] A euphemistic misnomer because the land was not "donated," Indian title to land was extinguished as a prerequisite to the Oregon Donation Land Act that awarded Indian tribal territory to incoming White men settlers.[99] The Oregon Donation Land Act excluded African Americans and Hawaiians and attracted White settlers to the Umpqua, Rogue, and Willamette valleys.[100] By 1855 when the law expired, approximately 30,000 White immigrants had entered Oregon Territory, with 7,000 eligible White people making claims to 2.5 million acres of land. With land expropriated from Natives attractive to White settlers moving West, Oregon's population boomed from 11,873 in 1850 to 60,000 by 1860, the influx almost exclusively White by legal design.[101] The Oregon Donation Land Act that usurped land from Native tribes, disallowed African Americans and Hawaiians from homesteads, and welcomed White settlers, drastically re-shaped the demographics of Oregon before it reached statehood.

Racial ideology and political maneuvers upended the sovereignty, lifeways, and territories of Natives. "Indian hating" peaked in response to challenges of colonization and was "acute when Anglos saw Indians only as obstacles."[102] During the mid-1850s, many tribes of Western Oregon—including the Umpquas, Athapaskans, Kalapuyans, Molallas, Chastas, and Chinookans—were removed from their ancestral homeland to reservations.[103] The Rogue River War (1855) broke out as area tribes defended their land from White incursion. To accelerate the removal of Native Americans in areas coveted by White newcomers, President Franklin Pierce signed an executive order establishing the Coast Reservation, more than 1 million acres housing 27 different western Oregon tribes.[104] In response to unregulated settler use of land for mining that wreaked ecological damage, a critic at the time called these violent practices "Squatter Sovereignty."[105] By 1875, the US government shrank the land base of the Coast Reservation and eventually terminated it, the Indigenous people residing there relocated to the Siletz and Grand Ronde reservations.[106]

The deterritorialization of Natives continued. In 1954, President Eisenhower terminated the federal protection of Native American tribes, as stipulated by prior treaties. Land not owned by individuals became property of the federal government.[107] Consequentially, individual land ownership is a Western concept outside of Native cosmology and practice, a cultural difference the US government weaponized for territorial gain.[108] Beginning in 1973 under President Nixon, a decades-long process of restoring federal recognition of tribal sovereignty was initiated. However, federal recognition did not restore tribes' former reservation lands.[109] Land usurpation for permanent settlement of colonial newcomers is a key feature of settler colonialism.[110]

The presumption of White supremacy is the through line of racial politics in the Oregon Territory and early statehood. As with history relating to Native Americans, early Oregon history concerning African Americans is characterized by government action and popular sentiment aiming to achieve a White state. Likewise, in the nation, anti-Black animus pervaded Oregon politics. Oregon holds the distinction of being the only free state admitted to the Union (in 1859) with a Black exclusion clause in its constitution.[111] More than a decade prior to statehood, legislators passed Black exclusion laws in 1844 and 1849 that threatened free Black migrants with corporal punishment, jail, and forced labor if they did not leave.[112] Public whippings of up to thirty-nine lashes every six months was the legal punishment for Black people who defied the exclusionary law that criminalized their presence.[113] Approximately two-thirds of the towns in Oregon were "sundown towns" that relied on coordinated violence (such as the Klu Klux Klan in the 1920s) and vigilante violence to chase out African Americans.[114] In 1857, Oregon voters (White men) prohibited both slavery and the presence and in-migration of Black people.[115] An overwhelming majority of voters (89 percent) approved the Black exclusion measures.[116] These vote outcomes signal a desire to exclude *all* Black people, irrespective of free or slave status. The Black exclusion clause was repealed in 1926, and in 2002, racialized language of "negroes" "mulattoes" and "whites" was removed from the Oregon constitution.[117] Even with stilted demographics, redlining enforced residential segregation and racial discrimination in public establishments was widely practiced (including Jim Crow signage) until passage of a state public accommodations law in 1953.[118]

While African Americans are an exceptional case illustrating the depths of nationwide commitment to Whiteness, the intensity of which should not be understated, policies were cast widely to disenfranchise additional categories of non-White people. The Oregon state constitution banned any "Negro, Chinaman or mulatto" from voting.[119] Poll taxes were enacted by the Oregon Legislature in 1862 requiring that each "negro, chinaman, kanaka [Hawaiian] or mulatto" pay a tax of five dollars to their county of residence annually, a policy meant to discourage these groups from moving to Oregon.[120] The Alien Land Law (1923) prohibited Chinese and Japanese newcomers from owning or leasing land. Amplifying nationwide political sentiment of the time, Oregon restricted the immigration of people who were excluded from US citizenship eligibility, ensuring the limitation at the state level.[121] In 1866, in an effort to preserve monoracial White families, the Legislature outlawed racial intermarriage, prohibiting White people from marrying African Americans, Chinese, Hawaiians ("kanaka blood"), and people with more than half American Indian ancestry.[122] An Oregon law outlawing Black-White marriage had been enacted four years earlier, so the "multiracial expansion of prohibitions on marriage" stretched to cover additional races to preserve Whiteness and White supremacy.[123] This expanded Oregon anti-miscegenation law regulated marriage from 1866 until its repeal in 1951.

Oregon legislators used the Naturalization Act of 1790 to leverage its own statewide immigration restrictions, with the national level influencing the state level. Yet we also observe the reverse line of causation where state racial politics influence federal law. In 1870, a proposal was floated at the federal level to remove the section of the Naturalization Act of 1790 that restricted naturalization to "free White persons." Resistant to Chinese-born immigrants being elevated to citizens with voting rights, Oregon opposed race-neutral alterations to the law. Oregon Republican Senator George Williams insisted that the law explicitly exclude people born "in the Chinese Empire."[124] The resulting amended federal naturalization law (the Naturalization Act of 1870) limited US citizenship to White European immigrants and people of African nativity and ancestry and barred foreign-born people of Asian descent. Here we witness Oregon politicians agitating for immigration restriction at the level of national law.

Anti-Chinese anxiety across the nation gave rise to the 1882 Chinese Exclusion Act which barred the immigration of people from China into the United States for ten years.[125] Mobs used violence to force out Chinese people, including in Oregon, where the murder of thirty-four Chinese miners and acquittal of the alleged perpetrators in 1887 took place.[126] In 1892, the Geary Act extended the Chinese Exclusion Act for another ten years. These legislative acts sharply reduced the Chinese population in the United States. Because these policies fulfilled their intended goals of cutting off the immigration of an "undesirable" group, they spurred later immigration restrictions against other groups (Middle Easterners, Indians, Japanese), codified in the Immigration Act of 1924. Later, in the 1950s and 1960s, the two democratic Oregon senators (Wayne Morse and Richard Neuburger) advocated to liberalize immigration. Tellingly, a host of letters to these leaders from their constituents opposed immigration and refugee acceptance on the grounds of racism and xenophobia.[127]

At the same time, the United States extended its empire across the Pacific in pursuit of trade relations with Asia. Its geopolitical interest there led the United States to expand its influence in Asia and the Pacific Islands through missionaries, teachers, diplomats, and health-care workers.[128] Hawai'i and other Pacific Islands figured prominently in the United States' quest to develop international trade and commerce. The US Navy built up military defenses in Hawai'i (annexed in 1898), Guam, Samoa, and the Philippines, an imperial policy meant to maintain an open door to China trade.[129] The Oregon-Pacific Rim relationship remains important, a Department of Defense report in 2019 touting both economic and military connections in the Indo-Pacific.[130] In the 1980s, Oregon's Governor Atiyeh established relationships with Japan's business leadership to expand its export economy and encourage investment in Oregon.[131] Now, with one in five jobs in Oregon connected to trade, China is Oregon's largest export partner and accounts for more than 20% of export profits, followed by Japan, Korea, and Malaysia.[132]

In terms of domestic relations, in 1921, the Ku Klux Klan (KKK) established an Oregon chapter, one believed to have the highest per-capita membership in the country.[133] The highly influential group infiltrated city, county, and state policy through officials including the governor, the mayor of Portland, the Portland police chief, and the Multnomah County sheriff.[134] By 1922, the KKK held its first parade in Eugene and burned a cross atop Skinner Butte, overlooking downtown. Pressured by agricultural interests and the KKK, in 1923 the Oregon legislature passed the Alien Land Law which banned Japanese and Chinese nationals from purchasing and leasing land in Oregon. Having grown to a membership of almost 40,000 in three years, the KKK as a site to harbor bigotry diminished in Oregon by 1930 due to bad press that swayed public opinion, as well as corruption and lack of leadership.[135]

In the 1980s, neo-Nazi skinhead organizations cropped up across Oregon. A chief goal of an offshoot of the Aryan Nations (the Order) was to declare a "territorial sanctuary" in Oregon, Washington, Idaho, Montana, and Wyoming, based on the belief that "the Pacific Northwest . . . is the true Promised Land on which an Aryan racist state must be established."[136] A flyer sent to thousands of people recruiting "all White Patriots" for the purpose of "declaring a territorial sanctuary"[137] conflates Whiteness with patriotism and nationhood and exhibits settler colonial notions that the dominant White class has the power to "declare" land-based boundaries and impose meanings on usurped Indigenous territory. This quest to devise a White-only state is part of Oregon's history that informs its demographics, culture, and holdover sentiment.

Contemporary research conducted in Portland—Oregon's largest city—coins the term "ambient racism" to refer to the subtly isolating and exclusionary characteristics that are "baked into" the culture, built environment, and daily interactions in this purportedly progressive majority-White context.[138] The long-running effects of exclusionary policies cast a pall on present-day Oregon, from the racial demographics of the state to level of (dis)comfort racialized populations feel in the environment.

Research as Liberatory

A belief in the transformative power of human agency and a desire to fan political will to create social change in the direction of racial justice by shedding light on inequalities undergirds my research philosophy. Research documents disparities, gives voice to the subjugated, and can serve as a foundation for deeper understanding and a basis for alleviating harms. I am inspired by Du Bois, among others. A believer in the power of social scientific study, Du Bois exhorts that rather than presume knowledge "a priori" (in advance of fact or experience), "the least that human courtesy can do is listen to evidence."[139] Sociologist Aldon Morris, a noted Du Boisian scholar, writes that Du Bois viewed social science as a "weapon of liberation" that records inequalities, agitates for change through activist and professional channels, and "reshapes" how the oppressed see themselves.[140] Positioning social science research as liberatory is a clarion call to include oppressed people in research agendas and to insist that research illuminate social problems—as diagnosed by the people living them—and seek to remediate those ills.

In elevating the voices of the racially oppressed, I draw from standpoint theory which posits that knowledge is not objective but subjective and shaped by where its originators sit among hierarchies of power. Standpoint epistemology questions the bases of so-called legitimate knowledge and is attentive to distortions created by power imbalances. Standpoint theory invites all people to be theorists; "lived experiences as a criterion for credibility" is a welcoming stance that makes accessible the ability to assert "knowledge claims."[141]

Standpoint epistemology supports "talking with the heart [which] taps the ethic of caring."[142] As an alternative to knowledge claims that cloak themselves in universality and objectivity, standpoint theory grounds itself in the partial, specific, contextual, and experiential. Patricia Hill Collins explains, "the ethics of caring suggests that personal expressiveness, emotions, and empathy are central to the knowledge validation process."[143] My research philosophy includes this ethics of care in three ways: First, I subvert racial power dynamics by positioning people of color as knowledge-holders. Second, in "relational interviewing" that relies on interaction and interpretation, I aim to foster rapport so interviewees feel comfortable sharing details about their lives with me.[144] Third, through active listening, engaged responses, follow-up questions, analysis, and write-up, I aim to affirm people's emotions and experiential knowledge. With these threefold goals undergirding my interview style, I center marginalized voices and build more comprehensive understandings about how race and coloniality in the United States operate, engender counternarratives, and affect lives and futures.

Power dynamics infuse how research has been conducted, informs what counts as theory, and has distilled into "epistemic exclusion" of less powerful groups. Theorist of empire and postcoloniality Julian Go argues that early "*social* exclusion" of scholars of color in sociology led to "*epistemic* exclusion."[145] Lingering consequences include a sociological canon that exalts Anglo-European men thinkers (who often studied other White people) whose works are judged to speak to universality and, conversely, the troubling accusation that scholars of color (who may study communities of color) indulge in subjective "me-search."[146] A pathway out of this exclusionary epistemic structure is to situate the particularity of *all* knowledge projects and diversify the sociological canon. "Perspectival realism" holds that "scientific knowledge is always partial and incomplete, because it is always perspectival."[147] This tenet reminds me of the child's game where children are asked to close their eyes, feel, and then describe the portion of an elephant's body they touched: an ear, a tusk, a leg. Despite the children's distinct descriptions of their assigned elephant body part, their observations are indeed accurate and valid; they simply are operating with a unique set of sensory data. Pertinent to this book, I heed Go's call to "seek a transformative epistemic pluralism."[148] This means taking a standpoint theory or perspectival realism approach which acknowledges that all knowledge is situated, and then using critical race, intersectionality, and race-as-relational insights to gain a better view of how racial status manifests in varieties of belonging. In centering theoretical frameworks and empirical foci that are typically de-centered, this work aspires to be Du Boisian in that it is "unapologetic in its emancipatory aim," to borrow the words of Itzigsohn and Brown, authors of *The Sociology of W.E.B. Du Bois.*[149]

Burdens of Belonging is based on interviews with seventy Oregonians of various racial backgrounds. Interviews are a gateway into people's experiences, their truths. Interviewing is storytelling, from interviewee to researcher. Interviewing is also a precursor to researcher storytelling: An objective of data analysis is to place interviewees' voices near others to better hear the chorus and variations of life-based stories. Storytelling based on interview narratives transports readers to alternative vantage points from which to view and contemplate life in an unequal nation. I join critical race scholars who capitalize on the power of storytelling:

> We each occupy a normative universe or "nomos" (or perhaps many of them), from which we are not easily dislodged. . . . "Everyone loves a story." The hope is that well-told stories describing the reality of Black and brown lives can help readers bridge the gap between their worlds and those of others. Engaging stories can help us understand what life is like for others, and invite the reader into a new and unfamiliar world.[150]

In placing differently racialized people's stories in relation to one another, this book demonstrates that belonging and a host of experiences within the nation, from (de)valuation to safety to goal formation, are conditioned by race and coloniality.

Overview

Taking up varied topics, the following chapters' central concerns are stitched to the overarching argument that belonging in the United States is colored by racial and colonial status. Belonging that is filtered through racial and colonial hierarchies translates to burdens shouldered by people of color. White people are excused from these burdens. A lesson is inscribed in the fact that the themes covered in this book are wide-ranging: race is omnipresent, its influence saturating all social domains.

Burdens of Belonging takes inspiration from W.E.B. Du Bois and, in the vein of emancipatory sociology, is committed to excavating subordinated knowledge and working toward racial justice. Pushing back against a White-dominated sociological canon, I deliberately present arguments and data pertaining to respondents of color first in each chapter, followed by White respondents. In upending Whiteness as prioritized and unnamed (yet positioned as universal), I make the point that ideology put into action can call into question and destabilize power hierarchies.

Taking a historical view, chapter 1 denaturalizes "being a problem" by asking how and why communities of color have been *constructed* as a problem. Highlighting settler colonialism and global imperialism, chapter 1 argues that the nation has actively constructed non-White groups as social problems and second-class citizens via policies and practices. Discussing Pacific Islanders alongside Native Americans as Indigenous, this chapter demonstrates how settler colonialism subordinates, invisiblizes, and traumatizes people well after "conquest." Additionally, the global imperial efforts of the United States, including foreign wars, contribute to the formation of "military-racial opponents" of certain Asian American groups who, generations later, feel the effects of vilification. But top-down construction is not absolute. "Double consciousness" feeds what I call "critical colonial consciousness," a decolonial perspective that illuminates coloniality. Critical colonial consciousness is a mind-set and agentic response to colonization that identifies colonial linkages between the past and present in an effort to resist settler colonialism, affirm the knowledge of the oppressed, and move toward liberation.

Chapter 2 empirically investigates W.E.B. Du Bois's rhetorical question: "How does it feel to be a problem?" This book interrogates national belonging—yet belonging, non-belonging, and marginalized belonging are experienced locally. Revealing a non-White/White divide, national rhetoric and local interactions affect respondents' sense of membership at both levels. Respondents of color perceive that their racial group is seen as a problem by society, messages of undesirability delivered via the themes of physical appearance, language, land destruction, and population change anxiety. In reaction, respondents of color use counternarratives to contest the exclusionary status quo by rejecting problem status as well as, conversely, committing to "continue to be a problem" for the sake of social change. Pulling another thread from Du Bois, I extend double consciousness as a contemporary *intersectional* phenomenon pertaining to respondents of color. Alternatively, because Whiteness sits at the apex of the racial hierarchy, White respondents did not resonate with "being a problem" in the original Du Boisian meaning. However, a newfangled understanding of Whiteness as a problem emerged where White respondents who see Whiteness as a problem at the *individual level* felt blamed, whereas those who see Whiteness as a problem at the *structural level* were able to critique White supremacy.

Focusing on American identity, chapter 3 delves into how Whiteness continues to be understood as quintessentially American. In contrast to White respondents whose racial identity aligns with the "ideal" American prototype and are thus undisputed Americans, respondents of color used facts such as birthright citizenship to claim American status or attempted to divorce Whiteness from American. This chapter explores barriers to belonging that respondents of color encounter that spider across realms, from spatial (majority-White landscapes) to history that shapes the present (slavery/anti-Blackness and colonial status) to institutional (legal status) and interactional gatekeeping. Examining racial formation processes, the chapter moves on to demonstrate the collective and relational processes that create groups and install divisions. Finally, with power to act, respondents of color create belonging in multiple ways: They establish "concentric circles of belonging" (curated supportive networks), argue to diversify the meaning of "American" and thus broaden the embrace of belonging, and adopt a global or decolonial view that decenters the United States as the apex of belonging.

Chapter 4 investigates the educational system as a racialized institution that brokers belonging, fostering White comfort and non-White discomfort. Grounded in respondents' experiences in schools, this chapter breaks down the "multi-level messages" (institutional, community, and interactional) occurring in schools that, imbued with settler colonialism and systemic racism, produce comfort for White people and discomfort to people of color. Tapping into the racialized emotions of comfort and discomfort, this chapter examines how emotions signal power relations and how racialized organizations prop up the racial hierarchy. Attentive to the spatial dimension, the chapter also documents the experiences of people of color who are racial "misfits" on a predominately White campus, amounting to feeling both invisible and hypervisible. In sum, through policies, lack of structural and curricular diversity, and the normalization of Whiteness, the educational system casts people of color as problems and ultimately leads people of color to *experience* problems within education. Comfort and discomfort is a color line.

Moving into embodiment, chapter 5 details the "embodied burdens" that snag people of color. Highlighting racism and colonialism as social determinants of health, embodied burdens result from the subjection of people of color to harms due to living in a settler colonial society that valorizes Whiteness. White people can assume that institutions will protect their health and safety. In contrast, burdens of belonging for people of color include their safety never being guaranteed, the requirement of navigating racial stress, and exposure to colonial and racially influenced traumas that downgrade their health and well-being. Attending to place, I coin the term "anticipatory racial stress" to refer to the state of being perpetually on alert to detect and respond to racism, particularly in environments where one's racial group is read as "out of place" (e.g., people of color in majority-White contexts). This chapter argues that negative health markers, intergenerational trauma, and safety concerns all function simultaneously as *symptoms* and *reminders* of the subordinated status of respondents of color in the United States' racial-colonial system.

Chapter 6 conceptually links a person's "racial biography" (the racial character of lived experience) to the development of their goals. The dividing line drawn between White respondents and respondents of color, differences in racial biographies produce two distinct types of goals: organic goals and acquired goals. Respondents of color developed "organic goals," or goals directly informed by real-life racial knowledge and experience. Owing to witnessing racism against their family and community, White-passing people of color also develop organic goals. Racial oppression is directive: Emotions stemming from racialized experience steer respondents of color toward life and career aspirations that are indelibly marked by racial inequality. In contrast, White respondents' goals were delinked from race. For the select White respondents whose goals included racial concerns, they were "acquired goals," or aims picked up through observations from an outsider-looking-in viewpoint on racial oppression. Goal formation is influenced by racial status.

Finally, the conclusion reviews the multilayered ways that race infiltrates life experience to shade sense of belonging in the nation and contour everyday life and future aims. Manifestations of subordinate status, burdens of belonging are ingrained into the lives, perspectives, and bodies of people of color in the United States. Race is knitted into the fabric of society, qualifies belonging in national and local spaces, and conditions the embodiment, comfort level, experience, and aspirations of individual lives.

1

Constructing a "Problem"

Settler Colonialism, Global Imperialism, and Critical Colonial Consciousness

Racial groups do not preexist as problems but are *constructed as problems*. Settler colonialism and global imperialism, both infused with racism, spur ideologies, policies, and practices that build the case for communities of color to be viewed as problems. Digging into government action to denaturalize the "problem" status thrust upon respondents of color, this chapter takes a wide-lens view to examine the structural processes that actively produce different social valuations based on racial and colonial status.

Siletz tribal member Beau Landon refers to "the Indian problem" as direct evidence that Native Americans have been classified as a problem. Beau remarked, "'The Indian problem' was a thing that was said and talked about, so yeah, I see where he's [Du Bois is] coming from there. . . . The Indians were the problem for westward expansion, colonialism, [and] Manifest Destiny. It was like someone [a US Army officer in the Civil War] said, 'The only good Indian's a dead Indian.'"[1] Inhabiting desired land, Natives posed a problem for White colonial settlement. Native Americans were collectively labeled an "Indian problem" to justify state-imposed genocide, removal, forced assimilation, oppression, and invisibility. "Problem" status is actively constructed and then justifies racial domination.[2]

Social scientists often declare that "race is socially constructed," referring to its lack of biological or genetic basis, but, as race scholar Ruha Benjamin reminds us, "we often fail to state the corollary, that racism *constructs*."[3] Powerful forces—such as genocide, forced assimilation, slavery, war, appropriation of land, and exploitation of natural resources—establish a racial-colonial hierarchy. Settler colonialism is a lens through which one can fruitfully read US history and contemporary race relations. Domination takes on a distinct form when White settlers intend to establish a new home and sovereignty over the land permanently—in settler colonialism, there is "no spatial separation between metropole and colony."[4] Access to territory is an "irreducible element" of settler colonialism, after which the "elimination of the natives" is pursued.[5] Seized land on which settlers sought self-government was "treated as *terra nullius*, unpopulated land, while the Indigenous nations and communities [were] reduced in numbers by genocidal warfare."[6] The establishment of the US empire-state was a settler-colonial project based on the elimination of Indigenous North Americans and the imposition of a modernist property regime that transformed land, people, and resources into ownable items.[7] From the outset, the state has been a perpetrator of violence and injustice.[8]

White settler power is cemented into the institutions that organize US society. Theorist Patrick Wolfe emphasizes settler colonialism as structure: "settler colonizers come to stay: invasion is a structure not an event."[9] Illustrative of settler colonialism influencing contemporary institutions is the criminal legal system, which has been called "a legacy of colonialism" by virtue of its "reproduction of colonial logics [that are] part of the broader culture of control."[10] Settler colonialism requires normalization and invisibilization, further evidenced by its conferral of full citizenship upon White people and marginalization of people of color.[11] As a pillar of settler society, "settler colonialism should be seen not as an event but as an ongoing structure."[12]

With respect to global imperialism, W.E.B. Du Bois viewed US imperialism as originating in slavery and conscripting racism to justify imperialism.[13] Viewing the state in racialized terms, Du Bois connected dispossession with the production of difference. Pressing for attention to imperialism, Du Bois insisted that the nation was racialized, concentrated power among White people, and "defended existing race relationships within . . . national boundaries and internationally through colonialism and imperialism."[14] In short, racism reinforces imperialism.

Via settler colonialism and global imperialism, the United States constructs people of color as problems and lays a foundation for conquest and domination. By using the theoretical bracings of race, settler colonialism, and global imperialism for this chapter, I aim to render visible their interrelationship and avoid the pitfall of offering an analysis of race that sidesteps colonialism and in so doing "extend the discourse of Indigenous erasure that itself is a central mechanism of colonialism."[15] With this corrective in mind, this chapter argues that settler colonialism as "ongoing structure" and global imperialism, both undergirded by racism, "make" racial groups into so-called problems.

Settler colonialism and imperialism are political tools that built the nation and demarcate belonging in the present era. Undergirding the nation, settler colonialism and imperialism mark the lines and ranks of belonging. Yet history does not overdetermine the present. Resistance efforts reframe people of color as knowledge-holders whose critical colonial consciousness cuts to the quick of settler colonialism, denuding this federal effort as an inequality-producing machination.

A goal of this chapter is to denaturalize the "problem" status that has been thrust upon people of color. This chapter excavates "counter-memory."[16] According to George Lipsitz, counter-memory "looks to the past for the hidden histories excluded from the dominant narratives. But, unlike myths that seek to detach events and actions from the fabric of any larger history, counter-memory forces revision of existing histories by supplying new perspectives about the past."[17] Being cast as a problem is a feat of settler-colonial and imperialist governmental engineering. With settler colonialism and global imperialism shaping lives in profound ways, hearing from people deeply affected by them illuminates how these forces manifest today and the consciousness they conjure. Historical and contemporary power relations brew dissatisfaction among the oppressed, which stimulates power-aware perspectives, including critical colonial consciousness. Attending to a fuller view of history, as articulated by non-dominant groups who hold counter-memory, allows for connecting-the-dots between the past and the present and a "bottom-up" unsettling of master narratives, or "history as written by the victors."

Living with Settler Colonialism

Native Americans: "On the Other Side of History"

Settler colonialism architects Native Americans as "problems." As an ongoing project, settler colonialism continually recasts Native Americans as "problems": "So far as conquest remains incomplete, the settler state rests—or, more to the point, fails to rest—on incomplete foundations."[18]

The incompleteness of conquest requires the colonial state to continually apply pressure to dominate subjugated populations, constructing and reconstructing problem status via multiple means. For example, the racialization and minoritization of Native Americans does harm in that these frameworks overlook that Indigenous people are "dual citizens" of the United States and Indigenous sovereign nations.[19] Indigenous respondents are aware of historical antecedents facilitating their oppression, insight that informs their critical colonial consciousness.

Displacement came up early in my interview with Evelyn Xus (Coastal Chumash). She answered my first question about where she grew up this way: "My first home was in the canyon . . . that my dad and my uncles had reclaimed. . . . It's where the oil refinery is now." Native American respondents whose tribes had been deterritorialized—the goal being "to clear the lands of Indigenous people so that settlers can replace them"[20]—perceived that the US federal government constructed them as problems. Evelyn explains the construction of Natives as problems as a framing that plagues her: "If I'm viewed as a problem based on being Native, it's because *I'm still here*. There's not that full claim to the land [for White people]. There's still a reminder . . . if I'm still here. . . . That's problematic for so many people and they don't like to think about it." Native presence interrupts White conquest. For "White-constructed larger society," as Evelyn put it, Native presence is a problem. Conquest is incomplete.

Conquest is continuing in the present moment. Part of the settler colonial mission is to allege that people of color are problems and then treat them as such, fulfilling the prophecy. The economic, sociocultural, and political foundation of the nation constitutes an "ongoing colonial process."[21] A Native working in higher education, Evelyn volunteered the idea of colonialism as ongoing: "It's still happening. It's not like settler colonials have gone anywhere. [laughter]." Evelyn explains settler colonialism as "this idea that somebody is occupying another area actively and trying to transform it into what they want, and with disregard to the folk that have lived here for thousands and thousands of years." As an example of takeover and "disregard," Evelyn mentions cave paintings recently uncovered near Malibu, California that were "totally wrecked," a "complete loss" that "can't be brought back." Willful destruction of Native culture is nothing new but the *continuing* quality is notable.

Erasure is a consequence of Natives being cast by settler colonial logics as problems. Native erasure has seeped into the public consciousness. Evelyn is constantly misrecognized as not Native American. This lack of recognition as Native rests on the false assumption that Natives have been annihilated, recorded only in the annals of history. This denial of Native existence is a symptom of settler colonialism, diminishing the presence of Native lives. Evelyn's misrecognition illustrates Native invisibility:

> People are always looking at me, like trying to figure out what I am. (Laughter) And they're like, "Are you Mexican? Are you Middle Eastern? Are you East Indian? Are you Southeast Asian?" . . . Nobody ever thinks I'm Native. Unless I'm in a Native space with other Native people, people don't think I'm Native. . . . Even if I'm wearing a Native shirt and jewelry . . . it never crosses people's mind that I might be Native.

Given her regional placement (American Indians and Alaska Natives constitute 1.1% of the Oregon population, as compared to Alaska, which is the state with the highest proportion of American Indians and Alaska Natives at 14.8%[22]), this misrecognition is tied to a local violent history and the assumed death of Native people and culture. I asked Evelyn how not being seen as Native makes her feel, to which she replied: "It's kind of frustrating because it's just a reminder that *people think we're gone.* [laughter] They think we're gone and that we don't have a place here. . . . It's almost like people waiting for us to disappear."

An iteration of troubled Native-US government relations, Evelyn brings up the Dakota Access Pipeline in Standing Rock, the site of protests in 2016 concerning the re-drawing of a pipeline route that critics contended was an environmental hazard and threatened tribal sovereignty.[23] Again linking to the *ongoing* and *present* quality of colonialism, Evelyn highlights common refrains she heard during the pipeline protests: "Just get over it. That [treaty] was a long time ago." Evelyn retorts sardonically, "It doesn't matter that these treaty rights are protecting these lands." Contemporary political struggles over land constitute re-injury for Native Americans, very public reminders of land and resource theft.

Beau Landon concurs that the long history of colonial relations is present in everyday life, a fact perceptible to oppressed people like him but unacknowledged by most White people. Beau says, "[history] *does* matter, *to me*." Counterposing his view with dominant narratives of history, Beau contemplates:

> People would rather just forget about it—America as a whole, White people. Just like America wants to forget about slavery. You don't hear slavery talked about. Black people remember it, but White people would rather not remember it, and they would be like, "Wow, it was long ago. I didn't have any slaves." But that Black person's like, "Well, my grandpa was a slave. It wasn't that long ago. I knew that person." And so if you're on the White side of it, you don't want to remember that; and it's easy to forget because it was a lifetime ago. But I think, on the other side of history, it's still very much present. And it's important . . . because it was bad, and it sucked, and it has caused a lot of long-lasting traumas . . . that are still going on.

The phrase "on the other side of history" poignantly illustrates how dominant and subordinate racial statuses have distinctive viewpoints. The compatibility of Native and Black experiences under a White supremacist state suggest the durability of a non-White/White divide and how racism has architected relations. Like Evelyn, Beau addresses "White comfort" (a theme developed in chapter 4) in pointing out how White people minimize racism, which is an affront to his experience "on the other side of history."[24]

Another example of settler colonial relations precipitating trauma, Beau addresses animosity between his "Indian" school and the neighboring White school. The "big rivalry" turned on race and colonialism. At sports events during high school, the opposing team from the White school waved signs saying "cowboys killing Indians." How Americans "play Indian" is tied to how the country views Indians and, in this case, this "playing" displays genocidal fervor.[25] Pulling on a trope of death by conquest, these White students played on settler colonial politics to express rivalries in a manner that reminds Native Americans of their decimation by White settlers. Settler colonialism is not over but is continuous and functions to portray Indigenous people as problems, legitimizing their subordination.

Adding Pacific Islanders: Indigenous Invisibility

Native American and Pacific Islander respondents spoke in earnest of erasure and invisibility. While not usually theorized together, this qualitative dataset suggests that, given their status as Indigenous populations who suffer(ed) colonial rule by the United States, there is solid reason to theorize Native Americans and Pacific Islanders side by side. Native Americans and Pacific Islanders, as Indigenous groups, share similarities such as de-territorialization, colonization, and usurpation of land and natural resources. Combining these Indigenous perspectives is novel because they are typically cordoned off by discrete "Native" and "Asian/Pacific Islander" categories which blind observers from connecting their experiences. Colonization and attempts at erasure conjoin Native American and Pacific Islander experience. Invisibility is a colonial inheritance that Indigenous respondents roiled against as they painfully spoke about the loss of their home territories, ways of knowing and being, and lack of recognition in White spaces.

The United States maintains colonial relations with territories (including Puerto Rico, Guam, the US Virgin Islands, American Samoa, and the Northern Mariana Islands), offering inconsistent constitutional rights. For example, US citizenship, rights to trial by jury, and congressional representation by a non-voting delegate vary across territories. The US government constructs Indigenous populations as problems by not providing readily comprehensible identification cards for all of its citizens, in particular those who live in US territories. Calling herself a "territory citizen," Mariana Palacios, of the Northern Mariana Islands, says pointedly: "I don't think I'm seen as a problem because I'm not even seen. That's that." She emphasized the importance of her territory citizen status, a settler colonial construct, as doing the work of erasure. Even in official bureaucratic spaces, like the Department of Motor Vehicles (DMV) and post office, she is forced to explain her existence. Lack of knowledge about US territories that reflects US priorities over who counts renders Mariana invisible in official White spaces:

> [Personnel at the DMV] were like, "Northern Mariana Islands, do we accept that?" They were like, "What do we do? . . . Is it official? Is it legit?" I

was like, "It's a [US] territory so you should be able to accept it." [laughs]
But it's still like, "Do we accept the Mariana Islands? Is that a thing?"
And then also sending packages, I have to clarify a lot. Like, "No, it's the
United States. So, you should not . . . say it's international. "

"Territory citizen" is tantamount to secondary citizenship status.
Mariana must act as an interpreter to make herself visible and legible.
Absent educational curricula, the media, and political leaders informing
the public about "territory citizens," Mariana is troubled to make herself
visible when society's institutions have failed to do so.

"The invisibility of being a Native person now is really intense," declares Evelyn Xus. Lessons on her erasure began as a child in school.
Whitewashed versions of history left out her people, heritage, and perspectives on history. She attended public school three days a week and
then was homeschooled in the southern California mountains where
she lived the remaining days of the week. Evelyn describes the clash of
knowledges:

> EVELYN: Just having to deal with the [public school] curriculum was
> always a challenge because we were taught something different at
> home (chuckles).
>
> JVT: What were the differences in the two systems?
>
> EVELYN: . . . Thanksgiving and Columbus [laughter]. . . . Also . . . this
> romanticized notion of us being a people of the past, too. . . . There's
> barely blips of Native people in history books as it is.

Eclipsing Native populations from representation in formal curricula
expunges them from common knowledge. Following US government
attempts at exterminating Natives through genocide, territorial dispossession, Treaty nullification, and withholding federal tribal recognition
comes deletion of Natives in educational curricula. Even opposition
to former president Donald Trump's "build the wall" (on the southern
border with Mexico) refrain, which claims that the United States is a
"nation of immigrants," sidelines Native Americans. Despite preced-
ing the formation of the United States, Native Americans are erased by
this erroneous statement. Evelyn protests: "We're *not* a nation of immigrants." A commitment to ignorance and nation-building mythology
obscures Natives.[26]

Tying into blood quantum rules of hyperdescent that restrict access to Native authentication due to racial mixing,[27] Pacific Islanders complained of death of their people and culture. One way for Indigenous people to be invisiblized is for them to die off. Malia Kealoha, who is Samoan and born and raised in Hawai'i, calls her Indigenous people and culture a "dying breed": "Polynesian in general, we're like a *dying breed*, yeah. We're a dying culture, definitely dying language. Everything's dying [laughter]." Oral tradition, in combination with intermarriage and geographic dispersion, threaten to diminish cultural ties. Even Malia, who dances a "traditional Samoan sequence," does not know the "meanings of the motions."

Racial categorization is another mechanism that erases Indigenous people. Pacific Islander respondents complained about being incorrectly subsumed by an "Asian/Pacific Islander" category. This nomenclature does not honor their indigeneity or status as colonial subjects. Malia speaks to categorization: "Us being grouped with Asians—'Asians and Pacific Islanders'—why are we even grouped like that? . . . If you actually take the time to see the identities of Asians and Polynesians, we shouldn't be grouped [together], that's not fair." Racial categorization is political—and to be collapsed into a larger category is to be made invisible.

Adding Latinos to a Settler Colonial Framework

I find it generative to put Latinos alongside Native Americans and Pacific Islanders in a discussion of settler colonialism, so long as indigeneity, conquest, and land seizure are pertinent themes. Traditionally a blind spot in Chicana/o Studies is Mexicans' and Chicanos' violent participation in settler colonialism, a history obscured by a fixation on Spanish and then US conquest of Mexico.[28] It is important to acknowledge Latinos' position as oppressor, not only as the oppressed, yet there is value in interrogating Latinos' alignment with Natives based on continuing subjection to colonization.

Who is considered Indigenous? This question is complicated in the context of racial and ethnic categories across the globe that homogenize variation. Even for those with obvious Indigenous roots, "claiming indigeneity is a fraught process," particularly in countries like Mexico and the United States that have "a long history of colonial exploitation and nationalist projects intended to assimilate and erase Indigenous practices."[29] Latinos are an amalgamation of colonizer (Spanish) and colonized (Indigenous). Like all aggregate racial/ethnic terms, "Latino" is a broad umbrella term that hides important variations, including nation of origin, ancestral heritage, indigeneity, and racial status. There is also the question of physical appearance and whether Latinos are racially coded as Brown/Latino, White, Black, Indigenous, or another category. Even as there is a difference between White-passing Latinos and those who are labeled as Brown/Latino (or another variety of non-White), Latino sociology and Native Studies can learn from each other through the useful conduit of settler colonialism. This section utilizes narratives from Latinos who expressed settler-colonial viewpoints to show the overlap between Natives, Pacific Islanders, and Latinos.

Settler colonialism constructs Indigenous communities as problems for the purpose of gaining political, economic, and social power for White people. Many Latino respondents with Indigenous ties are aware of exploitative relations that constructed them as unworthy, foreign, and socially (if not legally) outside the bounds of American membership. Maggie Rose, a twenty-eight-year-old US-born Chicana, calls her birthright citizenship as American "dumb luck." She mulls over her privilege and the limits of that privilege when existing on land desired by settler colonists:

> I'm absolutely [a] US-born citizen. And that as a privileged identity . . . feels really important. But when you . . . look at the Repatriation Act [in the early 1930s], for example, they started kicking Mexicans out that were US-born citizens and I'm like, "Hello" [says with Mexican accent]. So if Oregon decides to kick up . . . racial segregation, they're not gonna care if you were born here or not. . . . You're just going to be Mexican.

The relocation of people and redrawing of territorial borders is central to settler colonialism. Maggie is leery about how a history of "repatriating" (deporting) people of Mexican descent, even the US-born,[30] may repeat. The importance of usurpation of land and forced movement or deterritorialization of people remains pressing for the colonized.

Borders are geopolitical constructs. The US-Mexico border as a site of transnationalism in the early nineteenth century that Mexicans moved across freely has transmogrified into a site of "border spectacles" (apprehensions, detentions, and deportations)[31] and enforcement that drives migration toward the hostile Sonoran Desert.[32] Maggie speaks to the fluidity of the US-Mexico border and how people living on the border are treated as disposable:

> The border of Texas has been moved in and out. . . . That's why when I think of what it means to be American, it feels so flimsy. My . . . family . . . [is] from new Laredo and old Laredo. Old Laredo's on the Mexican side . . . and new Laredo is on the Texas side . . . but it used to be the same city or the same land. . . . It absolutely feels like all of this is so flimsy. . . . Mexican bodies in the United States [are] seen as disposable or movable or not important. . . . I wonder how Indigenous people think about these things—the [narrative that the] United States [is] like barren land.

Maggie suggests a solidarity of settler-colonial experience between all people native to territory now labeled as part of the United States. To elude colonialists' grasp of land and authority, Maggie calls on her family's far-reaching ancestral roots that ground her presence on land that predated the United States. Maggie challenges White people who ask her "where she's from" to rethink their assumptions, thus destabilizing notions of Mexicans as immigrant "problems":

> There have been times when—for the sake of being ornery—a White person has been like, "Well, where are you from?" And [I answer and . . .] they're like, "No, but where are you *really* from?" . . . I'll say, "We're from Texas before Texas was Texas." And they don't know what to do with that information. . . . Mexican bodies are seen as something peripheral that can be moved or excluded very easily.

People who inhabit the borderlands are made peripheral via settler colonialism that devalues, de-centers, polices, and ejects them from land.[33] Maggie does not submit to the settler-colonial assumption that White people are entitled to land they came to occupy by violence:

I don't necessarily feel super native or Indigenous to this land as much as: "This land doesn't belong to you." [chuckles] . . . Had we drawn the border somewhere else this could still be Mexico. . . . It's more this retort back to think about what you're asking me and how that [is] situated in the context of history of violence and war. It almost feels like positioning people to reconsider themselves. I usually only get that sassy with White people.

Engaging a conflict theory mindset where White people are the privileged group and Indigenous people are the dominated group, Maggie roots her family lineage in a time that antedates White settler arrival in order to widen historical perspective. Non-Latino people of color also witness the anti-Latino power play of settler colonialism. Vietnam-born Minor Hun said to a White coworker who was airing grievances against Mexicans: "The only thing [different] about the Mexican from you and me is that . . . they didn't even have to come on any boat to come over here. This is their land from the beginning." Even as some detect the sleights-of-hand that privilege White settlers, settler colonialism works through governmental and interpersonal avenues to construct Indigenous populations, including Mexican-origin people, as problems.

Black People within a Settler-Colonial Framework

Black respondents spoke ardently about the legacy of slavery and long-running anti-Blackness and yet they, too, are wrapped up in a settler-colonial framework. Rather than rely on a simple binary of settler/native that overrides status differences, the term "subordinate settlers" describes various minoritized positions.[34] Theorists of settler colonialism Eve Tuck and K. Wayne Yang explain that the United States operates as both a settler-colonial nation as well as an empire and brings "dispossessed people . . . onto seized Indigenous land through other colonial projects."[35] Colonial projects include enslavement, military recruitment, labor recruitment, and displacement or coerced migration. In this way, colonial subjects—who are displaced by external colonialism and racialized by internal colonialism—occupy stolen Indigenous land, even as they are people (settlers) of color who are subordinate to White settlers.[36] Settler colonialism, as a structure, "links" the racialization and treatment of groups of color.[37] A private property regime that converts people and territory into ownable, sellable, and transferable property is a similarity between the enslavement of Africans and African Americans and the usurpation of Native American land.[38]

While Black respondents did not speak overtly about settler colonialism, it nevertheless works in conjunction with systemic racism to frame their experience. As a youngster, John Blaze was enrolled in a majority-White school where he was one of two Black students. He recalls: "I drew myself with green eyes . . . and less Black features." As an adult, John's status as a "subordinate settler" more clearly emerges. His *subordination* as a Black man is evidenced in his heightened chance of being a victim of police brutality. He told me about a traffic stop, saying, "My wife was freaking out thinking I'm going to get shot." At the same time, John's *settler* status is revealed in his presence on unceded Indigenous land and his past service as a military police officer where he enforced the laws of the settler-colonial nation-state. In sum, suffering racial oppression while also occupying Indigenous land and adhering to (even upholding) the bureaucratic-legal structure of the settler-colonial nation shows the paradoxical position of subordinate settlers.

As an African international student from Sudan, Bogga Deta has an outsider's viewpoint on settler colonialism. She wishes that Americans would "admit right up front" Native American genocide and displacement and confess that White people are all settlers—immigrants like her. Bogga ponders the question, "What's an American?" She counterposes Native Americans with "people from outside who just came in but they got more rights because they were more powerful." Bogga calls out White settlers' claim to rights, asking, "*Based on what*?!" Slotted into this settler-colonial system, Bogga becomes a subordinate settler who is subjected to anti-Black racism and Islamophobia, as discussed in chapter 5.

Global Imperialism: The Making of Military-Racial Opponents

Settler colonialism and global imperialism are militarized manifestations of the desire for cultural and territorial domination. These nation-state philosophies, followed by expenditures and military operations, reveal priorities. Historian Roxanne Dunbar-Ortiz lends insight: "In the United States the legacy of settler colonialism can be seen in the endless wars of aggression and occupations; the trillions spent on war machinery, military bases, and personnel instead of social services and quality public education."[39] A Manifest Destiny–style abiding belief in White supremacy undergirds colonizing and imperialist ventures. A White supremacist ideology serves as a self-reinforcing cycle of (pseudo) justification for domination: People of color (interior or external to the nation) need to be "saved" or "civilized." This logic perpetuates imagery of "backwards" or "savage" people of color, both domestic and foreign, which generates and legitimates unequal material conditions.

A nation constructs military-racial opponents of people (racialized others) in locations it seeks to annex or dominate. I use the hyphenated term "military-racial opponents" to suggest that many military actions are executed with race, racial meanings, and ethnic difference as motivating factors. In addition to race *precipitating* labeling nations and populations as antagonists, using the term "military-racial opponents" after wartime underscores the racial *effects* of global imperialism and military intervention that linger. Elements of history persist.

Global imperialism constructs military-racial opponents out of domestic populations with origins in countries where the United States has had conflicts, making a generations-later population seem a racial anathema to the country. Obstructions to a more White nation, military-racial opponents are living relics of the United States' global imperialism enterprise. Racial-colonial power dynamics transmit the message that while these non-White populations may exist *in* the nation, they are not *of* the nation in the same way as White Americans. For Americans of color deemed military-racial opponents, their resulting burdened belonging is a drag on their American membership.

US military aggression waged in foreign countries that were Asian American respondents' ancestral homelands casts these Americans as villains undeserving of US membership. "Orientalism" is the act of defining the West as "dominating, restructuring, and having authority over the Orient."[40] The framing of the West as superior to an inferior East (Orient) is foundational to a logic of war because nations marked as inferior are seen as "posing a constant threat to the well-being of empire."[41] Undergirded by this White supremacist and West-is-best ideology, the United States justifies "being in a constant state of war to protect itself from enemies."[42] This mentality extends beyond wartime to include domestic racial tensions that cast immigrants of color and their US-born descendants as "forever foreigners"[43] as well as threats to the nation.

Asian Americans who were born in or have ancestral ties to countries with which the United States has been at war felt they were seen as enemies of the state at times. Paul Lee, whose family migrated from Vietnam to the United States as "boat people" in 1979, wears a pained expression as he tells me that his family split up and immigrated to two different nations due to the United States' military intervention in Vietnam. He insists that the war should be called "War in Vietnam" rather than "Vietnam War" to stress that the war was not instigated by Vietnam but driven by US policy tied up in the communist Red Scare. Paul believed he was viewed as the very embodiment of a US enemy. He felt jeopardized by being collectively racialized as Asian American where nation of origin is secondary to being framed as a military-racial opponent from *any* Asian nation. Paul borrows from Japanese American history to express anxiety about being coded as a holdover enemy due to foreign wars: "I am at risk of being interned too."

I extend here what Asian American Studies scholar Yen Le Espiritu theorizes as "militarized violence," that is, "the raw, brutal, and destructive forces that Western imperial powers unleash on the lands and bodies of racialized peoples across time and space."[44] Moving through time and space, militarized violence shadows subjects and can continue to wreak harm even years later, for example by being viewed as an enemy of the state (even as other racialized connotations may coexist, such as the "good refugee"). A manifestation of militarized violence, Paul is conceived as a military-racial threat and worries that a foreign policy directed at *other* national origin groups will capture him, too. Paul explains the vulnerability he feels under the Trump administration: "Current policies . . . [are] impacting me. . . . [We could] engage in warfare. . . . There's even a risk of being interned . . . with what's going on [Trump's 'zero tolerance' separation of Central American asylum seekers], you know? . . . There's that fear of . . . what can happen." Immigration policies profoundly shape the sense of belonging for the groups targeted by those policies, and yet people from groups *not* in the crosshairs of policy can also feel their effects.[45]

Crisscrossing racial groups, "non-belonging" or being "constituted as Others who don't belong on a symbolic and material level" is at issue here.[46] I asked Paul about the relationship between his fear of being incarcerated and the fact that he's Vietnamese and not Central American like the families being separated at the time. Paul replied:

> It's . . . kind of exaggeration . . . but . . . it's a possibility that can happen. I think especially [with] the current conflict with North Korea—the current [Trump] administration [is] not going to tell the difference between Chinese and North Koreans, or whatever. They're just . . . going to be seen as Asian [chuckles] . . . or people of color. They're going to put them in a category. . . . There's no limits to what they can do now in terms of policy.

As a "a theorist of racialized modernity," Du Bois's thoughts on "self-formation under conditions of racialization"[47] aid in understanding how people of color—even "honorary White" people—are compelled to "wrestle with constant dehumanization but [also] . . . glance into the white world"[48] (what Du Bois called "second sight"). Encompassing second sight, double consciousness or "always looking at one's self through the eyes of others"[49] requires that racialized subjects both comprehend and respond to their degradation. The chasm separating one's own vision of one's self and the nation's vision obliges people of color to reckon with the discrepancy. This reckoning is yet another reminder of non-White people's marginality: They are burdened with navigating a racially stratified system that pigeonholes them into constraining categories such as military-racial opponents. Because of the long shadow racial-military history casts, physically resembling an enemy combatant of the past countermands benefits Asian Americans may draw from "honorary Whiteness" or a model minority stereotype.

Hawaiian-born Luis Waimea calls himself "Japanese" despite being US-born because he is subject to racial profiling and microaggressions in Oregon. The Japanese internment [Executive Order 9066 (1942)] when the US government removed Japanese Americans from civil society during wartime continues to have relevance for him. His own immediate family was not interned but, he tells me, "some of the families in . . . my hometown [on the Big Island] . . . got interned." The fact that the United States would intern Japanese Americans who did not commit crimes against the state but racially resembled military opponents distresses Luis. Given the historical backdrop of Japan and the United States bombing each other during World War II, Luis believes his racial group is cast as a devalued enemy. In answer to my question about "how valued do you feel in US society" he chuckles and says, "Not at all," and then laughs some more. He expands: "Racially, I don't feel like we're valued at all. . . . Other than bringing good food to this country. . . . We [are] just looked at as immigrant workers. . . . It's heart-wrenching to say, but it's my truth." In this conception, Japanese Americans are "color capital" or sources of cultural objects such as food that White people fetishize and consume.[50] As White people acquire cultural resources through consumption, an imbalanced relationship based on "consumptive contact" that benefits the White group and keeps subordinated groups "physically and socially distant enough to preserve White comfort and institutional control" ensues.[51]

Luis's conception of how "Americans" view Japanese Americans is grim: He feels as if he inherits the infamy of a state enemy. Luis explains: "Honestly, outside of food, I don't know what other value people think that Asian Americans or Japanese Americans brought to this country other than war: World War II. . . . Japanese bombed Pearl Harbor and just because of the association, you're all of a sudden the enemy." Luis was not alive during World War II, but that fact does not abate his feeling of being unjustly read in the mold of a declared enemy. War history darkens his ability to feel at home in the United States. He winds back to how the Japanese internment affects him today, saying with exasperation: "What this country did to us as citizens!" Despite not yet being alive, Luis feels empathy for his Japanese forebearers ("us"), vicariously experiencing immense frustration. US citizenship no foolproof guard against racial antipathy, Luis concludes that the Japanese internment is "very troubling. . . . It's not about the length of time—it's the principle!" The US government forcibly segregated citizens based on the assumption that being of Japanese descent made one an enemy combatant and un-American. That Japanese Americans were once viewed as an incarcerable social problem is an obstacle to Luis feeling valued and welcome. Being positioned as a military-racial opponent casts a pall on belonging. Research on later-generation Japanese Americans concurs that "a stubborn understanding of Japan and Japanese people as the other—as the enemy— . . . [leaves] little allowance for a distinction between Japanese and Japanese American."[52]

Racial history that penetrates collective memory can affect people living after the events in question. Twenty-year-old Japanese American Yumiko Hoshiko uses her grandmother as a cautionary tale about racial animus in the United States: "When my grandma was younger, yeah, [Japanese Americans were considered a problem] because you just had to be Asian to be considered a danger and a terrorist." Perceiving race to be a sociohistorical construct and historically contingent, she contrasts her grandmother's experience to her own, two generations later: "But now people just think I'm going to be some rich Asian business owner who . . . raises my kids to be poets and piano players by the time they're four." Racial meanings can shift . . . and shift again. Asian American respondents were wary about internment reoccurring. When I asked Yumiko, "Do you ever worry that [internment] can happen again?," her one-word reply was: "Absolutely." The dangers of historically marked racial meanings are never fully quelled, even "discredited racial scripts . . . always available for use in new rounds of dehumanization and demonization."[53]

Even as Yumiko is subject to racial connotations very different from those projected onto her grandmother, family memory can keep alive recollections of racial targeting. Yumiko says she is not excluded from society but in the same breath says she needs to "stand up for [her Japanese immigrant] grandma" who was interned for two years in Colorado during World War II. She reflects on the historical moment that her grandmother experienced: "Everyone just told her that, 'Only your appearance makes you a terrorist and makes you a danger to the people you're around.'" Family relationships are conduits through which intergenerational family memory is passed and, in this way, US acts of war remain salient for descendants of those deemed enemies of the state.

Pamela Yamaguchi (Japanese American) similarly wrestles with the federally mandated internment of Japanese Americans during World War II. Pamela ruminates on change in racial meanings over time: "They're willing to incarcerate us and then we're 'almost White.' That doesn't make any sense to me [laughter]." Witnessing a "180-degree" change between her parents' lifetime and her own, Pamela is wary of the vicissitudes of race relations. To steady her identity, Pamela focuses on resilience as a route to pride and membership in the US community: "[Japanese Americans] stuck it out—and not only survived it, but came back and argued against it, and went through the system and got redress and reparation." In 1988, President Reagan signed the Civil Liberties Act to formally apologize and compensate more than 100,000 people of Japanese descent who were incarcerated in internment camps during World War II with $20,000 each. This law won congressional approval after a decade-long campaign by the Japanese American community.[54]

"Critical Colonial Consciousness": A Response to Colonization

In *Pedagogy of the Oppressed*, Brazilian educator and philosopher, Paulo Freire, put forward the idea of "critical consciousness" (conscientization, or conscientização in Portuguese). Critical consciousness "refers to learning to perceive social, political, and economic contradictions, and to take action against the oppressive elements of reality."[55] Critical consciousness makes it possible for people to be "responsible Subjects" (knowers and actors, as opposed to "objects"), conscientização enrolling them "in the search for self-affirmation."[56] Freire decried the "banking" style of education wherein students passively "receiv[e], fil[e], and stor[e] the deposits" and proposed instead interaction, inquiry, and praxis.[57] While Freire was referring to educational systems as institutions that structure knowledge, settler-colonial and imperial ideology and practice similarly construct reality. As a decolonial perspective that illuminates coloniality, critical consciousness has the potential to disrupt oppression:[58]

> [C]ritical consciousness would result from their [students'/subjects'] intervention in the world as transformers of that world. The more completely they accept the passive role imposed on them, the more they tend simply to adapt to the world as it is and to the fragmented view of reality deposited in them.[59]

In adapting Freire's "critical consciousness" to refer specifically to colonialism ("critical colonial consciousness"), I aim to underscore the liberatory potential of revealing and analyzing *colonial* dynamics, interrupting colonial relations and structures, and affirming the knowledge of oppressed people.

Action invites reaction. Settler colonialism provokes response. Critical colonial consciousness refers to Indigenous, colonized peoples' response to the construction of their group as a social problem vis-à-vis settler colonialism. Reflecting lived experience as colonized, critical colonial consciousness refers to colonialism as constituting a primary "mental schema" through which information is processed.[60] For those employing critical colonial consciousness, a power-aware critique of colonialism is a primary mode for processing information, making meaning, and making sense of the world. Critical colonial consciousness is a lens available to colonized people that leverages their familiarity with colonialism into a critique that reveals their oppression as architected by racist history and foregrounds their humanity, subordinated standpoint, and right to self-determination.

Critical colonial consciousness is a manifestation of "living history." History reverberates in and shapes the present. History is "alive" in the sense that it carries influence well after events have passed, this idea compatible with the "ongoing" quality of settler colonialism. Critical colonial consciousness is an agentic response to historical and contemporary oppression that vigorously questions why societal arrangements are the way they are and, at its fullest, offers alternative, emancipatory visions. As an orientation that actively interrogates reality and social hierarchies, past and present, critical colonial consciousness is a mindset and mission. Critical colonial consciousness stems from, skillfully assesses, and battles against colonialism.

Many Pacific Islander respondents displayed critical colonial consciousness: Colonialism is a framework they are familiar with and they use it to see and explain the world around them as they work toward liberation. Malia Kealoha (Hawaiian, Samoan descent) recaps the conquest and colonization of native Hawaiians: "[Captain Cook] was . . . taking and taking [from] the native Hawaiians. . . . We were illegally overthrown—our queen—[and] we were illegally annexed. . . . We shouldn't have gotten illegally overthrown. That's not okay [chuckle] to just come over and be like, 'Okay, now this is ours.'" Malia is not alone. She tells me of her best friend: "Any time someone brings up Captain Cook or the overthrow of the Queen, she will just cry. She just gets so emotional about it. . . . She's just so aware of it and [it] always just ring[s] so true to her." History ringing true to colonized people suggests that not only is history not over, but it presently inspires critical colonial consciousness. I asked Malia whether the overthrow of the

Hawaiian queen seems like recent history to her. She assented, "We still have active protests. . . . There's a . . . group of native Hawaiians that don't believe we should be a state and we should still be a monarchy." Displaying critical colonial consciousness, Malia says of colonization: "We . . . got power tripped."

Kaulana Tamata, who was born in American Samoa and spent her youth in Hawai'i, spoke cogently about colonialism that she sees as ongoing through US militarism, imperialism, and the subordination of her people. Kaulana speaks from a place of critical colonial consciousness when she emphasizes the linkage between settler colonialism, land, and the contemporary racial order:

> [In Hawai'i] . . . I grew up with colonialism—the businessmen coming and taking over the land hasn't changed. . . . In Hawai'i, we have . . . this mountain that's very sacred to us called Mauna Kea. Astronomers have . . . [been] wanting to put in a *huge*—absolutely ridiculously huge—telescope on our mountain that could affect our water supply. And Hawai'i's water supply is through the ground . . . We can't get it anywhere else. And, we fought . . . so much and yet . . . it was approved by the Supreme Court. And we've had so many people fight for that mountain because it's sacred to the culture and to the people, and yet nobody cares.

Kaulana refers to the Thirty Meter Telescope for which the Supreme Court of Hawai'i approved a building permit atop a contested site of the volcano Mauna Kea. The Thirty Meter Telescope is the largest contemplated in the Northern Hemisphere. Hawaiian activists, some of whom staged protests and blocked access to the construction site, have opposed the telescope on grounds that it interferes with cultural and religious practices and pollutes the natural space.[61] Thirteen telescopes already sit atop Mauna Kea. The settler-colonial dynamic comes into focus when one recognizes that Mauna Kea is considered "ceded land" that belonged to the Hawaiian kingdom and that the telescope would be built by an international collaboration (United States, Japan, China, India, and Canada) with little to no direct input from native Hawaiians.[62] The controversy can be read as settler colonialism playing out on a volcano, complete with a push for Western science up against Indigenous land rights and religious and cultural practices.

Colonialism continues. As environmental sociologist Kari Norgaard writes:

> [S]ettler-colonialism is ongoing today through land management policies. For just as colonialism is not a single event of the past, we must think beyond the notion that "land theft" and land dispossession are single events of the past. Instead, colonialism is an ongoing process that takes place through the alteration of land . . . and the alteration of relationships between people and the more-than-human entities known as nature.[63]

Regarding the Thirty Meter Telescope controversy in Hawai'i, Kaulana's reference to the Supreme Court as a governing body upholding oppressive colonial practices clarifies that settler colonialism is embedded in and propped up by the nation's institutions. Kaulana stresses the intertwined relationship of past and present colonization as she says with exasperation about the authorized telescope construction atop Mauna Kea:

> "Who cares?" This is what I've learned. Like, who cares about what we want? Who cares about how we feel? Because obviously nobody. Because who's asking the people the questions on how it's going to affect the people? No one. They're just doing . . . what they want. And it's just upsetting because . . . *it just never ends.* . . . Whether we believe it or not, this is a very White world—like, who are the leaders of this country? . . . White people. Who makes the decisions? White people. We are fighting for all these little wins and we're trying . . . to run for leadership. . . . But who really is making the decisions? And it's upsetting. Because it's just not fair. Yeah. And that's why it makes me worry for the next generation.

Between "it just never ends" and her "worry for the next generation," Kaulana is certain that settler-colonialism dynamics will perpetuate unabated because the settler-colonial racial state shows no concern for the subordinated.

Land has a part in Kaulana's narrative as a resource confiscated for Western scientific development. For Melanie Rodriguez, land is a political lightning rod after the US government responded neglectfully to a natural disaster. Melanie draws on her father's homeland of Puerto Rico to underscore that Puerto Ricans' second-class status is a consequence of colonialism. She points out evidence in the governmental structure: Puerto Ricans are US citizens but lack voting power and voting representation in Congress. Melanie believes that "Latinx people are certainly seen as a problem" and face the "brunt of bad treatment, stereotypes, and [are] looked down upon." She uses Hurricane Maria that devastated Puerto Rico in September 2017, which killed approximately 3,000 people and exacerbated preexisting health inequities,[64] to argue that settler colonialism applies to Latinos:

> The hurricane. . . . People [Puerto Ricans] are expecting help. . . . They're tax-paying people and they want . . . [the] perks that come with being a tax-paying member of society. And they're not getting help, really. . . . They're not getting help that they should be getting. . . . [They are] citizens who can't vote. . . . The hurricane . . . stirred the pot, so to speak, [and] brought a lot of things to light. . . . I think that aid that was offered after [Hurricane] Katrina [in New Orleans in 2005] . . . should also [have been] applied in this situation. . . . Now . . . people have to seek . . . refuge and have somewhere to live and [the message is], "Well, don't come here [continental US]"—and they're citizens. They're full citizens [laughter] of the United States. . . . "Coming here" refers to . . . just another stereotype or perception around migration that *those people* don't belong here.

Puerto Rico was annexed as a protectorate in 1898 and people born on the island are US citizens by birth, making their movement to other parts of the country internal migration.[65] Yet the US-Puerto Rican relationship is a settler-colonial one. This "colonial/racialized citizenship" presupposes and perpetuates a notion of the island of Puerto Rico and Puerto Rican people as inferior and excluded from Whiteness.[66] In this settler-colonial relationship, the social dimension of citizenship and belonging is reserved for White people. From a settler-colonial perspective, federal aid to adequately respond to Hurricane Maria is an unnecessary indulgence. Melanie draws an explicit imagined comparison: "If Puerto Rico was an island of well-behaved Irish White people, would they receive different treatment and funds and help when natural disaster struck? . . . I think that if that were a group of White people on an island this wouldn't have played out the [same] way. . . . I think there would be all of the aid that a group of people could need." "Well-behaved" is a loaded term because it suggests that Puerto Ricans are not read as such by federal authorities, perhaps due to their economic dependency (a result of coloniality), agitation for state-hood, or failing a benchmark of Whiteness. Furthermore, nearly half of Americans do not know that Puerto Ricans are US citizens—a fact that makes the death and destruction in the wake of Hurricane Maria "a domestic disaster, not a foreign one."[67] This knowledge is consequential because Americans were twice as likely to support aid to Puerto Rico if they knew that Puerto Ricans are citizens (80% support) than if they did not (40% support).[68] In sum, race and colonial relations are to blame for differential treatment which, in this case, amounted to a higher death toll that could have been avoided.

Even the built environment of Oregon reflects settler colonialism. Built environments are human-made constructions imbued with culture. Mariana Palacios, a college student from the Northern Mariana Islands, is pained by a lack of Pacific Island culture in her university environment. The mainland is "not tropical, not colorful" and lacks "cultural symbols" of her home and history. Mariana talks about how built environments replicate racial orders: "When I walk around [in Oregon] I'm like, 'Damn, this world is built literally for White people. . . . Oh, it must be so nice to walk around and feel welcomed. . . . I wonder how that feels.'" Built environments reflect racial orders. Buildings can, indeed, be racist.[69]

Drawing on critical colonial consciousnesses that links the past to the present, Mariana explains the difference in built environments between her island home and Oregon:

> Most [structures] are built of concrete [on the island] and so it was really weird to . . . hear people's footsteps [in Oregon]. . . . That's so weird. [Chuckles] I can't really hear anyone move through a house where I'm from. They're all one-story and there's a lot of symbology ingrained in public buildings. There's a latte stone—that's . . . a symbol of our people. It is . . . this huge 16- to 20-foot pillar made of limestone that ancient people carved that . . . would serve as the foundation of ancient homes.

Via visual and audio cues, Mariana can see and hear that her Indigenous culture has been trumped by Euro-centric architectural design and aesthetics in Oregon. Everyday exposure to colonization reflected in the built environment reminds Indigenous people of their cultural exclusion and the ongoing, structural quality of colonialism. It is Mariana's critical colonial consciousness that allows her to see and critique the power relations constructing reality, rather than passively consume them.

Settler colonialism expressed through language, dance, and naming pressures also invites critical colonial consciousness. Kealohalani Teo is a Pacific Islander woman, born in Oregon, who found solidarity in a Pacific Islander organization in college. Colonialism is a regular topic of conversation among her Pacific Islander classmates:

> Within our group meetings . . . we use "colonialism" a lot more than any other group that I've ever been a part of. That is something that we really resonate with. . . . We definitely, normally tie everything back into that [colonialism]. . . . Just wanting to go back to your cultures [is] . . . *radical*. . . . To think about how much pain that [colonialism] caused your ancestors . . . because [language and dancing hula] were outlawed.

That colonialism is "definitely, normally" part of everyday conversation seeking to explain contemporary life illuminates the "critical colonial consciousness" that is foundational to Indigenous respondents' mindsets. Kealohalani argues that settler colonialism forcibly revised the Hawaiian language, the "problem" being that Indigenous language was not valued enough to be preserved: "it was almost eradicated, it was almost gone. . . . Even the Hawaiian language . . . [now is] influenced by White people: there's a traditional Hawaiian language and then there's this Hawaiian language that came after [colonization]."

Critical colonial consciousness troubles the casting of oppressed groups and their cultural practices as problems. Rejecting the present social problem framing as illegitimate, critical colonial consciousness works to undo the construction of colonized people as problematic, unworthy, or base. Critical colonial consciousness operates by voicing and validating counter-memory, refusing Whiteness as a "natural" dominant group, and bucking pressure to assimilate to White norms.

Kealohalani observes Whiteness as an unmarked and unnamed category that occupies a location of structural advantage: "Whiteness becomes the norm. . . . Everyone else is different from you [and] you're just the 'normal person' if you're White." Kealohalani resists the momentum of settler colonialism that augments Whiteness and diminishes Indigeneity. Having attended years of schooling in a predominately White suburb of Portland, Kealohalani "took back" her ethnicity after high school: "[I felt] resentment for all of those people that . . . took it away from me by telling me that I should have been Whiter." She anchors present-day assimilationist forces in colonization:

> Immediately when I started . . . to take back my own ethnicity . . . that . . . caused a lot of "I was White" [projections from others]. . . . A lot of people . . . in the Pacific islands have experienced a lot of their culture just being literally . . . *stripped away*—told, "You can't dance, you can't speak, you can't. . . ." Those things still . . . manifest themselves in different ways, like being uncomfortable with people expressing their culture.

Anglo-conformity pressures flow from colonization. Using a critical colonial consciousness lens, Kealohalani (whose real name is Anglophone) suspects that her Pacific Islander mother's intermarriage to her White father led to her non-Indigenous name. This postulation squares with research finding that among intermarried couples involving Hispanics, the father's ethnicity outranked the mother's ethnicity in influencing the naming of children.[70] Daughters are more often given non-translatable (non-ethnic) English names,[71] a gendered decision that implicitly positions boys and men as carriers of tradition that may not align with girls' and women's desire to be such bearers of tradition. Kealohalani reflects on the impact of having an Anglophone name (in real life): "I get nervous . . . will I be able to give my kids Pacific Islander names? [. . . Not having a Pacific Islander name] makes me upset. . . . That's another way . . . of taking someone's culture away from them. I'm feeling like mine was taken away from me." Naming holds symbolic significance.[72] Flexing a critical colonial consciousness, Kealohalani concludes that her real-life Anglophone name is emblematic of cultural erasure. She questions the ability to revive Pacific Islander culture in her future children. Yet, Kealohalani reclaims her Pacific Islander heritage by participating in an ethnic organization and in her selection of a pseudonym for this book that reflects her heritage.

Resistance to settler-colonial conditions and power arrangements is key to critical colonial consciousness. Leles Talbot, a Native American (Miluk Coos) woman with long white hair pulled back in a bun, illustrates resistance well. As we conducted the interview over video-conference, she sat at a desk in front of a large, brightly colored Native American blanket hanging on her wall. There are two chief facets to Leles' deployment of critical colonial consciousness: her legal work pushing for federal recognition of her tribe and her professional effort advancing Native American curriculum.

Federal recognition of Oregon tribes was terminated by the Western Oregon Termination Act of 1954.[73] Leles' infancy coincides with federal termination of her Miluk Coos tribe: "I was just . . . *days old* when my tribe was terminated and so that means no recognition by the Federal government. I grew up saying, 'I'm tribal, I'm Indian' with the entire government saying, 'No, you're not.'" With two warring perspectives on tribal sovereignty—the federal government one of denial and a tribal one exemplified by her father who "was very very active in railing against termination"—Leles developed a consciousness that was critical of colonialism. Consequently, Leles strove for "restoration" or federal recognition of her tribe. Leles views her Native community's plight through a colonial lens and endeavors to attain justice.

Leles' trajectory illustrates how critical colonial consciousness can be leveraged to change institutions. Leles was steeped in a settler-colonial model of education, her teachers lacking Indigenous knowledge and peddling deficit thinking.[74] She became skeptical about formal education when it erased her experience as Native American. Possessing what immigration scholars call a "dual frame of reference"[75] that refers to having two national or cultural points of comparison, Leles rejected the colonial or deficit model of education that quashed her community's power. Distrustful of the colonial influence that pervades the US educational system, she embarked on a mission to represent her community by investing in education by, for, and about Native Americans. Leles begins chronologically, referring to her own education as a child:

> I've always . . . thought that . . . Native people were truly forgotten. When I was little, in elementary and junior high, the books I read about Oregon history and Coos Bay history said my tribe was *extinct*. . . . So where is my

place as a tribal child in my tribe's hometown? My tribe was terminated in [mid-1950s] . . . and then we were restored in '84, but the history books said that my tribe was extinct, that we were all gone.

Settler-colonial education depicts Native Americans via demeaning images that legitimate the colonial project of extinction. Leles remarks: "It was always a *deficit-based history*. It was always 'sad about those poor Indians' and . . . 'they were dirty Indians' or 'they were drunken Indians.' There's always some negative adjective attached to Native Americans."

Settler-colonial theorist Patrick Wolfe writes, "the role that colonialism has assigned to Indigenous people is to disappear."[76] The goal of disappearance can be accomplished through genocidal annihilation, dispossession of land and ecological violence, and erasure. Leles discusses how the settler-colonial project infiltrated the educational system and attempted to stamp out Native culture and invisiblize Native people: "When we do things like [lessons on] Ellis Island, 'Where's my place?!' You know, I'm standing here waving at everybody [for attention]. . . . [No one is] ever saying, 'How do you feel as a removed Indian?'" Having worked toward restoration for her tribe, Leles beamed that restoration was a "*huge* positive, a huge step in the right direction."

Countering Native "disappearance" is a challenge to settler colonialism that constructs Native Americans as a problem to be "fixed" via literal or symbolic extermination. In her career as an educator, Leles uses her critical colonial consciousness to envision and plan education that recognizes Native American presence. She teaches for the betterment of Native and non-Native youth alike by getting "the real history out." Resisting the tide of White-centric education, Leles aspires to "help [students] to turn their thinking around or give them different dimensions to Lewis and Clark or . . . Sacajawea." Leles was enthused about Oregon Senate Bill 13 "Tribal History/Shared History," passed in 2017, that "directs the Oregon Department of Education (ODE) to create K-12 Native American Curriculum for inclusion in Oregon public schools and provide professional development to educators. The law also directs the ODE to provide funds to each of the nine federally recognized tribes in Oregon to create individual place-based curriculum."[77] Leles emphasized, "not only is it the *right* thing to incorporate authentic and accurate Native American history, *it is the law*. It is the law."

Emphasis on "the law" here as a corrective is intriguing given the failure of the law to benefit all groups equally. Critical race theory holds that "racism is ordinary, not aberrational," suffusing even legal doctrine.[78] Laws are human creations and, as such, they absorb the prejudices of their authors and wreak repercussions that echo across time. In addition to critical race theory that arose from the premise that racism is endemic to society, "TribalCrit" emphasizes that "colonization is endemic to society" and pays special attention to Native Americans' marginalization by virtue of colonization, law, politics, and race.[79]

While federal and state government have been sources of egregious harms,[80] laws may be an avenue to institute change. This possibility of law working *in favor* of marginalized communities is open to debate, yet Leles believes that legislation can be wielded to help, not only hurt. Oregon is one of a handful of states with legislation mandating Native education. Leles effused about Oregon Senate Bill 13: "I see that as such a *huge* positive step. . . . So many times we teach Indian as old-timey: 'They're dead, they were gone, they—we—wore leather and feathers.' But this curriculum brings us as Native people into contemporary society: they talk about our tribes today, our land, our place, our presence, our partnerships. It is so phenomenally wonderful." Multicultural education can be a product of, as well as *generate*, critical colonial consciousness. "Unlearning" colonial thought is central to decolonization and inclusive education. Leles says that the decolonial challenge is that "so many teachers have to *unlearn* what they were taught, or parents have to *unlearn* what they were taught." The "Tribal History/Shared History" legislation in Oregon provided money to tribes to design their own curricula, aiding self-determination. Tribes now have decision-making power over what and how to teach about themselves, the lesson plans they design provided to the state for use by school districts. Leles lays out her response to critics who rely on racial resentment to shore up exclusionary education:

I hear people—especially White people—say, "Well, history is being rewritten." Bullshit! History is not being rewritten. History is being *accurately written for the first time.* And I always make a point when people say I'm trying to "Brown-wash history," . . . I say, "No, it's a balance. We're mixing Brown and White for once."

Revising history after reexamining the historical record and reinterpreting storylines to represent communities of color more accurately is a goal of critical race theory.[81] Revisions that incorporate countermemory are correctives to "hierarchies of credibility" that "distort reality" by trumpeting master narratives and discounting the viewpoints of the less powerful.[82] As an emancipatory tool born in reaction to colonization, critical colonial consciousness lifts the perspectives of the marginalized, counters erasure, unmasks colonial ideologies, and can alter institutions.

Addressing both institutions and culture, a "fight to decolonize," as Ross Reece (Karuk/Hupa/Yurok) phrased it, is predicated upon a critical colonial consciousness. Ross wants to go "backwards" to live in harmony with the landscape, to live sustainably and in spiritual connection with land. Unlike other minoritized groups' sociopolitical struggles for equality and inclusion, Indigenous orientations favor "autonomy and separateness" that honor tribal nation distinctiveness.[83] Given Ross's Indigenous, decolonial intention of saving tribal communities from cultural and literal annihilation, I posed the wrong question when I asked to what extent Ross felt included in, or excluded from, US society. My very question presumed the United States as the primary national frame of reference. Ross establishes his tribal identity as the one he is grounded in and invested in protecting:

> I don't feel included nor excluded from the United States. . . . Because the United States was recently . . . institutionalized . . . I feel like . . . the US mainstream society is excluded, and sometimes included, in my culture and my lifestyle. So, it's a kind of opposite . . . I think it's a good way . . . of relating back to who you are and what exactly the history is here.

Calling the United States "recently institutionalized" positions it as a younger country with a shorter history than those of tribal nations. Using critical colonial consciousness that is rooted in Indigenous history and perspective, Ross positions Natives as the decision-makers who determine how much US influence to allow. Pushing back against US colonizing influence underscores Native endurance. Possessing a critical colonial consciousness that keeps an Indigenous interpretive framework at the ready is affirming for Ross: "[It] does help. . . .

It's pretty much just disallowing . . . the United States to say that . . . they have accomplished colonization. . . . It's a way of saying that's not true, that we're still here doing . . . our cultural ways from before contact. I think it is a transfer of power." This "transfer of power" centers Indigeneity and declares the United States as a White settler-colonial nation intent on White cultural dominance.

Double consciousness feeds critical colonial consciousness. Ross contends that ideas about Indigenous lifestyles have been "twisted and turned [and] made into a false reality of who we are and that's where the stereotypes come from." In response, he leverages critical colonial consciousness to imagine a liberated future: "We're here and we're not just some mythical idea or creature." Ross's tribal roots form the basis of his critical colonial consciousness which, in turn, informs his engagement with White-dominated institutions. He refers to his overwhelmingly White college context: "The White man's world . . . [is] what I'm dealing with now. . . . There's another world that's doesn't want you to succeed." Much like Du Bois's reference to the "other world," Ross's phrase "another world" refers to a White power structure implicated in his marginalization and his ensuing double consciousness.

Coming from a rural area comprised of 95% Native people, Ross experiences White institutions as antithetical to his Native culture and knowledge base. The process of schooling "subtracts" from his cultural foundation, an assimilationist agenda divesting students of color of their cultures and languages.[84] Language loss has been institutionalized. Native languages have been declining for decades; of 245 known Indigenous languages in the United States, sixty-five are extinct and another seventy-five are near extinction.[85] Ross complains of institutional disregard: "I can't go and learn my language within the institution. . . . That's . . . a force that doesn't want me to succeed." In envisioning an alternative, Ross draws on Native practices: "Just basically to be outside. Not to be in a chair in a classroom. To be learning the ways of the wildlife that's out there. To know when . . . food is going to be growing up, what time of the year, and how much to gather. . . . The knowledge that we had was . . . severed." Coming from an oral tradition and experiential way of learning, Ross's decolonial vision rejects the Western tradition of classrooms. Favoring nature, spirituality, and hands-on learning, he utilizes critical colonial consciousness not only to criticize alienating institutions but to offer a decolonial possibility that resists his "disappearance" and adheres to Native epistemology and culture.

Expressions of critical colonial consciousness require engagement, or embattlement, with dominant structures and ideologies. Similar to Du Bois's concept of double consciousness, where African Americans are aware of White people's misperceptions of them, Indigenous respondents spoke of the disjuncture between themselves and wider society.[86] In order to exist with integrity or advance a decolonial agenda, Indigenous respondents referred to needing to "gear up to keep fighting" or get their "haka on." "Haka" refers to an ancient South Pacific (Māori) war dance traditionally used on the battlefield as well as at gatherings during peacetime. To invoke haka—as a ceremonial display of Indigenous people's pride, strength, and battle-readiness through rhythmic foot stomping and body slapping—as a precursor to engagement in a White-centric society is to invoke critical colonial consciousness in everyday life.

Conclusion

This chapter has argued that settler-colonial dynamics and global imperialism, both central to the founding of the US nation-state, drive the construction of people of color as "problems." The present is never fully divested from the past, historical elements influencing the present. Past maneuvers set in motion racist settler-colonial and imperial dynamics that have momentum and affect successive generations. From settler colonialism that aims to erase Indigenous people to global imperialism that creates "military-racial opponents" out of people of color with ancestral ties to foreign countries with whom the United States has had conflict, the state holds much responsibility for concocting racial inequality in the present era. Aware of their racial-colonial subjugation, Indigenous respondents exhibited critical colonial consciousness. Indigenous respondents optimizing critical colonial consciousness used colonization and systemic racism as frameworks to understand phenomena, enabling them to identify inequalities and articulate a need for societal reform. Spurred by double consciousness, critical colonial consciousness encourages counter-memory, resists colonization, and offers alternative visions for social organization.

History set the stage for racial inequality today. The settler-colonial and imperial mode of operation undertaken by the nation established a stilted racialized social structure that privileges the White racial category and dispossesses communities of color. Settler colonialism, usually applied to Native Americans, is a fruitful lens through which to read the oppression of additional groups with Indigenous histories, principally Pacific Islanders. Racial-colonial dynamics introduced burdens of belonging for groups of color early in the founding of the nation, a theme that percolates into the present. Indigenous respondents were adamant that racial-colonial history is not inert and left to the history books but alive and infiltrating present-day societal organization. Critical colonial consciousness illustrates the world-critiquing and world-building capacities that are a reaction to colonization and testify simultaneously to injustice as well as paths for possible transformation.

Settler colonialism and global imperialism installed a racial ethos, race relations, and institutions emblazoned with racial inequality that have much gravity today. People of color are not labeled as "problems" in a vacuum; they are deliberately constructed as such through "racial projects"[87] executed by nation-state policy and racial rhetoric that invest in Whiteness and disinvest from people of color. The next chapter explores how "American" is racialized and, in turn, how constricted notions of national identity racially stratify a sense of belonging.

2

Being a "Problem"

Getting the Message, Counternarratives, and Double Consciousness as Intersectional

In *The Souls of Black Folk*, W.E.B. Du Bois posed the self-reflexive question, "How does it feel to be a problem?" To assert, as Du Bois did, that Black people are viewed as a problem is a searing commentary on society's racial structure. Acknowledging that Black people in the United States have suffered an exceptional history of dehumanization, enslavement, and locked-up and locked-out status, this chapter moves beyond the Black/White divide to ask all respondents, regardless of race, whether Du Bois's line written in 1903 resonates with them today. Jo Paz, a twenty-one-year-old multiracial (Latinx/White), queer college student gives a layered reply. She is the daughter of an immigrant and feels "fairly excluded" because of her multiple devalued identities and her perception that Latinx women are exoticized, tokenized, and underpaid. She uses the term "Latinx" or "Latin-*equis*" to describe herself, saying, "Latin-*equis* . . . [is] just acknowledgement of all the intersections of what it is to be Latino. . . . Being Black but also Latino or . . . being queer, being non-binary, being a trans person. . . . Mixed-ness. . . . You're not *just* Latino, you're other things." Upon agreeing with Du Bois's assessment about being seen as a problem in the eyes of others, Jo responds to my questions, "How does it make you feel? What do you do with it?":

> It makes me feel (pauses) validity in my own unrest, I guess. . . . It am-
> plifies that I want to be revolutionary. It makes me . . . be part of diver-
> sity. . . . It makes me talk about these things. It makes me learn about
> colonization. It makes me dive into my history. It makes me be proud of
> my heritage. It does all these things because if I'm a problem because I'm
> not White, then I'm going to really be not White and fuck you. [Laughter]

Marginalization of people of color can be met with resilience, civic engagement, and political participation.[1] Jo's assertion about digging into non-Whiteness has the double intent of destabilizing White supremacy and re-valuing denigrated non-White groups. Jo re-brands her status *as* a "problem" into *being* a "problem" for a society that upholds a stilted racial hierarchy.

My objective in this chapter is to honor Du Bois's incisive query ("How does it feel to be a problem?") by examining its applicability to Black and non-Black people of color in the contemporary period. While the exact "type" of problem a person of color feels caged by varies by racial group, the type of problem matters less than problem status generally, for "when discrimination succeeds, it does not stop with one group but rather becomes generalized as a social principle and practice."[2] "How does it feel to be a problem" centers both feelings and problem status. I theorize feelings (racialized emotions) as not only meaningful "ends" or "outcomes" worthy of attention but also "inputs" that fuel action and contribute to embodied health or unwellness. I conceptualize feelings as indicators of structural location and conduits for action and reaction. When asked whether or not they perceive that their group is seen by dominant society as "a problem," respondents of color overwhelmingly agreed and expressed feelings such as frustration, anger, overwhelm, sadness, anxiety, and depression. The depth of agreement with Du Bois is notable, as is what comes next: counternarratives, double consciousness, and the contestation of oppression.

While Du Bois's sentiment is not intended to extend to White people—they produce the alienating gaze and benefit from society's racial structure—I ask this question of White respondents too, with the aim of capturing the full range of race-inflected replies. If I did not ask White respondents this question, one pole of a racial spectrum would be missing and Whiteness would continue to be rendered invisible.

Even as racial groups serve as a handy heuristic, they are not static constructs but are dynamic, with boundaries that are contested and in motion.[3] Some mechanisms of social control transcend racial boundaries, techniques of power that crisscross people within the "people of color" category revealing common experiences among racialized groups. I present material in this chapter by theme rather than by racial group for several reasons: first, to honor the in-flux quality of racial groups and boundaries; second, to avoid reifying groups as having certain advantages or disadvantages that all members uniformly possess; and, third, to make visible oppression and solidarity that cross supposed racial boundaries.

In what follows I flip the order of the usual "White/non-White" divide to a "non-White/White" one, providing material on respondents of color first. This arrangement inverts the White-centric practice of presenting findings on White people first and then tacking on findings based on people of color, which can be read as an afterthought.[4] This chapter reveals a stark non-White/White divide. The first three sections feature respondents of color. The first section enumerates techniques of power that convey the message that people of color are viewed as a problem. The second section hones in on counternarratives articulated by people of color, highlighting chief rhetorical responses that encapsulate two seemingly polar opposites: a rejection of "problem" status and an embrace of it as an avenue for social change. The third section elaborates Du Bois's term "double consciousness" by arguing that double consciousness is intersectional, respondents of color acutely aware of their positionality (and oftentimes, multiple marginality). The section on White respondents shows that inclusion is a racial privilege. White respondents had bifurcated reactions to the notion that their group may constitute a problem, from victimization narratives to critiques of White supremacy.

Getting the Message about "Being a Problem": Respondents of Color on the Non-White/White Divide

In Du Bois's terminology, the major "color line" is between White and non-White and yet smaller but still-significant color *lines* (plural) create group boundaries.[5] Summing up the sentiments of most respondents of color, Pacific Islander Sefina Sosene remarks: "In general for people of color, we're just seen as a problem." All respondents of color concurred that they were not racially privileged in the United States and most agreed with Du Bois's statement that their racial group is disparaged as a social problem. Respondents of color received the message that they are less desirable to the nation than people in the White category by way of four themes: bodily presence and appearance; non-English language; land destruction and imperial expansion; and population change anxiety paired with presumed cultural difference. These themes communicating devaluation rest on systemic racism and settler colonialism, these organizing structures scaffolding privilege and oppression.

Bodily Presence and Appearance

Physical appearance—skin color, hair texture, and hairstyle—provokes stares, surveillance, comments, and unwanted touching if a body is deemed unusual for an environment.[6] Unsolicited words and gestures mark boundaries between "us" (insiders) and "them" (outsiders). Respondents who complained of objectification, othering, and exoticization had their body judged as existing outside of Whiteness and occupying "problem" status.

White normativity—Whiteness seen as the racial and cultural norm in the United States[7]—is the root cause for why respondents of color are made to feel out of place. Light skin tone carries advantages such as social capital,[8] positive associations with income earning[9] and schooling,[10] and health.[11] Carrying a negative penalty, darker skin tone is associated with higher reports of racial discrimination and worse labor market outcomes.[12] Aware of light-skin privilege, people with darker complexions wrestle with self-esteem and self-efficacy costs in addition to the material taxes of stigma.[13]

Hair is also a racial marker.[14] Given the privileged status of Whiteness, respondents whose physical appearance diverges from light hair and skin are informed that their appearance is ill-fitting. Patrice Park is mixed-race Black/White and says she is perceived as African American. Her long black hair fascinates non-Black people:

> When I wear braids, I get a very different reaction from when I don't. People will touch my hair, or [exclaim], "Oh, my God, your hair is so beautiful." Blah blah blah blah. I'll just get attention [and] I'm not really sure if it's positive or negative. And then I'll get stopped a lot at the airport . . . because people think I'm hiding drugs in my hair . . . because of my bun. [Chuckles]

Patrice moves from being objectified and exotified to being marked as suspicious and potentially dangerous. Her Black body subjected to extra scrutiny, Patrice must prove that her body is nonthreatening: "I'll take out the bun and show you," she will tell Transportation Security Administration agents.

All respondents of color who came from more racially heterogeneous areas and moved to a predominately White location in Oregon felt less racially marked in their prior, racially mixed locale. Pearl Hashimoto (Japanese/White) was raised in multiracial Hawai'i and transformed into a visible racial minority when she moved to Oregon. Pearl's inclusion depends on geographic location: She feels included in Hawai'i, the US state with the highest multiracial reporting (24%),[15] a population comprised mostly of people of color, and a standard of beauty based on dark-skinned, dark-haired, larger-bodied people. According to Pearl, a national White beauty standard is negated by a majority-non-White population in Hawai'i:

> I never really wanted to be blonde. . . . A lot of Asian people in the mainland dye their hair blonde and they have light skin and they . . . get double eyelid surgery. That was never a thing for me because in Hawai'i what's beautiful is to be dark, have really long dark hair. . . . I never had [a blonde] frame of reference because everyone [in Hawai'i] had the same standard: . . . We're all dark. We all have dark hair.

In comparison to Hawai'i, where the beauty norm skews toward non-White racial admixture, in Oregon, Pearl detects that she is regarded as an outsider because of her physical features: darker tones and larger body frame. She relates instances of informal and formal policing of her body:

> People . . . yelled out of their car window at me to "go home to my country." . . . [They were] White men. . . . Always. . . . I got pulled over by a cop and he . . . asked me if I was smoking weed because my eyes were small (laughter). I was like, "Nope. This is just how my eyes are. I'm Asian."

In the largely White space of Oregon, Pearl is mistaken as an immigrant and put "into a box with a lot of propaganda" such as "you're a drain on society." To Pearl, these racialized judgments stemming from physical appearance make her, and others excluded based on physical cues, a "boogeyman." Being a boogeyman not only signals non-belonging but dehumanization: "You're like a fake person who just has all these characteristics . . . the worst of the worst. You get all of the negative connotations [but are afforded] none of what it feels like to be a *human* [laughter] who has [a] multilayered past." Bodies are judged as barometers of belonging.

Non-English Language

English is a prerequisite of belonging. Invested in by "guardians of English"[16] who desire to manufacture a White nation, linguistic ethnocentrism spurns non-English speakers, both US-born and foreign-born. English-only sentiments and policies regard monolingualism as a virtue, rejecting the ability to converse with multiple linguistic communities as a social good. Official English-only campaigns exploit the politics of resentment, raising the specter of linguistic separatism. English-only movements that have aimed to make English the official language of the nation are a thin veil for the fear of waning White supremacy, as journalist James Crawford notes: "Reaffirming our 'common bond' as Americans makes little sense . . . considering that English has rarely played that symbolic role in the past, except as a surrogate for racism or xenophobia."[17]

Centering Whiteness vis-à-vis the English language marginalizes people of color who speak languages other than English. Elijah Cortez, born in Mexico and now in graduate school in Oregon, refers to language as a way to police belonging: "I don't like . . . when people tell you, 'Oh, you have an accent.' '. . . Where are you from?' . . . I seriously don't like that because it's very stereotypical and we all have accents."

Pearl Hashimoto (Japanese/White) is assumed to be a non-English-speaking foreigner. Pearl, who is of Japanese descent, remarks wryly: "People look at my face and they're like, 'China. I don't know if you speak English'—especially people here [in Oregon]. They will not say hello right away because they're not sure if I'm going to understand them. I always have to go out of my way to be like, 'Hello. Hi. Yes, Hello.' [says with a distinctly American accent] [snickers]." Making linguistic overtures to prove her Americanness through English proficiency,[18] Pearl shows how language and physical indicators intertwine to make her "a problem" in the eyes of others. Even upon resisting incorrect assumptions, people of color are left holding the emotional bag of burdened belonging. After she told the above story, I asked, "So how does that make you feel?" Pearl replied, "Shitty. Always, always shitty." In turn, Pearl uses the English language to preempt marginalization: "Because if you don't basically roll out the welcome mat, you may or may not be served or looked at or acknowledged. . . . *You're not a player* because you're effectively on the side because they can't categorize you and so therefore you're in the periphery."

Like interpersonal communication, institutions also establish cultural norms. Bilingual respondents spoke forcefully about how schools compel English-language acquisition to the detriment of additional languages a child may know. Messages of value are delivered when one language is embedded in official curricula and others are dismissed. Consuelo Nodal, a bilingual (Spanish and English) speech language pathologist, says that she learned of her "problem" status due to her Spanish capabilities: "Because [students'] English skills are not at at 'adequate'—*they're* the problem. [School administrators] never saw the institution . . . or their method of teaching . . . as being the problem. It was the children." Consuelo implicitly asks, "Problem according to whom?" Like Du Bois, she identifies White supremacy as an arbiter of who is a problem.

Graciela Pinela relays a related tale about institutions force-feeding English rather than supporting multilingual youth. Born in Quito, Ecuador, Graciela is a fluent Spanish and English speaker who aspired to teach her son both languages. She was quickly inducted into the English-as-supreme culture: "When I first came to the United States . . . I had a pretty thick accent. . . . I got [a] tremendous, tremendous amount of discrimination because of my accent." The priority of knowing English in the United States, endorsed by schools and health professionals, worked against the intergenerational transmission of Spanish to Graciela's son, damaging his relationship to his Ecuadorian extended family and culture. She explains the difficulty of standing up against intertwined systems that prioritize English and extinguish other languages:

> We started speaking to [my son] in English and Spanish. And, here he is, three years old, and he's not talking. . . . He would do this babble that . . . was like his own language. . . . Speech therapy was recommended and . . .

the speech therapist . . . was like, "Do you speak to him in English or in Spanish?" . . . Both, really, like fifty-fifty. . . . [The professionals] were like, "Oh, he's just confused. . . . You need to choose a language." I was 24. I had no idea about anything . . . and no college education. . . . It was just like, "Well, you are the expert, so. . . ." And it felt really bad and wrong. . . . At first I was like, "Well, what if I just speak to him in Spanish, and then he goes to pre-school and then he learns English there?" And they were like, "No, no, no, no. . . . We suggest that you choose English. . . . This way when he goes to pre-school, he'll be prepared." And I was like, "Well, I want what's best for my son." And then they told me . . . "We don't have a speech therapist . . . who speaks Spanish and we would have to find somebody." . . . I was like, "Well . . . you are the experts, so. . . ." I mean, that was so racist. And it was terrible.

Repeating the refrain that she "just wanted what's best" for her son, Graciela was pressed into English-only instruction for her young son. Prioritizing the English language, the speech professionals were not equipped (and did not desire) to serve Spanish speakers. Schools were "weirded out" by a non-English language, causing shame for Graciela's son to the extent that he covered his ears when Spanish was spoken, effectively eliminating Spanish. Her son is English monolingual, and Graciela stresses the long-lasting impact of what she now identifies as "institutionalized racism": "To this day it affects me and it has affected my son's future: I was very sad because it has caused a lot of disconnect . . . in me bringing my culture to my son. . . . It [enforcement of English and loss of Spanish] did cause a lot of strife and shame, for sure."

Demanding English and squeezing out non-English languages sends a clear message about which speakers are valued. By way of comparison, studying multiple languages in school is required in much of Europe, with more than twenty European countries requiring the study of a *second* foreign language for at least a year.[19] In the United States, people of color who speak languages other than English—even when *in addition to* English—are frowned upon, whereas White bilinguals are admired for getting an edge in the global capitalist system.[20]

Bearing a non-English-sounding name is also grounds for problem status. Naming is an important cultural decision that signals racial, ethnic, or national identity and has long-term consequences.[21] Audit studies show a person's race, even inferred by a name, can adversely affect employment chances.[22] Bogga Deta is a Black woman from Sudan whose resumé reflects her international status. Although she has a Master's degree, she had trouble finding a job, a stumbling block she attributes to her foreign-sounding name. A Mexican-born friend advised Bogga, "You have to play the game right." She says:

> That means "Do not tell them who you are." . . . But . . . I want to say I'm an African. . . . But I was told not to do it, so I could get a job easily. And it did work. That surprised me. . . . I took [off] all the countries [from my resumé] . . . although the name of the university [in Sudan] is still there. . . . I had to . . . play the game.

The wisdom of a Mexican friend who had learned that names serve as shorthand for nation of origin and race shed light on Bogga's job search frustration. The job market advice to strip down her resumé that proved successful supports the cultural priority of English.

Land Destruction and Imperial Expansion

Destruction of the natural environment—and the ways of life tied to nature—accompanies settler colonialism.[23] Just like the people that populate the terrain, lands are not equally valued and preserved. Particularly in my interviews with Native Americans and Pacific Islanders, the theme of damage to native lands and lifeways of people indigenous to the area was strong. Respondents expressed sorrow over harm inflicted on the natural habitat and the disruption of cultural practices tied to the earth. The land is not vacant but home to people; injury to land is tantamount to injury to people of that land.

Indigenous people, both Native American and Pacific Islander, see their group as a problem in the eyes of White society because they are obstacles to the United States' imperial expansion. Karrie Matthews (White/Hawaiian/Chinese) grew up on the west side of Oahu, Hawai'i, and witnessed artillery practices that destroyed the natural habitat. Karrie saw the valley near her home go up in flames after live-fire training ammunition explosions:

There's a valley called Makua Valley [where] the military would practice. And many times as a child, my mom would get us all in the car and go fifteen minutes down the road because the whole valley would be burning. The whole valley burning flames. So hot because they would be practicing artillery. . . . As a child it was probably amazing to see, "Wow, the flames," you know? But the other side was like (crying), "Why are they doing that?" . . . It happened every year. Every year.

Ancient Hawaiians considered Makua Valley as sacred, the birthplace of humans and the point of departure for souls shedding human form for the afterlife. After the bombing of Pearl Harbor in 1941, the valley was placed under military authority and local residents were displaced from their homes. The fires Karrie beheld as a child, and that still touch her emotional core now, were US Army trainings that used artillery and dropped up to 1,000-pound bombs into the sea and valley.[24] I asked Karrie, "Did that make you feel like your land, and maybe even your people, were disposable or, your word . . . 'ruined'?" Karrie answers: "The land. . . . Island people were treated less than, say, the White people."

The lives of people whose cultures and foodways are based on the environment are altered when land is seized or natural resources extracted without concern for the balance of the natural world. Native American Ross Reece ruminates:

We see all these pictures of . . . Geronimo or Chief Joseph, and all of them . . . look . . . stoic and mean-looking. . . . Why they're not looking happy and why they're looking mean and just stoic [is] because of the . . . death and the killings and . . . stripping of their culture. . . . But before that . . . we were the happiest people ever and . . . we had a sustainability of the earth. . . . And today, we're killing the earth. . . . Back then . . . nature was a higher being than humans. . . . We were happy, we were . . . sustainable within the earth and the ecosystem.

When referencing Geronimo and Chief Joseph, Ross's language slips from "they" to "we," indicating that Native trauma reverberates in his life. Ross links the confiscation of Indigenous land to the literal and figurative death of his Native people and the overruling of their ecological knowledge. Of transhistorical importance, land has been pivotal to colonial projects and remains a vital resource for Native revival, healing, and decolonization and sovereignty that calls for return of land.[25]

Population Change Anxiety and Presumed Intransigent Cultural Difference

The Office of Management and Budget, responsible for drafting racial categorizations that appear on the Census, decided in 2000 to classify mixed-race individuals of minority and White origins according to the minority category.[26] This bureaucratic decision positions the minority side of mixed-race people as "[taking] precedence over the white side in the federal statistical system."[27] This "demographic illusion" skews population forecasts in the direction of racial minority population growth.[28] Projections of a decline of White demographic dominance are the source of racial resentment for some.[29]

White people's anxiety over changing racial demographics—the "browning of America"[30]—is another way respondents of color intuit their subordination. A related apprehension is the presumption that people of color are mired in inferior and unchanging cultures.[31] The problematic assumptions here abound: that cultural differences are always divisive; that White culture constitutes the agreed-upon core of the United States; and that cultures are impenetrable and do not shift over time. Attending to talk of "culture" is important because it can be a soft-spoken way to articulate racial concerns, biological racism masquerading as cultural racism.[32]

When Whiteness is upheld as the cultural center of the nation, people of color and the cultural diversity they carry is sidelined. Miguel Hernandez (Latino) resonated with being framed as a problem because of the growing Mexican population that the dominant group fears signals a death knell for White dominance:

> I understand what [Du Bois] means. . . . Like when people ask me what it's like to be a Brown person. . . . Being ostracized [in Texas], even though . . . there were *so many* fucking Mexicans . . . where I went to high school. White friends would ask me these ridiculous questions about . . . "What does it mean to be Mexican?" Or, "Did you all make tacos all day?" You know, shit like that.

Boundary marking is essential to questions such as "what's it like to be a Brown person?" While both men and women received this boundary-marking treatment, consistent with my earlier work on third-generation Mexican Americans, men were more consistently and sternly penalized for their Brownness, revealing a gendered quality to perception and treatment.[33]

Assuming cultural splits between racial groups, even if overblown or inaccurate, etch boundaries. In the case of US-born Mexican Americans, Edward Telles and Christina Sue's research finds that pitting "Mexican" against "American" is a false dichotomy that does not accurately represent the heterogeneity of this group that draws from both "Mexican" and "American" cultural reservoirs.[34] Miguel points out the irony of oppressing a group that comprises nearly the same share of statewide population (as of Census 2020, Hispanics were 39.7% and non-Hispanic White people were 41.2% of the Texas population)[35]—though fear of population growth may be fueling what Miguel calls "cultural segregation." For historical context, Jim Crow–like segregation of Texas prevalent in 1920–1940 was rationalized by White ethnocentrism.[36] Miguel's sense of "ostracization" is built upon a long historical legacy.

Cultures and people that are not deemed "American" are viewed as threats by those invested in Whiteness. Fears over cultural gulfs disregard long-standing trends of cultural amalgamations and cultural hybridity that occur over time, as seen in interracial marriage.[37] A narrow view of American culture as White glosses over varieties of Whiteness,[38] internal heterogeneity within all racial/ethnic groups that call the United States home,[39] and the fact that White people are susceptible to cultural shifts as well.[40]

Counternarratives from Respondents of Color

Respondents of color used two principal counternarratives in response to their categorization as a problem. Some rejected the idea that they are a problem. Others asserted that "continuing to be a problem" is a useful strategy to assert group needs and gain visibility. Another counternarrative is featured in chapter 3: the call to expand the definition of "American" to include more people, irrespective of race.

"We're Not a Problem"

Counternarratives challenge a dominant narrative. One reply to being cast as problematic is to reject the allegation. Many people of color view White supremacy as the *real* problem. A pervasive "white racial frame," or "overarching worldview" that "impose[s] or maintain[s White] racial identity, privilege, and dominance vis-à-vis people of color," characterizes the racial climate in the United States.[41] In response to a White racial frame that damns people of color to problem status, people of color renounce that categorization and thereby undercut White supremacy.

Beau Landon (Native American) points out that the assessment of who is labeled a social problem rests on the perspective of the accuser. Pulling on perspectival realism,[42] Beau asserts: "I think in the current atmosphere, White supremacists, or White people are looked at as the problem now. A White person probably wouldn't say that. But I think from the viewpoint of a person of color, it's the establishment that historically has been White that's been screwing things up for all the people of color." Beau flips the script of Natives being cast as a social problem by identifying White supremacy and its adherents as a social problem. His answer challenges the premise of the question ("How does it feel to be a problem?") by examining who gets to ask the question. By wresting power from White power holders, Beau inverts power relations and gives voice to his standpoint.

Native American Leles Talbot underscores that it is only according to dominant society that her group is seen as a problem. Leles transgressed expectations of Native girls' silence as a youth: "When I was in school and I'd say, 'My tribe's not extinct,' . . . that was seen as . . . bad. . . . Things would be so much easier if I would just shut up. Well, who's it easier for, you know?" Perspective is at play here. Leles' perspective, as Native, disagrees with the master narrative of Natives as problems:

> I don't think as nations we see ourselves as a problem. Oh, sure. The prob-
> lem is how you see us. From . . . tribal people, [we] are persevering. . . . The
> problem is the world around [us]. I think the White government would
> love if all the problems went away. If we would just act White. If we would
> just get over it [there] wouldn't be any problems. . . . I still go back to that:

it's their problem. Yep. Yeah, it's White people's problem [when they] keep trying to change us or [tell us], "Get over it."

Rejecting problem status and calling it out as a tool of social control manufactured by a White, Western standpoint is one way to butt against oppressive master narratives.

Shayla Pierre offered a structural critique of problem status, emotions accompanying her words. She remarked, "I'm proud [to be Black] but it kinda sucks, I'm not gonna lie. It doesn't feel good." She continued with a structural condemnation: "You made us the problem!" Categorizations such as "problem" are outgrowths and reinforcers of racial inequality. Shayla attends Black Lives Matter movement events and approves of peaceful protests like football player Colin Kaepernick's "taking a knee" during the national anthem at athletic events. Shayla repudiates Black subjugation: "I'm 'stepping out of line' to show you this is not the line I'm meant to be in." This imagery of a line conjures up human-imposed notions of rank and tidiness. Shayla disputes the very existence of the line (racial hierarchy). As the previous chapter argued, problem status is imposed, not innate.

Some respondents of color clutched respectability politics, rooted in claims of deservingness, when they dismissed problem status and asserted that they are contributors to society. This trope of worthy contributors to society may especially pertain to groups of color castigated as a criminal element or financial drain on society. Candi Perez's conception of Mexicans as "hard workers" is a "moral hierarchy of worth" claim commonly used by Latino workers to underscore their economic contributions.[43] Candi offers a retort to anti-Mexican discourse:

> I can definitely see [my group labeled as a problem] more now with . . . Trump trying to make us look bad. . . . He was saying that the Mexicans were just drug cartels and "they're bringing in all of the bad people." . . . Let's say a Mexican got caught with drugs: they would make that *such* a big deal. . . . There are other races doing that, but once they get caught it's not a big deal because they're not the "problem." Mexicans are because Trump is saying we are the problem. I feel like we're not the problem because there's so many millennials that are trying to better themselves and do exactly what their parents came here to do: become somebody

and progress in life and make something of themselves. . . . The good ones are overlooked, they're not paid attention to. Then everybody says, "Trump was right," but that's just one person out of thousands of students or workers not doing that [illegal activity]. Personally, I don't think we are a problem. If anything, I feel like we're a group of hard workers, picking up the slack of everybody.

Discussing the Mexican-born as students, workers, and law-abiding contributors to society, Candi argues for "defensive inclusion"[44] that utilizes hard work and an economic notion of Americanness to rebut the dominant discourse that her group is a drag on society and a problem. Repudiation of the problem framing is followed by re-framing the group in a positive light.

"Continuing to Be a Problem"

"Continuing to be a problem" is a counternarrative that flips being a problem from a constraint to an opportunity. Continuing to be a problem asserts non-White subjectivity, experience, and groupness, and demands attention on those grounds. "Problem" groups do not conform to the proscriptions set forth by White-structured society. Picking up on this vein of non-submission, some respondents of color offered "continuing to be a problem" as a way to assert themselves and battle marginality. In this formulation, "continuing to be a problem" is a rallying cry and strategy for calling attention to inequalities and collectively agitating for change.

Evelyn Xus (Native) views continuing to be a problem as a life-or-death proposition. She sees being a problem as tantamount to Native Americans' continuing existence. In response to my question about Du Bois's line in *The Souls of Black Folk*, Evelyn remarks:

I think it feels like, "Yup!" [Laughter] . . . That resonates a lot on different levels, but it also . . . makes me feel like it's important to continue to be a problem. [Chuckles] . . . Because if . . . you're not . . . the problem per se, as that quote goes, then, do you exist anymore? . . . Not as in you disappear, but do your people exist anymore, if they're not [a problem]? . . . If they're . . . just absorbed?

From a Native perspective, Evelyn's use of "absorbed" connotes forced assimilation as a way to diminish culture that runs counter to White dictates. Part of a multi-pronged state effort that ran alongside genocidal projects,[45] assimilation or absorption is a strategy of elimination.[46] In terms of racial formation, nations respond to social movement demands through a strategy of "absorption" whereby they adopt demands in moderate forms in order to pacify threats.[47] I followed up by asking Evelyn, "What does it mean to want to continue to be a problem? What does that look like?" Her answer is grounded in Native epistemologies and practices that resist "absorption" by the racial state: "Just to continue the teachings and our ceremonies and our ways and our connections to land and pass those on, and also to continue to be a voice." Envisioned this way, the very lives, livelihoods, and voices of Natives are counternarratives to a dominant White cultural norm.

Fifty-one-year-old Mongolian, Vietnamese-born, US veteran Minor Hun worries that the "model minority" stereotype encourages Asian passivity. Minor does not think Asian Americans are cast as problems because they "do not create waves—that's *why* the model minority myth exists." But he dislikes this orientation and argues that Asian Americans collectively need to "be a problem" in order to challenge discrimination. Minor rejects the pacifism associated with Asian Americans and favors confrontation: "I feel like Asian people should . . . make themselves a problem. . . . They should be in people's face in these racist . . . societies. They . . . should make themselves heard." Minor hopes Asian Americans will surmount the image of a mollified model minority who is "busy trying to do whatever they can to see the White majority . . . nod their head with approval and acceptance" and instead "fight." Minor indicts the model minority stereotype as an enticement for a high-achieving segment of the Asian American population to accept honorary Whiteness and relinquish race-specific complaints. Pushing against the dominant narrative, Minor entreats Asian Americans to be a visible problem that grabs attention and demands remedies to injustices.

The impulse to reject categorization as a problem or embrace the problem status for the sake of uplifting communities of color are not discrete, opposing options. People can engage both counternarrative strategies. Consider Desirée Robinson (Black), who expressed a range of desires in response to "being a problem" in the Du Boisian sense, from wanting acceptance to embracing *all varieties* of Black culture rather than risk derogating any Black subcultures. Desirée spoke of the "abstract stress" of being Black: "We don't have any room to F-up. . . . We're behind the line, anyway." Bridging the counternarratives that reject problem status or coopt that terminology for the sake of group empowerment, Desirée straddles both:

> Being Black, it's so complicated. You . . . want to be an example. You want to show that we're—you're—good enough. . . . But then, honestly, some days, you want to embrace the whole . . . of being Black, and if that means rap music, gold chains . . . I want to be all of that too and be able to show that and be able to be okay . . . with every facet . . . there is to being Black. And whether you like it or not, whether you think it is beneath us or not . . . I'm gonna do it. . . . I'm gonna . . . be loud. And sometimes I just want to . . . show you how proper and . . . smart I am. . . . It shouldn't be about . . . my skin color. . . . But we get all of these stigmas put on us all the time. . . . My [White] ex[-boyfriend] even said to me, "You have to be one of the good ones." And I'm like, "You're an idiot. . . . There is no 'good ones.'"

Here Desirée vacillates from wanting to "be an example," which suggests conventional success, to embracing "every facet" of being Black in order to eliminate intra-group hierarchical divisions that cast some subgroups or behaviors as superior to others. This democratizing instinct deconstructs the notion of "good ones" and pushes back against value-laden judgments that condemn some subcultures. Using Desirée's phrase, to "push back against all that" (including respectability politics) is to agitate for respect on the Black community's own terms, in all its variations. In holistically honoring the internal diversity of Blackness, Desirée is "continuing to be a problem" (in the eyes of White society) by advocating for acceptance and equality of all versions of Blackness. In continuing to be a problem, respondents of color are arguing for rethinking how being "problematic" can trouble the status quo in favor of social change. Continuing to be a problem is a stratagem to vocalize inequalities and demand respect and visibility.

Double Consciousness as Intersectional: Respondents of Color on Positionality

Coining the term double consciousness, Du Bois wrote that African Americans are:

> born with a veil, and gifted with second-sight in this American world—a world which . . . only lets him see himself through the revelation of the other world. . . . It is a peculiar sensation, this double-consciousness, this sense of always looking at one's self through the eyes of others, of measuring one's soul by the tape of a world that looks on in amused contempt and pity.[48]

People of color who share in being labeled social problems share in double consciousness, for "the veil creates different subjectivities on different sides of the color line."[49] I illustrate here that double consciousness is fundamentally intersectional. Double consciousness as intersectional arises from being viewed as an *intersectional problem*, multiple hierarchies structuring this framing. Double consciousness as intersectional builds out double consciousness to show how additional axes of oppression operate *in combination with* racial subjugation. Double consciousness is contoured and complicated by multiple forms of marginality.

Intersectionality holds that several dimensions work "together in diverse and mutually inter-influencing ways" to create the conditions of social life.[50] Arguing that double consciousness is intersectional illuminates how racial oppression operates in nuanced ways when in combination with added axes of domination. Du Bois laid the groundwork for this elaboration, writing on the confluence of race and socioeconomic status, some crediting him with being a forefather of intersectionality.[51] Yet others find Du Bois's theorization of gender to be weak, leaving ample room for complication.[52] Over time, gender and sexuality have been woven into double consciousness, that is, "gendering double consciousness"[53] as a means to understand gendered racism.

Drawing attention to overarching racism, sexism, and classism that shape lives, there are parallels between Du Bois's double consciousness and Mexican American lesbian feminist writer Gloria Anzaldúa's "mestiza consciousness."[54] Anzaldúa conceives of "mestiza consciousness" as a "consciousness of the Borderlands" that finds resourcefulness in hybridity and malleability in "racial, ideological, cultural, and biological cross-pollination."[55] Like double consciousness, the ability to "juggle cultures" and have a "plural personality" is emblematic of mestiza consciousness.[56] Both thinkers theorize at the overlaps of oppressions, with Anzaldúa offering robust commentary on gender and sexuality which are underdeveloped in Du Bois's work.

Double consciousness and mestiza consciousness are both "epistemological constructions" that "emanat[e] from experience" and "illuminate experience."[57] Being subject to multiple oppressions are "common threads" that "bind" the work of Du Bois and Anzaldúa and underscore collective racialization processes.[58] As a guiding principle, both leverage experience and standpoint to better understand and theorize collective life. Double consciousness and mestiza consciousness also examine the interplay between oppression, oppressed subjectivity, resistance, and collective struggle.[59] For the purpose of holisitic comprehension of racialized people, all relevant forms of double consciousness and mestiza consciousness should be interrogated, as anything less risks yielding "an incomplete understanding of self-formation."[60] Theorizing about what Anzaldúa called *"los intersticios"* (intervening spaces between "different worlds" one inhabits) validates the existence within, and perspective stemming from, these liminal spaces.[61]

Double consciousness—or, mestiza consciousness—as intersectional recognizes that race functions in tandem with additional systems of oppression such as gender, sexuality, class status, religion, nationality, skin tone and more. Double consciousness remains a salient concept because it reveals the development of subjectivity—subjectivity being "the forms and patterns of understanding, thinking, and feeling about the self, other people, and the world we live in."[62] Racialized subjectivity is compounded by additional social systems that mete out advantage and disadvantage.

Double consciousness as intersectional is illustrated by Xavier Bow, a genderqueer Black person, who confides, "I think about queerness and race every day." Xavier tells me that they are uncertain why onlookers are intensely curious about them. Race and gender are inseparable in this conundrum: "Sometimes people will just be staring and I'm just like, 'Is it because of my hair? Is it because [laughter] of the fact that I'm a Black person in Oregon? Is it because [you] can't figure out what gender I am?'" Calling this predicament of public inquisitiveness "shitty," Xavier is left to guess whether their race or gender presentation is being disciplined by stares and loud conversations. By virtue of the "huge reaction to me just trying to live my life," Xavier is informed of multiple, intersecting hierarchies that others judge them to be transgressing.

Daliah Gansler (Mexican/Maltese/White) is race conscious as a result of seeing her Mexican-origin mom suffer slights. Because of her light skin, Daliah says she is "White-passing" ("I am so light that people just see the face value: 'Oh, she's a White chick'"). But Daliah's physical appearance belies her political commitments: She aligns herself with oppressed groups more than to Whiteness. Resentful that "marginalized people" are treated like "hot garbage," Daliah identifies with her maternal-line Mexican heritage, contributing to her intersectional double consciousness. I had asked how valued she feels in US society, to which Daliah replied:

> On a scale of one to ten, one being like the least valuable and ten being the most desirable, probably I would say a six. . . . I'm also a queer woman. . . . Double whammy. . . . I mean, *I* think I'm worth the Hope diamond (laughter) but . . . [in] society as a whole . . . I might not be as desirable.

Double consciousness is a multifactorial, intersectional state of being.

As a nonbinary masculine-presenting transgender person who identifies as Latino, Miguel Hernandez's double consciousness is attuned not just to race but also gender. Miguel catalogs their social value on a sliding scale as they review their identity categories: "As a man, I feel extremely valued. As a Brown person, not so much. As a trans person, not at all." These intersecting systems all contribute to Miguel's varying sense of social value and double consciousness that are both crosshatched by multiple hierarchies.

An indicator that double consciousness is intersectional, gendered racism spurs awareness of multiple axes of domination. Gendered racism is the negative synergy between racism and sexism that denigrates people of color and simultaneously upholds hegemonic White masculinity and femininity as a "normative standard."[63] For women of color, gender and sexuality inflected their double consciousness through gendered racism that dismisses or fetishizes them. Pacific Islander Keolohalani Teo remarks, "Me and my friends get annoyed . . . at how much men don't gravitate toward us . . . especially men of color. . . . We often get ignored . . . so our value is diminished." Vulnerable to decreased self-esteem by way of racialized beauty norms,[64] Keolohalani refers to Eurocentric beauty standards that affect not just women of color but men who, in her words, "internalize these things when they are looking for a partner"—and men's preferences then circle back to affect women of color. Activating the racial hierarchy, heteropatriarchy figures here as an arbiter of social value, adjudicated by heterosexual men's desire. Sexuality threads through gendered racism.

Whiteness as the prevailing standard of beauty, racial stereotypes, and sexual racism that fetishizes groups based on race influences interactions and is embedded in media such as song lyrics.[65] Yumiko Hoshiko (Asian American) recalls, "When I was younger, I used to hear songs that would fetishize Asian women. . . . I was like, 'Oh I'm special.' . . . But now, it's like, 'Fuck that, man! That's *so* messed up! . . . You don't care about me and about my identity." With age, Yumiko's intersectional understanding of double consciousness—how she and the multiple groups she holds membership in are perceived and treated by dominant groups—has strengthened. Over time, she perceives with greater acuity how the "other world" views Asian American women and she rejects the typecasting and tokenization of them.

Double consciousness as an intersectional optic where people of color possess "second sight" to see themselves the way dominating groups see them can affect behavior. Abdullah Jibran is US-born of Middle Eastern descent. He contends with gendered racism inflected with anti-Muslim animus that fomented "racialized surveillance" post–9/11[66] and positions Muslim Americans outside the national imaginary.[67] Doing "impression management"[68] to mitigate negative controlling images based on perceived race, gender, and religion, Abdullah repeats five times in the interview that he "censors" or "should censor" himself. Despite his legal standing in the United States, Abdullah perceives that his Muslim, Middle Eastern, and male identities collide to curb his constitutional rights. He publicly decried the Muslim travel ban and fundraised for legal funds for unaccompanied migrant children and believes his actions would be approved more often if he were White:

> [It's] my First Amendment right to say that . . . I think the system . . . is not right. And I feel really intimidated to say that because I will be perceived . . . [as] a Middle Eastern disgruntled angry man. They will say, "He doesn't like it here. He should go away. He doesn't belong here." . . . Maybe I should censor myself—and that's the hard thing. . . . [Chuckle] I should preface [this] with . . . I love my country and I love this community and I love the system and that's why I want to change it. Now, if you use this [example] in your book [and identify me as] White rather than Middle Eastern—which under the federal categorization is true—I might be called patriotic.

Contemplating how the same actions would likely be applauded if he were a White man, Abdullah's experience as a Muslim American man beleaguered by gendered racism and anti-Muslim sentiment exemplifies intersectional double consciousness. Speaking fervently about "First Amendment rights" (free exercise of religion, speech, press, peaceable assembly, and ability to petition the government for redress of grievances), Abdullah admits he would be quicker to dissent if he were a White man and Christian. He asserts his love for this country, fending off skepticism about his loyalty. Not socially defined as White (despite how the Census classifies him), Abdullah censors himself based on his "second sight." With an acute sense of intersectional double consciousness, including how people "presume [his] intentions," Abdullah ponders: "Do I have the right to dissent? And what's the level of dissent that I could establish and still be called patriotic?"

Again showing how intersectional double consciousness can direct emotions and delimit behavior, Praveen Kumar, a dark-skinned international student from southern India, remarked, "I was a little afraid [to come to the United States] because everything they show in the news is . . . students getting shot and security being tighter if you appear to be a Muslim. So my family made sure I took off all my beard and mustache and looked as innocent as possible." Due to global media, Praveen and his family learned of US-based gendered racism and acquired "racial baggage" even before setting foot on US soil.[69] In reaction, Praveen curated his body to avoid scrutiny upon entry to the United States at the airport.

As intersectionality scholars have long posited, race is co-constitutive of multiple axes of domination, conditioning the experience of race, racial subjectivity, and double consciousness. Double consciousness is intersectional, life experience modified by how social identities are arrayed in stratified social systems. This intersectional complexity affects the thoughts, emotions, and behaviors of people of color. Emphasizing that double consciousness is intersectional honors the ways in which racial subjectivity is punctuated, informed, animated, and made more complex by additional systems of domination.

White Respondents on Whiteness

White respondents disagreed with "being a problem" in the Du Boisian sense. They recognized that they sit at the apex of the racial hierarchy and feel comfortably included in the nation. Some White respondents stated that Whiteness is a problem. Such statements conveyed two meanings that operate at two levels: the individual (White people) and the structural (White supremacy). First, White respondents who perceive White *people* to be accused as responsible for racial inequality expressed White victimhood in an era of ebbing power. Second, White respondents who perceive *systems* of power as disadvantaging people of color and advantaging White people critiqued White supremacy as a structural problem. The chief divide is whether White respondents view the proposition that Whiteness is a problem as referring to *individuals* (and thereby places blame on them *personally*) or referring to a wider *structural problem* that is a *public* concern. If the notion of Whiteness as a problem is interpreted at the individual level, the person feels implicated in wrongdoing and responds by voicing victimization. If, however, the association of Whiteness with racism is seen as a *structural* problem *external to the self*, then White respondents could condemn White supremacy as a public problem. Externalization of the problem was a necessary stepping stone to criticizing systemic racism. This section draws from White respondents to reveal a number of themes: Whiteness as tantamount to national inclusion (even if White privilege can be "downgraded" by other identity features), White respondents as feeling victimized, and White respondents as critical of White supremacy.

White Privilege as Inclusion—but Downgradable by Intersecting Statuses

Du Bois was a forerunner in viewing Whiteness as a structural location in a system of domination. In Du Bois's words, White supremacy manifests in an "assumption that of all the hues of God whiteness alone is inherently and obviously better than brownness or tan" and motivates "ownership of the earth forever and ever, Amen!"[70] Beyond an identity category, Whiteness is a system of power that sustains Whiteness as a normative, default category to which other groups are compared. Whiteness can be defined as both "a racial identity and a dimension of social structure that privileges whites as the dominant group."[71] Whiteness as a structural location of privilege and a normative category feed into the "subtle omnipresence of whiteness."[72] Combined, these features of structural advantage and normativity position White respondents to declare themselves included in US society with ease.

All White respondents perceive that Whiteness grants them automatic inclusion in the United States. Aware of her White privilege, Lizzie Rhodes stated, "I don't feel actively excluded because I don't feel targeted by anybody or anything. . . . I'm White and so people don't feel the need to argue with me." Whiteness is an escape hatch from racial targeting and a route to social power. Kathleen Post believes that nothing is off-limits by virtue of her race: "Going off the privilege [theme], I've never . . . felt like there were certain things that I couldn't necessarily do because of my race. . . . I was never like: 'Oh! That's gonna be a tough field for me to get into because I'm White.'" Zeke Luck addresses how White people are socialized to expect White privilege: "I feel included as a White person, yeah. . . . I think that sometimes I don't realize what my privilege gets me and it's just so ingrained that I don't even see it. I *totally* believe that." White privilege as "ingrained" speaks to how White privilege is instilled as an expectation for White people.

Most White respondents acknowledged White privilege ("the often unseen benefits of occupying a structurally rewarded position in society"[73]). Yet, not all White privilege is created equal. Since Whiteness does not exist in isolation but coexists among multiple social identities—all carrying degrees of privilege and oppression—it can be amplified or downgraded. Whiteness is augmented or tarnished by social features such as gender, sexuality, class status, marital status, religion, and more.

Marie Varnum describes Whiteness as an "invisible barrier" that protects her. Yet, even with an invisible barrier of Whiteness that shields her from racism, Marie's White privilege is downgraded by her class and marital status: "I think that 'single mom' thing really put me on a different status level. . . . I do feel like being a White single mom . . . sucks but it could have been a lot worse if I was a woman of color." She adds body size to this equation. Marie uses self-deprecating humor to draw an image of herself: "I'm White and overweight. . . . I look like one of those women that probably just lived off welfare . . . with my little tank top on and my shorts that are too tight, my muffin top [stomach fat] hanging out [laughing]." Referring to Whiteness as the emboldened feeling of "the world is your oyster," Marie comments that, for her, "[The oyster] is kind of grainy with sand [laughing]." Marie's privilege is subtracted by lower-class status, body size, and single motherhood. Possessing oppressed identities acts as a counterweight that can downgrade White privilege.

Non-racial aspects of White respondents' identities can be seen as a problem. Two of the most frequently cited non-racial aspects of identity that respondents volunteered as being treated as problems by society are gender and sexual orientation. Women (cisgender and transgender) and people who identify as non-heterosexual or lesbian, gay, bisexual, transgender, and queer (LGBTQ) raised these complaints. Lizzie Rhodes lands on her status as a woman when she reflects on whether the Du Boisian "problem" question resounds with her:

> No. I would say that as a White person, I don't feel that at all. As a woman, I can definitely resonate with that. Yeah. Being a woman [I] definitely feel like the problem and it's like [you're being told], "Shut up. . . . Why are you making so much noise? . . . Why are you fighting for your rights?" So relevant. I feel that a lot. . . . Definitely as a woman you can identify with that a lot.

Lizzie delineates being a woman as a subordinated vector of her identity; she becomes a problem when she asserts herself around gender equality issues.

Chance Green, a White trans man, speaks to being a "problem" as a transgender person: "When I think about trans people, we're often created in this image of being a problem. That we don't fit into the bathroom correctly, that we don't have documentation of our gender that makes sense and is coherent with the data keeping systems, right?" Stressing the social construction of problems, groups are "created" as problems by the dominant group that holds the power of categorization.

White Victimhood: Subjection to Generalizations Does Not Feel Good

Some White men spoke of White victimhood. In a patriarchal White supremacist system, White men have reason to believe they should be accorded a double dose of privilege on account of their gender and race. White people regarding themselves as oppressed and under attack has been called "embattled victimhood"; in essence, they are "suffering because they are white."[74] A few White men respondents who took an individualist view of Whiteness felt that they are blamed for wrongs of White supremacy and they mourn the privilege White identity loses once it is decried as connected to a system of power.

Speaking at the individual level, Doug Miller was animated when he complained of being subjected to stereotypes about White men:

> DOUG: Some people *are* angry at me. A couple people who have
> worked [with me] . . . they *hated* me. Every small mistake that I made
> was just fuel for their fire and they hated me because I was a White
> man. They hated the owner of [retail store] who was an older White
> man as well. . . . Both of them were White women.
> JVT: Why were they hating you?
> DOUG: I don't know. . . . My best understanding is because I'm a White
> male oppressor because I was in a position of authority. I'm White
> and I'm an older man. . . . Suicides of White men are going up.

Doug raises contentious work relationships as evidence of victimization as a White man. Suggesting that White men are increasingly feeling dissatisfied with shifting racial and gender dynamics and discourses, Doug references climbing suicide rates. His telling risks distorting trends by abstracting his own race/gender category, however. Data from the Centers for Disease Control and Prevention show that suicide rates rose for *all* racial categories between 2011 and 2021 (and the percentage change was actually lowest for White people).[75] In his narrative, Doug points to defamation by group-based stereotypes as the reason for work tension. He is distressed about not being seen as an individual and mal-treatment, not unlike how respondents of color react to racial prejudice and discrimination. Accustomed to living at the pinnacle of racial and gender hierarchies, Doug is aghast when he is reduced to group statuses and treated as if he were a generalized representative of a group. This perspective on group-based stereotypes could have been an opportunity to be in solidarity with people of color who are often caught in nets of racial stereotypes, but it was not.

White victimhood creeps into Dylan Johnson's narrative when he claims that people overgeneralize about White people. When Dylan gets a taste of being homogenized based on his racial group—a regular oc-currence for people of color—he decidedly dislikes it:

> We [White people] kind of all get bunched together with—I'll use the president [Trump] for example—just 'cause we might look somewhat similar but don't have the same beliefs whatsoever. . . . Sometimes we all get grouped together. . . . When he's up there speaking . . . especially when it comes to a sensitive topic . . . a lot of people feel that that's the consen-sus of White Caucasians in America and it's . . . not.

For Dylan, even if he disagrees with Trump, their shared White racial status means that Trump's words are projected onto him unfairly. Dylan feels himself to be a victim of racial homogenization: "The repercussions are: 'Well, *you guys* all believe.'" Not unlike people of color who must positively distinguish themselves from a negative model, Dylan draws symbolic boundaries with Donald Trump: "I don't see things exactly the same as the president. I think he's his own circus act."

The parallels between Dylan's sense of White victimhood and the everyday experience of people of color being hemmed in by racist preconceptions were not lost on him. I asked him, "So how does that make you feel—having to respond to issues [of group stereotyping] as a White person?" He replied, "It makes me sad that other people perceive it that way, but then it also makes me look at myself and realize I do the same thing . . . in reverse, basically. . . . I'm just as guilty as the next person, although everybody likes to think they're open-minded." In this moment of self-reflexive insight Dylan does two things: He has an awakening about how he is wrong to overgeneralize about other people based on race while at the same time he positions Whiteness as similarly victimized by group-based assumptions. On the one hand, Dylan's self-reflexivity is instructive, as he recognizes he has work to do to bring his ethics in alignment with his actions. On the other hand, his view that Whiteness parallels the experience of people of color does not square with the power dynamics of White supremacy that preserves his structural position of racial privilege.

White Respondents Critical of White Privilege: The Problem Is White Supremacy

A substantial subset of the White respondents (principally women and people who identify as LGBTQ) sees themselves as engaged in anti-racist struggles and as allies to people of color. These White respondents take a structural view of White supremacy, seeing the system as overarching, already built, and predating them. Even as these White respondents recognize they benefit from the racial order (and some pondered aloud how to relinquish privilege), they cast a quizzical eye at their participation in the system, but without blame so much as a sense of agency to move toward justice. Many of these self-identified anti-racist White respondents work in social services or education.

A distinction between White respondents who took an individual versus system view of Whiteness was apparent, yet there was slippage. Respondents sometimes lumped together White people and racist structures. While this conflation of people and structures flags that White people benefit from White supremacy, analyzing people separately from structures allows for White people who are cognizant of racial domination and challenge it. Lizzie Rhodes shows how a structure of White privilege that conceals itself infiltrates individual thought processes when she says: "Whites are the problem in thinking that other folks are the problem. . . . So we are the problem, but we're not seeing it that way." As Marie Varnum notes, standpoint matters a great deal: "My Whiteness is not a problem for me, but it is a problem for other people." The White interviewees who brought the sharpest critical lens to Whiteness and White privilege were women (both cisgender and transgender) and nonbinary/genderqueer individuals. Being subjugated by gender identity, gender expression, or sexual orientation correlates in my data with identifying and calling out additional systems of oppression, even if one currently benefits from them.

White racial progressives do not adhere to colorblind rhetoric that minimizes racism with claims such as "the past is the past"[76] but, instead, acknowledge that racial discrimination is central to society. Even if White racial progressives feel hamstrung about how to best influence social change, their starting point is the admission that White supremacy is a problem. Tess Smith ponders whether Du Bois's question applies to her as a White person:

> Yeah, how does it feel to be a problem? Um, hmm. [laughing] I think [pause] that [pause] as a White person I *am* a problem. As a beneficiary of a system, I am a problem. And, and it's hard. . . . As an individual person I'm like, "Well no, I try really hard to do good things." But, I don't wanna say White people are a problem and not count myself in that. . . . I mean, an entire system was set up over time slowly to benefit specific people. And I still benefit from it. That's a problem.

White racial progressives expressed discomfort, regret, and even present-day culpability (such as being a beneficiary of an unequal system). Tess struggles to disentangle herself as an individual from the unfair racial system in which she is embedded; she speaks in personal terms ("I *am* a problem") even as she recognizes that the problem is the "entire system." In using the word "system" twice in the above quotation, she acknowledges her racial inheritance without feeling affronted by the idea that White people, as a privileged group, constitute a problem from the perspective of communities of color. Because Tess views racial inequality as a systemic public problem, acknowledging the White privilege she holds is not offensive to her. Tess collapses White privilege into human rights: "I guess privileges are privileges because they're not given to everyone. . . . I think a lot of the times the things that we say are White privilege are actually just basic human rights." In her view, White supremacy is the problem and an ensuing problem for White people is what to do about their unearned advantages.

For Nellie Locke, the problem of Whiteness is not locked in history, no matter the temptation for White people to minimize racism. Nellie balances critically assessing White privilege as a structural problem with trying to ameliorate race relations through individual action:

> You know how White people say, "Oh, I don't see color"? You can't say you don't see color because that's like [saying] you don't see all the hardships that [people of color have] gone through. So, I'm not going to say I don't see color and . . . half-ass that. I'm going to say, I don't see *enough* color.

This color consciousness is an attempt to correct for power evasiveness that obscures power structures.

White respondents who argue White supremacy and White beneficiaries of unearned privilege are a problem invert the usual narrative that disparages people of color as problems. Chance Green "flips the narrative" when answering the "how does it feel to be a problem" question this way:

> Yeah. In reverse, though, right? Like, White people are the problem, actually. White people are fascinated with solving the problems of communities of color without ever really being in community. . . . And we do this in very race-neutral terms: through school policies, through . . . debating in [my] county about adding another jail. No, I don't want more jails . . . because I know whose bodies are going to be put in that jail. So, no, I don't want another fucking jail. . . . We're trying to flip the narrative . . . like, how have White people created problems that now get . . . filtered back to communities of color to now fix?

Casting a wide net to include people, policies, and institutions, Chance shows how racism moves between people and systems, racism becoming institutionalized over time. Eschewing a divide between people and systems, Chance connects the dots between the past and the present:

> White people want to give ourselves a pass of, "Well, I didn't own any slaves," or "It's not my fault that Indigenous people were displaced and

killed." And it's like, "Okay, but, you didn't plant the cabbage and you still got to eat it, so. . . . [chuckles]. Right? You still got the goodies, right?" . . . We want to back ourselves out of the problem.

Even if White people who reap benefits of White privilege did not originate the system, they nonetheless garner advantage.

Among White respondents, women and LGBTQ-identified respondents were most likely to characterize White supremacy as a problem. Oppressed by other systems of domination (gender and sexuality), these respondents viewed racial inequality as resulting from a *system* of White supremacy. White women and White LGBTQ-identified respondents being overrepresented in critiquing White supremacy is in concert with the observation that working-class White women are more inclined to be "race traitors" and not endorse colorblind ideology,[77] likely on account of being familiar with gender and class oppressions. Even as experiencing oppression does not automatically translate to a certain consciousness (people may need a vocabulary and community to raise their consciousness[78]), the trend here suggests that subordination on one axis of privilege/oppression may position people to recognize other forms of oppression.

Conclusion

This chapter asks whether and why respondents of varying racial backgrounds believe that US society deems them a problem. A clear non-White/White divide cleavage emerged. Respondents of color receive the message that they are seen as racially problematic in numerous ways: non-White bodily presence and appearance treated as ill-fitting and unwelcome; the derision of non-English language use; land destruction directed by imperial expansion; and concern over population change and presumed intransigent cultural differences between White people and people of color.

Respondents of color used two counternarratives in reacting to the messaging that they are regarded as a social problem. Bucking dominant narratives that disparage people of color and uphold White supremacy, one counternarrative rejects the framing of people of color as problems outright and the other coopts the language of "problem" and proposes to *continue* to be a problem to facilitate social change. Since "problem" status is not cordoned off to racial status alone, this chapter argues that double consciousness remains a valuable tool for understanding social lives and demonstrates that double consciousness is intersectional, folding in additional axes of privilege and oppression.

In stark contrast to respondents of color, White respondents felt included in the nation based on race, even if some felt social demerits based on non-racial social identities. Whiteness is a source of privilege and an entrance ticket to automatic inclusion in the nation. Yet, White privilege is downgradable: Membership in one or more undervalued category (such as relative to gender, class, or sexuality) tarnishes White racial privilege. Not categorized as a *racial* problem, some White respondents pivoted to discuss how they are viewed as problems as women, working-class or poor, transgender, or a sexual minority. Whether White respondents view racism as individual or structural led to two distinct responses: White victimhood or a critique of White supremacy. Accustomed to advantage and on edge about being accused of being racist, a few White men begrudged what they perceived as a loss of status for White men, this diminishment of prestige a *personal problem* for them that augured a victimhood narrative. A polar opposite response was articulated by a handful of White respondents (almost exclusively women and people who identify as LGBTQ) who viewed White supremacy as a *structural problem*. They were critics of systemic racism. This individualistic-or-structural perspective split among White respondents demonstrates how gender and sexuality inequality suffuses mindsets: Sitting at a status apex leads to anxiety about status loss, whereas people with marginalized identities are more likely to detect subordination and denounce unfair systems.

3

On Being "American"

Belonging as Indexed by Race

Seamlessly claiming the title of "American" and being identified by others as "American" is facilitated or hindered by race. Consider a pair of vignettes. Jubilee Thompson is a twenty-five-year-old White woman with pale skin, blue eyes, and long, blonde hair. She describes a popularized image of American, as she sees it: "Somebody who's . . . White, strong, beautiful, and has money." She fits this description, as mirrored in her statement: "I don't feel like anything has ever prevent[ed] me from being a part of the US." Jubilee fits the reified image of a White American and sits in a privileged position. Intuiting a protective effect of Whiteness,[1] she continues, "If I called the police, they would come." She is confident the nation's institutions will work in her favor.

Malia Kealoha, a nineteen-year-old woman of Samoan descent born in Hawaiʻi, says that if Whiteness is a precondition for Americanness then she is an "outsider" due to her Polynesian background. The image of American she carries in her head is "the White population." Malia's physical appearance of chestnut color skin and long, straight dark hair with bleached-blonde highlights marks her: "I'm seen as an outsider. . . . It has its drawbacks. People will always look at you funny because you don't look like the majority of the US." Malia considers herself American because the United States is her place of birth. Malia calls herself an "untraditional American": "We're not the traditional Americans. . . . You probably wouldn't think of some little Filipino, Samoan Hawaiian girl . . . as the first image of being American. We're definitely the untraditional American or vision. . . . We're just not what would first pop into your head as an American."

Whiteness delineates inclusion in the United States. Whiteness has long been the "default" racial category in the United States.[2] Thus, White respondents most easily claim American belonging whereas respondents of color present an array of complex or qualified answers ("yes, but. . . ."). Such hesitations or justifications that respondents of color make are a burden of belonging to a nation that holds dearly to a White hegemonic core, even as demographics are shifting toward greater racial diversity. Among recent newlyweds, one in six pairs inter-married across racial groups and a total of 10% of married people have a partner from a different racial or ethnic category than their own.[3] In 2017, one of every seven births (14.1%) were to parents from different racial backgrounds, three-quarters of which were to White-minority parent combinations.[4] Yet the national imaginary remains White. Bur-dened belonging connotes membership that is weighed down by con-ditions and racial baggage, a peripheral status relative to a national identity that is exaggerated as White.

First, this chapter proceeds by establishing Whiteness as foundational to respondents' conception of an ideal American and types of belong-ing this sets up: undisputed Americans and fact-of-the-matter Ameri-cans. Second, the chapter lays out barriers to belonging that maintain a White/non-White divide: a majority-White landscape that naturalizes Whiteness as conjoined to Americanness, the ongoing legacy of slavery and anti-Black racism, colonial status that signals subordination to an imperial power, legal status that demarcates formal exclusion, and White gatekeepers who police racial boundaries. Third, I demonstrate that ra-cial formation (the process of racialization and racial group boundary development) occurs both collectively and relationally. Finally, absent Whiteness that is required for unbridled American membership, people of color in the United States are tasked with establishing their belonging. Respondents of color strived to create belonging in three ways: building relationships that constitute "concentric circles of belonging," arguing in favor of diversifying a definition of American that extends beyond Whiteness, and situating their value in global and decolonial perspec-tives that decenter the United States.

The "Ideal" Image of American as White

Whiteness Paired with Americanness

Whiteness in the United States functions as a structural location of privilege and is the default racial category against which others are measured.[5] To be White affords "the opportunity to be included in the civic, political, and economic life of the nation."[6] Whiteness is associated with Americanness, "Americanness" thus contributing to the self-esteem of White people, an effect not accessible to members of other groups.[7] As the introduction covers, there is historical legal precedent that enshrines Whiteness as a venerated, precondition of Americanness. Myriad laws and practices, from the 1790 Naturalization Act which established Whiteness as a naturalization prerequisite to Muslim bans and border walls, support this vision. It is no accident that the image of a financially secure White person infiltrates respondents' answers about the profile of an "ideal" American. Given this context, White respondents easily consider themselves American. In contrast, respondents of color rattle off justifications for being American (such as birthright citizenship) or they qualify what they mean when they say they are American (such as deliberately not adhering to a White-only definition).

The "ideal" American is envisioned as White—a message that is received loud and clear by all respondents, irrespective of race. Rachel Jones, mixed-race, answers the question, "is there an ideal type of American that the media or society generally portrays?" with: "If you're going real basic . . . I picture . . . White parents with the two and a half children, picket fence, two-story house, two-stall garage . . . blonde, blue eyes." Karrie Matthews, Hawaiian, simply says, "White people are American." Pearl Hashimoto, Asian American, refers to media: "It's always predominantly a White person [chuckle]. And then they throw in a person of color to spice it up [laughter]." "Spice" has an exotic implication, conjuring up imagery of faraway places that are geographically and culturally distant and, when applied to women, the term has sexualized overtones.[8]

Whiteness is central to dominant portrayals of Americanness. Kealohalani Teo puts it bluntly, "I don't think that I could ever be the face of America." I asked why not and she replied: "Because I'm not a White male. . . . Just imagining what someone who's American looks like . . . definitely it would be [a] White male, maybe a White woman. . . . Definitely Whiteness. And then a degree of attractiveness, but again based off of Western ideals." Even when vacillating about the centrality of women to visions of an ideal American, Whiteness remains the constant qualifier. An international student from Sudan, Africa, Bogga Deta sees Whiteness tied to American identity so tightly that she thinks *even citizenship* could not override her Blackness enough to make her feel American. Calling herself an "outsider to the US," I ask if anything could change that status. She replied: "If I get a citizenship that will make me an insider. And to be *fully American* is by me turning into a whole different person, you know? Yeah, become White, blonde." Even legal status would not be sufficient to make Bogga American—for "turning into a whole different person," physical features and all, is impossible. Secondary to being White, an "ideal American" has secured economic belonging and is understood as middle-class or wealthy.[9] Paul Lee, Vietnamese American, rank orders requirements of Americanness: "To be American . . . is really to be White. . . . Having a property is also a big thing. . . . So it's like: color of skin and property." Jo Paz, Latinx/White, links middle-class standing and English proficiency to a White prerequisite to Americanness: "Let's face it, they have White skin [chuckles], [are middle-class,] and they speak English well."

White People as Undisputed Americans

White respondents easily considered themselves American because they fit the racial profile. Marie Varnum outright laughs at my question that anyone might not consider her American: "[laughing] Not American? No. . . . I guess being a pale White person, you don't really hear that." Expressing an opinion that is unanimous among White respondents, Marie notes her automatic belonging by sheer virtue of her Whiteness. My conversation with Dylan Johnson lays out Whiteness as so commonly understood a requirement for Americanness that his identity as an American has never been questioned:

JVT: Do you consider yourself American?
DYLAN: [long pause] Well I guess, yeah. I've never been asked that question but if I didn't consider myself American, I guess I'd feel pretty lost.
JVT: Without it, you'd feel lost, so with it, you feel . . . ?
DYLAN: Well I think everybody kind of wants to feel a sense of belonging. . . . A sports reference . . . but you want to be on a team, you want to have that kind of camaraderie.

To follow Dylan's sports analogy, Whiteness is a jersey that instantly testifies to belonging.

Whiteness equals unparalleled belonging in the United States. Chance Green reflects on how their Whiteness "securely fasten[s]" them to the United States:

> When I'm in this United States, I don't ever really feel questioned. . . . I don't feel like my belonging is really up for debate. It's not. . . . Whiteness affords me to be securely fastened to the United States. . . . I have light hair and light eyes, and I'm pale, right? And so I'm seen as belonging here.

Continuing, Chance addresses the cognitive dissonance between the racial heterogeneity of the nation and what is idealized:

> Some of it is related to our *imagination* of, "What does an American look like?" Even though we know there's no "one look," right? *Logically* we know this, but our schema is different. . . . When I think about . . . what we *uphold*, I think this is blonde-haired, blue eyes, White guys.

Schemas are "mental structures that represent knowledge and process information" and they refer "not just [to] groups of categories, but a complex of information about the relationships among them."[10] This definition of schema is helpful in considering how a dominant schema (e.g., of Whiteness associated with US belonging) is outsized and shoves non-dominant categories of people to the periphery.

Fact-of-the-matter Americans

"Fact-of-the-matter Americans" are respondents of color who legitimize their Americanness as a "fact" due to birthright because their non-Whiteness makes Americanness feel tenuous. Birthright citizenship is an "egalitarian promise," a "color-blind and class-blind path to membership" that rest on ideals of inclusion and equality.[11] Despite birthright citizenship legitimized in the Fourteenth Amendment of the US Constitution, many respondents of color testify that their status as Americans feels conditional and peripheral. Yet because of birthright citizenship, these respondents of color claim the legal descriptor of American, even as they feel racially or culturally set apart. This sense of exclusion is in concert with work on Latinos from Chicago, Illinois, which finds "ethnoracial nationalism" ("race and/or culture determines who belongs")[12] but is at odds with findings on Mexican Americans in Los Angeles, California, and San Antonio, Texas, that maintain that ethnic (Mexican American) and national (American) identities are "highly compatible and complementary."[13] While many factors may be at play here, region may be one. Who makes up and takes up space? The former study was located in a site where Latinos were a numerical minority, whereas the latter study was located in spaces with Latino populations well above (even double) the non-Hispanic White population. While numbers do not tell the whole story, they color a place and clarify or obfuscate possibilities for meaningful belonging. Circulating in an "ethnic core" (an ethnic community and ethnic social structures) maintains or strengthens ethnicity, ethnic identity coexisting with a national one, rather than one antithetical to the other.[14] In my Oregon field site, restrictive racist history shapes the present demographics where the non-Hispanic White category overwhelms all other groups (at 76% and 77% of the population for the two city hubs where I conducted interviews). This "White space" context visually supports the notion of unquestioned Americanness as reserved for White people. Fact-of-the-matter Americans are respondents of color who claim Americanness by stating "the facts" (such as birthright citizenship), these factual assertions made in response to racial limits to belonging that are more obvious in a largely White context.[15]

Most respondents of color who were born in, or spent most of their lives in, the United States call themselves American. Yet they volunteer that they do not fit the racial mold. These respondents of color who asserted their Americanness trouble the White racial predicate of American identity and widen it to include themselves. Minor Hun, born in Vietnam and a US veteran, remarked: "I consider myself American . . . but . . . being an American . . . doesn't mean I have to wholeheartedly . . . [be] head over heels falling into . . . American culture. . . . Because it's a melting pot and I have a right to be . . . who I am as American: have my own tastes, have my own attitude and my own personality." Minor wants to be American and authentically himself in terms of race and culture.

Oftentimes, fact-of-the-matter Americans claim Americanness but eschew White cultural dominance. Pearl Hashimoto said, "Yeah, I guess," when asked if she considered herself American. She followed with, "Yes, I guess, but not in a way that I would be like '*America, fuck yeah.*' We don't really rep[resent] America [laughter]." Pearl refers to Asian Americans as excluded from race-coded imagery of the United States: "We don't consider ourselves to be the face of America."

Latinos, like Miguel Hernandez, talked about the difficulty of identifying as American because that title allies them with a country that houses anti-Latino racism. Birthplace and culture mark Miguel as American, yet they equivocate. Miguel is a fact-of-the-matter-American due to birthplace and culture, yet they are also on the receiving end of racial discrimination: "There are a lot of Americans who are like myself: Brown, born here, know what's going on in American pop culture and music, blah, blah, blah. But there are a lot of ways in which I don't feel like an American based on how White Americans treat me." This White exclusivity is also observed by Jo Paz (Latinx/White), who remarks, "So many Mexican American families that I know—their children are born here—feel so constantly attacked because people are questioning their citizenship all the time." Miguel and Jo imply that Latinos should be able to claim Americanness yet they do not possess full-fledged belonging by virtue of race.[16]

African Americans are well represented in the fact-of-the-matter American category. Xavier Bow says American is "not a primary identifier," and yet they would "check a box on a form" to indicate American if asked. Shayla Pierre chuckled at the question of her Americanness, saying, "Yeah, yeah. [chuckles] I mean I live here, I do what is asked of me." But then she moves on to loyalty to the administration, saying, "[For] some people being an American means you have to support [former] president [Trump], but I don't. And so, in some people's eyes, I'm not an American, but . . . yeah, I'm an American." Shayla's allegiance is filtered through her racial group affiliation. Because Shayla feels that her life is strongly shaped by her Blackness, she possesses a "linked fate" with other Black people in the United States.[17] This sentiment is in concert with survey research which finds that a majority of Black adults (81%) feel at least somewhat connected to a broader Black community in the United States and that being Black is extremely (52%) or very

(22%) important to how they think about themselves.[18] By comparison, only 15% of White adults (and 59% of Hispanic adults and 56% of Asian adults) see race as a central piece of their identity.[19]

Delinking Whiteness from "Americanness"

The linkage between Whiteness and Americanness did not go unchallenged. Some respondents of color questioned the very foundation of Americanness, an identity stemming from a nation built on Indigenous lands by African slave labor. This historicization of national identity subverts the fusion of American with Whiteness. In this alternative version of American identity, respondents of color articulate a multiracial and race-conscious Americanness that remembers and reckons with the fact that the nation was built on violently stolen Indigenous land by the toil of enslaved people torn from African homelands. In this rendering, the United States is not a supreme entity but a historical actor. Understanding the nation as historically constructed and with vested interests opens up space for respondents of color to be both American and non-White. Respondents disentangling Whiteness from Americanness are engaging in "politics of belonging" that challenge hegemonic political powers,[20] contest the reproduction of boundaries, and re-determine the bounds of the collectivity.

Leles Talbot (Native American) and Desirée Robinson (African American) ground their belonging in what is now the United States through ancestral lineage that predates the 1776 founding of the nation. As women of color whose ties to North American geography extend back several generations, the yardstick they use to measure claim to the nation is not Whiteness but existence, toil, and survival on the land. As Native American and African American, these women attest that the United States would not exist if not for usurpation of their ancestors' lands and labor. If anyone is American, they are.

In answer to the question "do you consider yourself American?" Leles replied, "I do. I consider myself *the first American*." She paused to let her words sink in. "I believe that foreigners came to my land and became part of my Americanism." Indigenous to these lands, Leles' Americanism predates the starting date of the United States. As "first American" she establishes her lineage and relationship to the land. Leles turns the tables on the "discovery of new lands" narrative by citing her ancestors' presence prior to the arrival of White settlers. She is clear in her Americanness: "I consider myself American. This is the country I live in. It's the country of my birth. I consider myself very loyal to the country." Leles stresses her Indigeneity and honors her multiple identities in introductions: "I identify in my tribal language first . . . and then I translate into English. . . . So I consider myself American and I consider myself 'first American.'" Leles is both a member of a tribal sovereign nation and the United States. In claiming both identities, Leles subverts the notion that there is room for allegiance to only one nation and she rejects the collapsing of Americanness into Whiteness.

A few respondents of color, like Desirée Robinson, staunchly held to the title American to claim space as Americans who are also people of color. There is a racial equality impulse embedded in staking claim to a country that one's own enslaved ancestors built. When I asked if Desirée considers herself American, she replied, "Yes. Super." Her fierce grip on American identity is a response to the African diaspora, slavery, and racial capitalism. Desirée continues:

> I've always had this connection to the fact that I am . . . part of . . . America. . . . I just hold that with me a lot. . . . I guess it may be subconsciously in my head like . . . my ancestors were brought here, they did what they could. And I'm here just like Joe Blow over there is from here. . . . They're not any more American . . . than I am. . . . Being a part of America was just always big to me.

Desirée refers to slave ancestors that she assumes she has because she's "African American and so it just makes sense." She grounds her claim to US membership in forced migration and generations worth of lineage. She implicitly calls for racial equality, marking her American status as equal to that of "Joe Blow over there" (notably, a masculine Anglophone name). Linking past to present, Desirée fast-forwards to the anti-Black racism she experiences and doubles down on her American status:

> Damn, yeah, I do feel even today in 2021 . . . a lot of people who are . . . non persons of color are on this kick like, "if you have any type of melanin in your skin, well, you should be grateful that you're an American."

And I'm like, "Nah . . . I'm probably more American than you are." Because . . . you talk about what . . . our ancestors went through . . . to be here—being brought or not—what they achieved while they were here and all of the issues that they dealt with. . . . Yeah, I'm American.

Descendants of slaves as "probably more American" challenges the primacy of Whiteness in conceptions of Americanness. In this rendering, it is by enduring hardship in the making of the nation that Desirée claims an irreducible status as American. The term "non persons of color" also de-centers Whiteness, centering instead "persons of color" and tacking on a "non" to refer to White people. This rhetorical technique puts people of color center stage. Another African American respondent who also assumed slave lineage, Tahj Hayes, remarked: "I know my ancestors died just for us. . . . I know somebody died for me just to sit in this apartment, to be able to go to school, to be able to have a degree, to be able to have a career. I'm celebrating my people as unapologetically Black." By hailing their enslaved ancestors, these African American respondents establish vital presence at the founding of the nation and proclaim their undeniable Americanness.

Barriers to Belonging

What is at stake in perceiving Whiteness as tantamount to Americanness? Belonging. Belonging is experiential and expansive.[21] Referring to positively identifying with a group, belonging is socially mediated.[22] In the context of societal organization that is hierarchical, infused with crisscrossing and compounding processes that privilege and oppress, capacity for belonging and impediments to belonging reflect unequal social power, including political representation, economic opportunity, and "cultural citizenship."[23] Reactions to the question "Do you consider yourself American?" varied by race. White respondents quickly said yes. Respondents of color expressed outsider status or Americanness that was burdened by conditionality and marginality. Chief barriers to belonging affecting people of color include: a majority-White racial landscape that naturalizes Whiteness as Americanness; the history of Black enslavement and present-day anti-Black racism; colonial status, especially affecting Native Americans and Pacific Islanders; legal status; and White gatekeepers who police the boundary line of Whiteness and non-Whiteness.

Majority-White Landscape Naturalizes Whiteness as Americanness

Local context (what geographers call "place" or "space") is an important driver of racial meanings, including the fusion between Whiteness and Americanness. Racism is a grounded phenomenon: Racism occurs in *places* ("where") as much as through processes ("how").[24] "Place" harbors cultural meanings that people invest in a specific geographic location. The racial project of Whiteness undergirds the spatialization of race and the racialization of space.[25] Examples of this dual phenomenon include plantations, prisons, and ghettos as well as segregated neighborhoods, schools, and workplaces. Space is an agent of racialization, influencing the creation of race and racial categories and the subjective experience of them.[26] This territorial logic of a "spatial imaginary"[27] extends to an *extra*-spatial imaginary that signals degrees of belonging in both a local community and an "imagined community"[28] of the nation.

Space and place are not inert but, rather, a crucible of racial dynamics that reveal power, stimulate or curb belonging, and influence the racialization of self and others. This section draws exclusively from respondents with affiliations (past or present) with either of the two research universities in my two field sites. The Oregon Public University system (to which University of Oregon and Oregon State University belong) has diversified over time, albeit student enrollment remains overwhelmingly White. From 2011 to 2020, student enrollment data by race for the entire Oregon Public University system show White student decline from 68% to 59%. Native American/Alaska Native, Native Hawaiian/Pacific Islander, and Black/African American student enrollment remain slim and steady across the nine years, at 1%, approximately 0.5%, and 2% respectively.[29] Asian American (5% to 7%), Hispanic/Latinx (6% to 13%), and the "two or more" race category (3% to 6%) saw gains in student enrollment in the 2011–2020 window.[30] It is in this continued majority-White environment, but with White student enrollment giving way to a slowly diversifying student body, where tensions around who has unquestioned authority to exist in a space play out on the ground. Sheer numbers do not automatically equate to belonging. Power is always at issue. Universities tend to endorse "diversity of convenience": They implement policies to increase the size of underrepresented groups but without redistributing power to support pluralism, a situation that can backfire and devolve into a hostile climate.[31]

For people of color who moved to Oregon from racially heterogeneous places, what are their prospects for "homemaking"[32] in their new, predominately White environment? What road bumps do they encounter in this relocation and adaptation process? This section demonstrates that majority-White towns naturalize the fusion of Americanness and Whiteness, a dizzying phenomenon for people of color who relocated to Oregon from more racially diverse locales.

Rosie Patel (mixed-race Asian, White, South American, Pacific Islander) refers to the racialization of space (including the racialization of *herself in space*) when she says plainly, "I never thought of my race being a problem until I moved to Oregon." She explains the "shock" of trading a racially heterogenous environment for a predominately White one:

> I think my shift from going from the Bay Area [California] to [Oregon town] was such a huge culture shock for me in a negative way. . . . Now I'm constantly defending my presence. Like, "No, no, no, I *am* an American citizen" [or] "No, no, no, I was *born* here." "No, no, no, I speak English, English is my first language."

To rebut assumptions about her foreignness, Rosie says "no" nine times in two sentences that replay scenes where White people are suspicious of granting her inclusion in "their" space. Rosie bitingly remarks about the minimal diversity she sees: "diversity is nothing without inclusion." In her assessment, her town "is not willing to include that diversity." When people in her community are "not willing to have conversations around race," attention is directed away from race as an organizing principle of social life and therefore precludes meaningful relations with, and belonging for, people of color. Insistence on colorblindness allows an epistemology of ignorance to strengthen wherein White people innovate "color-blind logics that foreclose . . . racially conscious learning."[33] Having attended a university in California where she felt "belonging because it was more diverse" and then living in the San Francisco Bay Area, where "everybody is mixed-race," Rosie was jolted by Oregon. She explains the impact of Oregon Whiteness on her: "[Brownness is] not something that I claimed before. . . . But, I'm finding myself having to claim that [Brownness] now. It's a forced kind of a claim. . . . It's a hard realization for me to see that people *only* identify me based on what they see as the color of my skin." Racialization shaped by place is a sharp injury for those coming from more diverse locations who must reckon with race anew in a majority-White space that naturalizes Whiteness as core and favored.

Racially heterogeneous geographies are not devoid of race, of course, but they offer a wider array of contested significations and boundaries of race because they are populated by a greater diversity of people. In fact, how people assess diversity is often based on both heterogeneity and representation (the share of specific groups, with particular attention paid to disadvantaged ethnoracial groups).[34] With greater diversity comes intra-group heterogeneity of enthoracial groups,[35] which works against the flattening of groups to single dimensions or distorted images. Perez Ochoa (Latinx) remarks on the power of race in place: "Growing up in Southern California, the schools I went to were super diverse and I really didn't see myself as a racialized being until I came to college [in Oregon]." Perez notes a dichotomy around their peers' colorblindness and the assumption that Perez is color conscious: "On one hand, [people are] not even thinking or caring about it [race/ethnicity] versus expecting me to think and care about it *all the time.*" Divina Garcia (Hispanic), also from California, feels like she "sticks out like a sore thumb," this hypervisiblity hitting her "the minute [she] stepped foot in Oregon." "The spatial nature of social life,"[36] including population demographics and regional histories, animates racial boundaries and scaffolds degrees of scrutiny and belonging.

African American Desirée Robinson has lived in multiple locations across the globe and finds Oregon striking for what she calls its "White blizzard," or exceedingly high White population. Desirée explains how Whiteness crowds out Blackness in Oregon:

> I joke with people . . . "I often say it's a blizzard." And they'd be like, "Oh, it's cold." It's like, "No, there's only White people here. That's why it's a blizzard." . . . I used to live in California, I've lived in Hawai'i. . . . I have not lived in a place that has percentage-wise so many Whites. . . . Everywhere

I see "Black Lives Matter" [signs] and blah blah blah. But, where are the Black people, though? Why are they not here?

Desirée's curiosity touches on early political campaigns to build Oregon as a White utopia, repercussions of Black exclusion manifesting in contemporary population demographics.

Some respondents of color recognized the historic and contemporary policies that countermand the popular phrase "Oregon nice." As Paul Lee (Vietnamese American) remarked, "People perceive [Oregon] . . . as a progressive liberal state, but . . . I think we pretend not to be racist but we have so many racist policies." Interviewed before Oregon's H2015 bill that allowed for undocumented residents to obtain a noncommercial driver's license with proof of legal presence was passed (2019), Paul expressed disappointment that Oregon was not keeping up with its neighbors (California and Washington) to enact this progressive policy. Paul next criticized Oregonians for "not acknowledging the history of Oregon being a racist state." He is bothered by the gentrification of Portland, noting with irony:

All these gentrified areas in Portland that used to be predominantly Black, or [have] poor refugees, and immigrants . . . now they're all gentrified with a lot of White folks taking over, buying property and opening up their businesses. . . . You see a lot of "Black Lives Matter" signs. . . . Most of the signs are in those gentrified areas. . . . "You put up the signs, but you were the one that pushed them out of here?" . . . So it was like, "You're welcome, but really you're not," you know?

This critique of signage that makes proclamations but lacks supporting evidence was articulated by another African American I overheard in public (not a respondent). On the subject of "Black Lives Matter" signs that dot White neighborhoods, this African American asked rhetorically, "Where are all these Black people whose lives you say matter?"

Luna Espinosa (Asian/Latinx) does not mince words when she connects a racist past to a colorblind racist present: "There's . . . a vacancy in Oregon of even asking any questions and I think that has everything to do with Oregon not wanting to talk about race because of its historical legacies in White supremacy." It is uncomfortable for White people to discuss the White supremacy that structurally advantages them and from which they draw calculable benefits. Stubborn colorblindness or an "epistemology of ignorance"[37] will not assuage racist injury. Luna points out the irony of White people in Oregon who shy away from discussing race in a place deeply marked by racial projects:

> If you can't reconcile that we were a sundown town or . . . that we have legacies like Chinese Massacre Cove . . . [where a] group of Chinese folks were massacred [in 1887] because White . . . pioneers who settled here believed . . . that they have the right to get rid of Black and Yellow [people]—they were considered Yellow people at that time. . . . That's history that's embodied.

Chinese Massacre Cove is a site named for the ambush and massacre of thirty-four Chinese gold miners by nine White men and boys in 1887; despite a grand jury trial, no one was ever punished for the murders. Luna's final remark ("That's history that's embodied.") can be interpreted multiple ways, from how racialized history is carried in bodies via stress and trauma (or its absence) to how "belonging" (or not) in a space is an embodied experience.

White respondents who grew up in White contexts were socialized to believe their racial background was unremarkable and "normal."[38] Many White respondents lived without recognizing they even *had* a racial identity until they circulated in a space with people of color. Unlike for respondents of color, race and racism was not dinner-table conversation, many White respondents reporting that their racial status was "never discussed." In these White families existing in largely White environments, Whiteness and its attendant privileges are rendered invisible. Hypersegregation of White people from people of color incubates a "White habitus" that geographically and psychologically limits meaningful relationships with people who are not also White.[39] Spaces themselves—that are wrapped up in racist histories, racial demographics, and racial climates—can animate cultures that are either welcoming or unwelcoming. It is commonplace to think of people as agents of inclusion or exclusion, yet this section uncovers that *places* are imprinted with historical (mis)deeds that influence present-day sociocultural environments, including the potential for people of color to feel as if they can belong in those spaces and be viewed as valuable Americans.

Slavery and Anti-Black Racism

Due to slavery and modern violence and exclusion bedeviling Black people in the United States, African Americans do not feel prototypically American.[40] African American Tahj Hayes invokes the transhistorical theme of anti-Blackness, bemoaning, "*We still have to fight to justify the point of living.* We shouldn't have to. . . . I do feel like we are excluded still. Like you are always constantly told that you don't belong here." Tahj dives into the history of anti-Blackness to frame the Black Lives Matter (BLM) movement as a protest against one of many iterations of injustice against Black people:

> The [BLM] movement really was spurred through video images of some-body being killed: Trayvon Martin. If you continue to go backwards into time, the Black Lives movement could really go all the way to 1619 when we were brought over here. We've been lynched for centuries—Black people. You've heard of Billie Holiday's "Strange Fruit"?[41] [Interviewer affirms.] So, when you see "strange fruit" hanging from the vines, it's just. . . . Hell, when you think about the Tulsa Massacre of Black Wall Street . . . or Rosewood, or you choose a city in the South from the late 1800s to the mid-1930s where Black businesses were destroyed and people were killed. Tulsa Riot—that was not a riot, that's a massacre. Black Wall Street is just 100 years ago . . . 1921. You had the KKK come through and destroy Black folks and we was fighting too, until we could fight no more. And they killed hundreds and thousands. So, yeah . . . these movements, that's just a continuation of our fight . . . it's just a new form.

Racist history weighs heavily on the hearts and minds of Black respondents who perceive racism, past and present, as a blockade to full, unbridled inclusion and belonging. Belonging is not determined by individuals alone; society mediates the relationship that Black people have with the nation and tempers their belonging. Tahj's narrative takes space seriously at the level of the nation. When a nation is the object of inquiry, the entire nation's deep and expansive record of hegemonic Whiteness and race relations history, replete with evidence testifying to anti-Blackness, becomes relevant to belonging today.

As Tahj indicated, slavery looms large in the lives of African Americans who are descendants of enslaved Africans and African Americans. Denise Lareaux holds slavery, anti-Black sentiment encoded in national symbolism, and her predominately White town in mind as she parses out layered meanings of belonging: "I do [consider myself American]. I mean, because I was born here. But do I feel . . . part of an inclusive America? Not so much. [laughs]" She expanded:

> You see all these people that are really patriotic with the American flag . . . and I just don't have those same feelings. . . . For African Americans, we were brought here against our will and pretty much forced to be here. And then we're told to basically assimilate and . . . fit in.

Denise details her family history of internal migration post-emancipation, which landed her ancestors in Oregon illegally:

> My family actually came up on the Oregon Trail. So, we've been here since the 1880s. So, my grandparents and great grandparents; they . . . fought to be here . . . because when they came it was not legal for them to be here. If you were over the age of eighteen, it was illegal for you to live in Oregon [as a Black person]. They had those exclusion laws. Yeah, and so, in that aspect, my family . . . felt proud that they made it and endured fear.

In answer to a question about whether she considers herself American, Denise highlights both legal exclusion and symbolic censure (forced assimilation) and expresses pride in her family's fortitude in the face of a racist regime. Denise cites laws as locking down her family in a caste-like racial system:[42] slavery and Oregon's Black exclusion laws (the first enacted in 1844 and the last repealed in 1926, fifty-eight years after it was legally invalidated following the Civil War in 1868).

Family history involving slavery does not need to be known to be impactful. Xavier Bow does not have records but "assumes" that their ancestors were enslaved: "[as an African American,] pretty much if you're here you have some of that in history, unless you're recently immigrated." Xavier argues that because slavery reveals the capacity of the nation to enact egregious harms, new tactics of harm against communities of color are no surprise:

> Just knowing how terrible this country was for so long and how it [slavery] was so accepted. . . . The atrocities that this country is committing . . . the children who are in internment camps right now . . . which is horrible. But at the same time it's like, "This is not new. This is how America is." [laughter] We've been doing shit like that for so long. . . . It doesn't surprise me in any way. . . . [Slavery] is something that I carry . . . from the past, but it's also like, I'm not seeing you guys [with federal power] do anything different. You're just kinda shuffling things around.

Hinting at embodied intergenerational trauma ("something I carry"), discussed more fully in chapter 5, history weighs down respondents of color. While Xavier addresses Blackness and the legacy of slavery, they emphasize that people of color are in the crosshairs of racist actions as a collectivity *and* as racialized subgroups, the racial state "shuffling" or rotating over time the communities of color at the crux of oppressive state machinery.

Colonial Status

Indigenous respondents (Native Americans and Pacific Islanders) belong to sovereign or colonized nations with a history that precedes contact with White European settlers. Colonial status enforces Indigenous respondents' second-class status with maneuvers like land usurpation, stripped sovereignty or voting power, and forced assimilation projects.

History pulses in the present, as was discussed in relation to settler colonialism in chapter 1. Native Americans Beau Landon (Siletz) and Ross Reece (Karuk/Hupa/Yurok) see the egregious harms exacted by the US government against their tribes as reason to hold lightly the title "American." Beau says that as a matter of fact he is American: "This is where I'm born." Beau addresses the tension that exists in being Native in the United States, asking rhetorically: "How do you be Native, and . . . *like* the government or the American society that not that long ago tried to kill you? I don't know. . . . You . . . can't really think about it too much."

Ross Reece shirks the term American as a self-descriptor because he sees it at as forced assimilation. Because of sustained efforts of conquest and genocide, the US government has positioned itself against Native identity, pitting Ross between opposing factions. Ross ponders my question about whether he considers himself American: "I don't know. . . . My people—it wasn't a choice to be American. . . . Forced assimilation . . . forced everything. Forced treaties signed and ratified. . . . I'm leaning towards more so 'no.'" Seeing "American" as the antithesis of "Native" grounds his opposition:

> When I see the flag, it makes me cringe sometimes. . . . Ideas of what it's built on. . . . There's a lot of good that [has] come out in the concept of the United States, but it's built on . . . murder and colonization. . . . As an Indigenous [person] . . . it's hard to say that I'm an American [when] . . . ideally they're forcing me to go away from who I am.

Ross's very sense of self is at stake in whether he calls himself American. Given the violent history of US government and Native relations, Ross sees these entities as incompatible.

For Native American respondents attuned to settler colonialism, the thought of greater "inclusion" in what they see as a White racial state is anathema to their Native identities. Native American scholar Jodi Byrd explains the tension between colonialism and inclusion: "When the re-mediation of the colonization of American Indians is framed through discourses of racialization that can be redressed by further inclusion into the nation-state, there is a significant failure to grapple with the fact that such discourses further reinscribe the original colonial injury."[43] Native American respondents spoke the language of decolonization to right their position in the United States, whereas other respondents of color utilized terminology of inclusion and representation.

In concert with Native Americans, Pacific Islanders resisted colonialism as they hedged about American identity. Kaulana Tamata retains distance by saying she is Samoan, not American. Kaulana distinguishes between American citizenship and American imperialism:

> KAULANA: When people ask me, "What are you?" I say, "Oh, I'm Samoan." [chuckles] . . . You can go deep on it or you can just be

literal. Like, "Okay, yeah, I'm an American citizen." Or, like, "Are you American? Do you have the American values?" . . . I'm just like, "What values?" [chuckles] . . .

JVT: So if you do "go deep on it," what's your answer?

KAULANA: I don't see taking over other people's countries as . . . right, like overthrowing Queen Liliʻuokalani. . . . Coming to other countries and pushing religion onto them . . . when everything else was perfectly fine before they came. . . . Bribing innocent people or taking their lands and trying to destroy their culture; I don't agree with any of it, which is what America has done from history.

Kaulana stands apart from the United States in terms of identification out of disagreement with extractive, annihilating colonialism.

While some Indigenous respondents view Indigeneity and Americanness as incompatible, like two ends of a seesaw (when one side goes up, the other side goes down), not all ascribed to that view. Other Indigenous respondents see their Indigenous and American identities as compatible and they use this dualism to expand White-centric definitions of Americanness. Kealohalani Teo resists the notion that racial status equates to exclusion: "'Just because you don't think I'm American doesn't mean I'm not.' . . . I absolutely still feel American even if others maybe don't perceive me that way."

Another Pacific Islander, Mariana Palacios, remarks, "I know that I'm an American, but I don't like it. [chuckles]" Mariana explicates how her status as a "territory citizen" is an embodiment of political marginality: "It's just the history of how I became an American and what my American status means as [a] territory citizen." Here Mariana refers to the Supreme Court's ruling in the *Insular Cases* (1901) which "made the innovative claim that the territories acquired from Spain *belonged to*, but were not *part of*, the United States."[44] Digging into the political alienation endemic to territory citizen status, Mariana remarks on her Latino partner's reaction to learning about her legal exclusion: "He was also upset . . . 'What? You can't vote for a president?' He was like, 'What? Your congressional representative can't even vote, can't even make bills, can't do anything?'" Mariana's status as a territory citizen dashed her dreams years earlier: "I wanted to be president when I was a kid. . . . And my mom had a tough conversation with me and was like,

'Sorry baby, you can't be a president. Your sister can because she was born in Hawai'i. But you can't because you were born in Saipan in the Mariana Islands.'" At a young age, Mariana expressed political career aspirations, but she is denied certain hopes because she was born in a US territory, not a US state. Colonialism demarcates "territory" versus "state" status. Mariana grimaced when she told the story of learning she was barred from occupying the Office of the President because she is not a full-fledged US citizen. She summarizes: "It feels othering. Yeah, it feels very much othering." Sharing a colonized status, Pacific Islander and Native American respondents speak plainly about state-enforced marginal belonging.

Legal Status

Lack of legal status is a hardship that wreaks many negative conse-quences. Formal legal exclusion leads to emotional and psychological distress,[45] lack of economic opportunities and blocked mobility,[46] and health risks such as stress and depression.[47] Beyond undocumented people themselves, undocumented status has a "spillover effect" and touches citizen family members, including citizen children.[48] There is a rich and growing literature on how legal status affects undocumented people and their loved ones. For the purposes of belonging, immigration and legal status concerns can bring about civic engagement as a reaction to being legally marginalized.[49]

I did not ask respondents about their legal status and yet a few vol-unteered that they were, or had been, undocumented. Lack of legal status particularly affected Latino respondents. Even after successfully pursuing legalization, psychosocial costs of being undocumented can endure.[50] Candi Perez (Mexican-born) was granted permanent resi-dency and yet she "forgets": "I'll be watching the news like, 'Oh my gosh, what am I gonna do?' I forget just because I've always had that fear. I guess it's just still in me. It's scary." Having lived nearly two decades without legal status and being vulnerable to deportation, fear became ingrained and is a default feeling Candi easily slips back into even after achieving legal status.

Beyond legal status, political rhetoric enforces labels of docu-mented/undocumented, criminal/law-abiding, and deserving/undeserving. Blanca Ruiz (Mexican American) refers to a "Trump effect" wherein Donald Trump's provocative speech renews "old-fashioned" racism and inflames others to act on their racial prejudice.[51] Blanca cites Trump's denigration of Mexicans as criminals, rapists, drug dealers, and gang members as whipping up racial animosity and making her feel wrongfully accused. She referred to Oregon Proposition 105, on the ballot in November 2018, that aimed to repeal the state's sanctuary status: "If you look a certain way, we're going to stop you and ask you, 'Are you . . . here legally?' . . . The news . . . is making it seem like people of color are *the problem*. . . . That measure, it's like, 'We have to enforce this rule because you guys are doing something [wrong]." As for Roberto Torres, a Mexican-born Deferred Action for Childhood Arrivals [DACA] recipient, he has to tune out media for the sake of his mental health: "It makes me sad." Listening to all of Trump's "nasty words" about Mexicans provokes a post-traumatic stress disorder reaction in Roberto. Roberto emphasizes, "I've *fought* to feel included."

White Gatekeepers Judging Non-Whiteness

In addition to a White racial *landscape* and racist political-legal *structures* that overvalue Whiteness, White *people* also draw boundaries of inclusion and exclusion, fitting and misfitting. Doing the work of White supremacy at the interactional level, these gatekeepers of Whiteness police boundaries by judging cultural cues and physical features as non-White. With national identity being a social phenomenon,[52] "American" coded as White is animated by people who interactionally inform respondents of color that they are "not White" and therefore "not American." Sociocultural cues, such as language, first name, and religion, in addition to color and ancestry, are important predictors of how White people classify other people.[53] Cross-racial exchanges that demarcate boundaries of belonging have consequences—they send signals of marginality that can become internalized, even as they may also be resisted. Identities and classifications that are thrust upon people by observers can profoundly impact self-concepts.[54]

White gatekeepers influence the self-title of US-born Mexican American Blanca Ruiz, who equates "American" with "White." Our conversation proceeded like this:

JVT: What's your preferred title? What do you call yourself?
BLANCA: Usually when people ask me, I'm like, "Oh, I'm Mexican."
JVT: . . . Mm-hmm. When you were saying "American" [before] . . . is there a particular race that you were thinking of as American?
BLANCA: Yeah, White. That's the first thing that comes to my mind, White.
JVT: So, is Whiteness . . . the reason why you don't say you're American?
BLANCA: I believe so.

The racial encoding of the title "American" has been so effectively transmitted to Blanca that she rejects that title on the basis of race. I asked Blanca if she had ever been told that she is not American. She left the door open in her reply: "No, not directly to my face. [laughs] . . . But people might say it behind [my back]." She was once informed by a White man that she was unwelcome in the predominately White town in southern Oregon where she lived:

When I was young, me and my mom . . . and my sisters . . . were going into the mall in our hometown. . . . When we walked in, this White guy was leaving. And he was like, "Oh, why [are] there so many . . . Mexicans in the mall today?" . . . I [thought], "Why . . . did he say that? . . . Are we not welcome here? . . . Is there an issue?"

Gruff interactions such as this pinpoint Mexican heritage as unwanted in public space coded as White. People who identify strongly as American (presumably the White man in this encounter) are more likely than those who are weakly identified as American to believe that American identity requires individuals to be US-born, live in the United States most of their lives, speak English, and be Christian and White.[55] This racial and cultural view of Americanness ensnares Blanca: She is informed that she is disqualified from being American because of Mexican heritage, which then affects her self-perception.

Latino belonging in the United States is burdened by racist stereotypes that cast Latinos as a permanent immigrant group,[56] foreigners, a cultural menace to a presumed White cultural core, and a criminal threat.[57] I asked Jo Paz (Latinx/White):

JVT: Has anyone ever suggested to you that you're not American?

Jo: [Firmly] Yes, many times. [chuckles.] I think especially [with] Latin-*equis* [Latinx] folks . . . there's this assumption that . . . you're probably not from here.

JVT: I see. So, who's making that assumption?

Jo: There's never been a . . . single Brown person who has asked me where I'm from . . . or asked me if I was a citizen. That question has never come up.

White interlocutors can appoint themselves gatekeepers who treat racial or legal status as a litmus test for acceptable civic presence. In these excerpts, both Blanca and Jo exhibit what Chicana feminist and cultural theorist Gloria Anzaldúa called *la facultad*, or "the capacity to see in surface phenomena the meaning of deeper realities, to see the deep structure below the surface."[58] An exercise in acute perception, *la facultad* boosts comprehension of barriers to belonging. In gaining a stronger grasp of exclusionary mechanisms, however, "we lose something . . . something is taken from us: . . . our safe and easy ignorance."[59]

White gatekeepers can excoriate people based on physical features such as dark skin color. Tahj Hayes (African American) has faced repudiation: "I've had people say, 'Go back to Africa, go back to this shithole [country].'" Tahj retorts, "I would tell them to go back to Europe." This repartee puts Tahj on level footing, this reply recasting the White interlocutor as a newcomer to Indigenous territory. Nevertheless, former President Trump fanned derogatory speech against African countries when he referred to African countries, Haiti, and El Salvador as "shithole countries."[60] Tahj's tale ties into what scholars have dubbed a "Trump effect"—that is, that Donald Trump's inflammatory speech encourages others to express their bias.[61] A nationally representative survey conducted in 2019 found that 59% of Americans say race relations in the United States are bad and 56% think that Trump has worsened race relations.[62]

A narrow, race-based definition of "American" excludes people of color from both Whiteness and Americanness. People of color are viewed as un-American or hyphenated Americans (with race/ethnicity as a demerit), but not "American" without a caveat. Emboldened by White supremacy stitched into the culture and organization of society,

White gatekeepers do interactional work to erect boundaries that cordon off belonging as being for White people only.

Collective and Relational Racial Formation

Racial formation is "the sociohistorical process by which racial categories are created, inhabited, transformed, and destroyed."[63] *Collective* racial formation casts nets over groups of varying sizes and contours. Boundaries (which are contested and mutable) can be drawn at various scales: around an aggregate "people of color" category as well as what are considered specific racial groups. A *relational* perspective holds that racialization does not occur "in a vacuum, isolated from other groups" but rather "relative to and through interaction with" other groups, making racialization trajectories "profoundly interrelated."[64] Thus, racial meanings and identities are always constituted through relationships.[65]

Racial formation is linked to "the evolution of hegemony, the way in which society is organized and ruled."[66] Collective racial formation and relational racialization operate simultaneously. This dual racial formation process (collective and relational) instantiates both a non-White/White divide *and* racial group divisions among groups of color. I demonstrate below the twofold operation of collective and relational racial formation. First, I show collective racial formation. I draw on narratives where respondents emphasized shared experience as people of color, followed by racialization that distinguished them as members of a specific racial group. Second, I explore the relationality of racial formation. Finally, I demonstrate that *both* collective and relational racial formation processes operate concurrently.

Collective Racial Formation: A Dual Process for "People of Color" and Specific Racial Groups

Racial formation works on collectivities of varying sizes and scales, including the "people of color" category as well as populations that are racialized as specific racial groups. Collective racial formation creates or re-instantiates group boundaries. With collective racialization creating or reproducing *multiple* racial boundaries (since people of color *also* belong to specific racial groups) the messaging of racial subjugation is doubled down on.

COLLECTIVE RACIALIZATION AS A "PEOPLE OF COLOR" UMBRELLA CATEGORY

A sense of sweeping collective racialization where people of color are positioned on a non-White side of a non-White/White binary pervaded interviews. This collective racialization as people of color is often indicated by mistreatment of specific groups that "add up" to comprise a people of color category. "Another day, another minority group," is how one respondent referred to ongoing rotation of racial targeting that zeroes in on specific racial groups from within the people of color umbrella. Similarly, Divina Garcia (Hispanic) identified collective racialization when she visualized communities of color taking turns in the crosshairs of national-level racialization:

> Minorities in America have gone through very similar stories in the sense that at one point or another we have been mistreated—racially identified and told that we're basically the worst of the worst. . . . [Working conditions during] the Cesar Chavez movement for Hispanics, Japanese people were . . . put in camps . . . during World War II, African Americans were put in slavery for hundreds of years. . . . We all have this similar struggle where at one point or another one of us were looked down upon and . . . told that we're not anything. . . . I think it . . . bonds us together.

The slippage between "minorities in America" who are "racially identified" reveals that racially marked groups constitute "minorities" more broadly. The "very similar stories" of mistreatment marks "minorities" as a meaningful collective. By seeing collective racial formation as a *dual* process (working on people of color and constituent racial groups), one can view how techniques of power may differ by group while also aggregating to dominate people of color collectively. "Bonds us together" is a multivocal phrase that refers to emotional affinity based on a shared status as well as to racialization processes that unify smaller collectivities.[67]

Jasmine Salazar (Mexican American) also addresses collective racialization leveled against people of color. Speaking to how class status, educational achievements, or occupational prestige do not safeguard against discrimination, Jasmine, who earned a Master's degree and works in public health, remarks: "I went to college. I have [African American] friends who are lawyers, they're doctors. . . . Unfortunately, there are much fewer of us. . . . As minorities, we have to stick together . . . and support each other." Collective racialization subordinates groups of color, inspiring Jasmine's sense of shared status with African Americans and need for solidarity.[68]

A power gap between White people and people of color signals collective racial formation. Sinbad Sanaa (Middle Eastern) conceives of the racial divide this way: "White comes first and everything else is next." Sebastian Cain (South Asian American) sees blunt, collective racialization processes washing out finer-grained gradations among people of color: "White American is . . . on the top, [with] . . . all other forms of American . . . tied for second." As a tactic of White supremacist domination, collective racial formation lumps together "people of color" as set apart from the structurally privileged location of Whiteness.

COLLECTIVE RACIALIZATION AS A SPECIFIC RACIAL GROUP MEMBER

In addition to collective racial formation reinforcing a non-White/White divide (even as categories in the US racial system is a subject of debate[69]), variations within non-White and White classifications add crucial nuance to the dichotomy. Collective racial formation that activates and crystallizes *specific racial groups* (even as these boundaries are debated, crossed, and blurred) is a useful lens through which to view finer-tuned processes of race-making.

Being cast as a member of a particular racial group—preloaded with meanings—is a common experience for respondents of color. Relative to an "American" (understood as White) who needs no descriptor, John Blaze, a Black man, quips, "As soon as you have a little pigment—a little melanin—you Latino American, you African American, you Asian American." Despite working a professional job that requires a law degree, John is regularly asked on campus if he is a football player. He recounted a time when, upon informing an inquiring stranger that he is not on the football team, the man pressed on, asking if John was on the basketball team or soccer team. Such racial group–specific and gendered racialization that reduces Black men to their physical attributes attempts to confine Black men to "controlling images."[70] In John's words, this includes being cast as a "sidekick, comedian, buddy cop, drug dealer, football player, NBA [player], [or] rapper"—none of which accurately describe him.

Controlling images foment the collective racialization of specific racial groups. A tool that reproduces racial, class, and gender subjugation, controlling images are intersectional depictions of dominated racial groups that spring from and maintain oppressive systems.[71] Controlling images are "major instrument[s] of power."[72] Originally conceived relative to Black people, controlling images pertain to other marginalized groups as well.[73] Divina Garcia (Hispanic) bristles at portrayals that aim to denigrate and dominate:

> There are ... *negative* stereotypes. . . . After I left home [Victorville, California] and came over here . . . there is that idea that . . . if you're Hispanic, you're . . . using the system, you're . . . not doing things legally. . . . [But] you can't classify a whole race, a whole culture, [or] even one individual on one stereotype.

Divina captures collective racialization targeting Latinos. She also addresses regional racial formation:[74] She surmises that people in Oregon may rely on controlling images to fill in knowledge gaps. Divina resists damnation of Latinos by rejecting the broad brushstrokes of collective racialization. And yet, she is sufficiently caught up in the collective racialization of her group to be aware of the meanings she needs to deny.

Much of this book illustrates and teases out the reasons for—and consequences of—collective racialization. Collective racialization that bolsters the boundaries of racial groups works in tandem with sweeping efforts to position "people of color" as an assemblage accorded less social value than White people. These dual processes, in combination with relational racial formation described below, redouble the force of delineating and hierarchizing groups of people.

Relational Racial Formation

In relational racial formation, group boundaries and meanings are developed in relationship to *multiple* groups, not just White as the dominant category.[75] A relational perspective acknowledges the jostling of "racial projects," the "discursive or representational means in which race is identified and signified."[76] Racial projects can rope in multiple racial groups and play off group relationships and consolidate (or test) meanings and boundaries.

Racialization occurs in relationship. Pamela Yamaguchi (Japanese American) recalls her mother advising her, "All those stereotypes about us, they're good ones, so keep them." Pamela zeros in on relational racialization in discerning different meanings cast upon groups engaging in equivalent behavior: "Some of the things that Mexican Americans would get denigrated for, the Japanese Americans were doing the same. I mean, the immigrant generation not learning very much English because they never went to school because they had to work: With Mexican Americans that was a bad thing, with Japanese Americans it was like, 'Oh, that's fine.'" Communities of color are racialized in relation to each other.

Interactions that shoehorn people into racist caricatures—while some escape surveillance—are conduits for relational racial formation. White people's freedom of movement and expression contrasts with racist limitations for people of color. Chinese American Emma Bentley was preparing for Halloween with White friends in her sorority who wanted to dress as princesses, recalling, "I was like, 'Oh, can I be this one?' They were like, 'Well, Emma, you don't look like that one. Why don't you be Mulan [a likely fictional Chinese folk heroine popularized by a Disney movie]?'"

Drawing out a gendered element of relational racial formation, Vietnamese American Minor Hun recalls a scene where he was viewed as a potentially threatening man of color:

> It was in the winter and we were [on a field trip at a ranch with my university as] part of a natural resource course. . . . I was wearing a navy-black beanie. . . . This [White] teacher . . . told me to take off my cap. . . . [We were] inside and other people were . . . still wearing winter knit caps. . . . I think the reason he probably made me take it off . . . [is] he thinks I look more like a street thug. And so, that's racist right there. . . . I . . . [get] angry at myself for not challenging him. Like asking him, "Well, why [did] you tell me to take off my cap? But then you've got all these other students right here wearing their cap?"

While the racial backgrounds of the other students are not noted, the racism that is coded into this everyday interaction[77] to which Minor is subjected is *in relation to* other students who evade monitoring and censure. Minor being singled out for a sanction when other students are not signals his disadvantaged racial position relative to his peers at the largely White institution.

Relational racialization is also shaped by additional social categories. With respect to nation of origin, research has shown that Black immigrants strive to distinguish themselves from African Americans to preserve positive reputations such as hard workers and that employers hold cultural stereotypes that favor immigrants over the native-born.[78] Etundu Lobengo, a twenty-five-year-old international student from the Democratic Republic of the Congo, stresses how accentuating his foreign-born status elevates him relative to African Americans in the eyes of non-Black Americans. As a Black African, Etundu complained that class, age, and student status all pale in importance to race in the United States: "There isn't really room for me to be myself because the first thing that they look at is my skin color." Etundu suffered great mental anguish as he learned about US-based anti-Black racism and adopted coping strategies such as "wearing bright clothes or never walk[ing] behind someone." Yet relational racial formation emerged as significant. Etundu drew on nativity, language, and accent hierarchies to access prestige given to Black foreigners but not native-born African Americans. Etundu speaks to both his *collective racialization* alongside African Americans as well as *relational racialization* where his status elevates in relation to African Americans:

> African and African American: they both *see* things the same way, but . . . we don't *experience* things the same way. . . . We will both be . . . perceived as a threat because of our skin color but instead I start speaking French or just speaking English with my accent [and] people will know that I'm not from here. So, they will . . . say, "Okay, he's a good one." But they [my African American friends] will still bear that weight of being the "bad apple."

Nativity, language, and accent can modulate racialization and reveal splits in how subgroups are cast relative to each other. The cachet he garners from speaking French equates to, as Etundu says, "perception . . . being changed." Perception change due to multiple reference groups being harnessed—against whom comparisons are made and judgments of social "worth" are rendered—illustrates relational racial formation in action.

Status hierarchies operating within one's racial group reveals that racial formation occurs not only in relation to *other* racial groups but also *within* one's racial group. This in-group dynamism exposes racialization as intersectional, reflecting multiple social locations. Quincey Bernabe refers to how her mother's intertwined statuses as an immigrant from the Philippines play into relational racial formation: "Anti-immigrant. Filipinos . . . I've been told [are] at the bottom of [the Asian] food chain. . . . And you're a *native* Filipino . . . so you're at the *very bottom* of the Filipino food chain." The relational racial formation here concerns immigration status, Filipino identity within the Asian category, and Indigeneity relative to non-native Filipinos and Asians more generally.

Even as a race-as-relational approach divests itself from comparing to Whiteness, Whiteness remains an overused comparison point. A mixed-race medical student, Rosie Patel notes that health research reifies race and a racial order. Indeed, race scholars have pointed out that it is problematic to use causal language when stating a "race effect" which treats race as an unalterable individual characteristic rather than how "society *responds* to an individual's racial identification."[79] Seeing the White category used as a typical point of comparison in public health research, Rosie reflects on how medical reporting by race distills messages of value:

> In research . . . we're always comparing every minority group to the White group. . . . We say that . . . the White population is . . . the ideal and we're gonna compare *everything* else against that. We do that with socioeconomic status, we do that with health. . . . As a society we place [the] White group at the top—because otherwise why would we compare everything to a lesser, moderate group? We wouldn't do that.

A relational racial formation approach accounts for relationships among multiple racial groups, and yet Whiteness remains a sturdy and over-weighted vector of comparison.

A relational understanding of racial formation remedies the shortfall of viewing race-making as happening only along a non-White/White dichotomy. By investigating beyond the two poles of the racial hierarchy, we can see how "binary thinking . . . [can] hide the way dominant society often casts minority groups against one another to the detriment of each."[80] A relational view helps lay bare how racialization processes simultaneously target and crisscross various groupings, all while undergirding White racial dominance.

Collective and Relational Racial Formation

As shown, racial formation occurs at two *collective* levels: one that encapsulates people of color generally and another that is racial group–specific. Both collective processes of race-making are *relational*, meaning-making bouncing off multiple reference groups. Racial formation as collective and relational shows racialization to be multiscalar, layered, and complex.

Native American group formation is reliant on collective meanings relative to other groups. Beau Landon (Native American) describes his view of the US racial order:

> It's hard to rank *who's hated more* because it's . . . phases. When I was in high school . . . and now again, Mexicans were the big issues: "stealing all our jobs, crossing the border" and stuff. And then . . . it's Black people who are the issue, all this gun violence and cops. . . . You don't really hear about Natives too much, but [if so it's] always an alcoholic Indian.

Boundaries around collectivities are clear here and yet the relational aspect, while less crisp, functions at the level of defining what one group *is* by virtue of what it is *not*. The above quotation draws on "controlling images"—the aim of which is to discredit and dominate communities of color—which animate racial boundaries.[81] As a relational project, White supremacy has relied on "logics of sorting, ranking, and comparison that produce and naturalize categories of racial difference necessary for the legitimation of slavery, settler colonialism, and imperial expansion."[82]

Whiteness is also a collective and relational project, advantage built from the oppression of other groups.[83] Dylan Johnson, a White man

who says his father was racist, learned the term "White privilege" a year
before the interview in the course of a conversation with a Puerto Rican
friend. Dylan recounts:

> We were talking about cops and getting pulled over and different sce-
> narios we had in the past with being stopped. He . . . [commented], "Well,
> you don't have much to worry about. You have White privilege so that's
> why you still have your license and I don't." And I was like, "Huh?" . . . I
> wish I never would have heard that term because now . . . if I get pulled
> over, it always makes me question what would happen if I was a different
> race. How things would pan out.

This newfound awareness pierces the ignorance that often shrouds and
normalizes White privilege. The emphasis on uneven consequences
based on race ("how things would pan out") points out potentially lasting (devastating) effects of racialization. Dylan's guilt over being granted
White privilege because he is a member of a racialized collective arises
after a cross-racial conversation revealed collective and relational elements of empowerment and disempowerment: Unearned White
privilege is relative to, and counterpoised against, the equally unearned
disadvantage of people of color.

Collective and relational racial formation happen simultaneously.
Collective racialization as non-White functions relative to Whiteness,
and then more specific categorizations within the overarching "people
of color" group are constructed in relationship to other groups. More
complex than a two-tiered system of non-White/White, collective racial formation is a dual process that also activates distinctions that are
subsumed by the "people of color" category. Relational racial formation
shows that racialization bounces off of multiple reference groups, from
racial groups to which one does not belong to subgroups within one's
own racial category. Relational racialization is contoured by vectors such
as nation of origin, gender, and language. These multiple and layered
racialization processes show the extensive cultural investment in ranking people of color rank beneath Whiteness in the national imaginary.

Establishing Belonging

Even as belonging is socially mediated, it is also an active category, people endowed with the agency to establish belonging. As a creative, active process, "belonging is not a fixed category but rather one we have agency over."[84] Moves to generate belonging showcase people's ability to create welcoming local environments and possibly even change the contours of society and boundaries of group membership.

Concentric Circles of Belonging

"Concentric circles of belonging" captures how respondents of color carved out space for themselves in local social networks within a larger society that devalues them based on race. Belonging is contextual. Concentric circles of belonging evokes the visual image of smaller circles that widen into bigger circles, just as a stone tossed into water casts ripples that widen from point of contact. Relationships where people feel valued, cared for, and respected as knowledgeable create a sense of belonging. Even as a workplace characterized by collegial relations is a source of belonging, that is not to say that racism or poor work relationships do not sour the job. Nevertheless, many respondents referred to workplaces as more familiar spheres where they are appreciated, as opposed to the anonymity of predominately White public spaces.

Respondents of color offered bifurcated answers when I asked about how valued they felt in society. First, at the national level they felt devalued on account of race (but more valued if they were educated or employed). Second, many respondents of color recouped self-esteem by claiming that they were valued in their local environments among friends and peers. Luis Waimea makes these points: "As far as on campus, I feel like I bring value because of my experience. But racially . . . I don't feel like we're [Japanese Americans] valued at all." So, like ripples in a pond, the wider circle of the nation discounts people of color and yet inner circles represent everyday life among chosen families or in supportive workplaces. These local networks can offer belonging in a way that the national level does not.

"It changes," is the way Pamela Yamaguchi (Japanese American) explains how included she feels in US society. She describes what I call concentric circles of belonging:

> I've worked here [university] for a long time, so in terms of local cam-
> pus, I feel included. . . . People know who I am. But there are times
> when I don't [feel included]. . . . I was at the coast this weekend [one
> hour away] and I got denied service at a bakery. . . . So, I feel included
> in my local community.

Traveling to a different town equates to becoming more anonymous and
the risk of being treated according to group-based categories rather than
as an individual rises. Sebastian Cain (South Asian American), who
complained of strangers judging his accent, echoes Pamela's sentiment:
"Thankfully . . . because of the [diversity] work I do, I'm surrounded by
people who are generally more accepting than others. But in society in
general . . . I've just gotten . . . desensitized to the way people react to
me." Pitching his workplace as a counterpoint to wider society, Sebastian
feels more valued among his work colleagues. Given his employment in
diversity work, Sebastian self-selected into a work environment with a
higher likelihood of being valued.

Yet working in a niche sector that centers diversity is not required
to feel belonging in a work community. Lily Chuang (Asian American)
works in drug and alcohol recovery, a community that sustains her.
Counteracting the societal exclusion she feels ("I do feel excluded a little
bit because . . . I'm Asian and I have tattoos all over"), Lily experiences
concentric circles of belonging at work: "[Inclusion] *does* depend. For
the most part I feel included only because I'm really big in the recovery
community. . . . I think if I were to step out of it . . . there could be some
exclusion [based on] appearance . . . just straight appearance." Keeping
herself in the recovery community maintains Lily's "sobriety [and] sense
of belonging." Networks of sustained relationships contribute to inclusion, a status that does not travel into different social spaces.

Jo Paz (Latinx) broaches the idea of concentric circles of belonging
as she narrows down the width of the community, moving from exclusion to inclusion. She points out that sexuality, being the daughter
of an immigrant, and her racial identity combine to produce multiple
marginality:

> I think in US society . . . I feel . . . fairly excluded. [chuckles] . . . I feel
> that . . . bodies of immigrants are not allowed to feel American. So, for

that reason, I feel fairly excluded. And then when I think about my own queer identities . . . same. I feel pretty excluded. And then the ways that I feel included . . . the LGBTQ+ community makes me feel included. Latino/Latina/Latin-*equis* [Latinx] communities make me feel included. Places like [my college campus], where I can be part of [a multiracial group], make me feel included.

Especially for those at the crux of intersectional identities that are subordinated, feeling included locally coexists with exclusion as the national level. Having communities does not equate to feeling comfortable everywhere locally, yet these inner circles are where respondents of color felt safe, known, and comfortable.

Concentric circles of belonging denotes having a familiar community where a person of color feels valued. The direct, interpersonal nature of professional and personal relationships suggest that people of color are viewed as unique individuals. Not all professional or personal relationships fulfill the desire for belonging, but this theme suggests that absent wider-scale wholesale belonging, smaller environments can satisfy that need for mutual relationships in a local domain. Graciela Pinela (Latina) uses the term "chosen family" and offers it as a glimmer of hope: "I've got a fantastic chosen family. . . . [I] feel . . . embraced in the way that America is supposed to embrace all of our differences."

Diversifying "American"

Since American identity is predicated upon Whiteness, immigrants and people of color have been expected to assimilate to enter the mainstream and be American. Race strongly influences the prospects for mainstream incorporation, a premise that has given rise to literature on the racialization of immigrants and people of color. Threading the needle between the immigration and race literatures, it is important to note that the idea of the mainstream was originally grounded in "a *composite culture* evolving out of the interpenetration of diverse cultures and beliefs."[85] Over time, this "more flexible and open-ended" notion "receded into the background" and succumbed to a homogenized Anglo-American middle-class host society.[86] This later version of "mainstream" that has become synonymous with middle-class Whiteness is reflected in respondents' understanding

of an "ideal" American. Many respondents of color refuted a racial criterion for American membership and argued that a racially heterogeneous
population, and subsequent multiculturalism, provide grounds for an
inclusive expansion of the connotations of "American."[87]

Scholarship on Mexican Americans argues that an "ethnic core" con-
sists of an ethnic community and ethnic social structures that exerts its
own "gravitational pull."[88] The ethnic core is not an isolated entity but
interacts with the mainstream, and vice versa. Even as the ethnic core is
complementary to the mainstream (these entities are not mutually exclusive), the ethnic core is a "counterbalance" to the mainstream in that
it "counteract[s] the pull of mainstream assimilatory forces."[89] A major
contribution to the understanding of multiracial, immigrant-receiving
societies, the concept of an ethnic core heralds racialized communities
as "unsung reference groups"[90]—that is, meaningful local communities
of color that have been dwarfed by a singular focus on a White-centric
mainstream. Local context matters. In my prior work on whether Latino
interviewees consider themselves part of mainstream US society, I found
that those living in a racially heterogeneous area pointed to their local
environment to argue in favor of a *multiracial* mainstream, whereas
those living in a predominately White context did not make the same
argument.[91] Region and racial demographics are contextual factors that
shape sense of inclusion.

Turning to respondents of color interviewed for this book, most
spoke cogently about making "American" more diverse and inclusive of
non-White people and cultures.[92] Respondents of color were invested
in this diversification because their unquestioned belonging hinges on
it. Divina Garcia (Hispanic) roots her meaning of American in racial
diversity rather than Whiteness, "defensive inclusion" that insists that
the United States is a multicultural society.[93] To Divina, the meaning
of American is "having a love for our country and a people that are just
very diverse." Her multiracial emphasis derives from having spent her
youth in southern California among Latinos and African Americans.

Actively revising conceptions of belonging, respondents of color endeavored to expand who is perceived as American. Malia, who remarked
earlier that someone like her (a "little Filipino, Samoan Hawaiian girl")
is not "the first image" that comes to mind when thinking of American,
argues for multiracialism:

Being American isn't just one thing. . . . It's whatever you make it out to be because . . . we're not just people from Europe. We're talking about . . . other communities coming in and playing a role. . . . We're just newer to being American because we're the fiftieth state [Hawai'i]. So . . . we're the newest Americans by definition.

Malia refers to her birth state of Hawai'i that was granted statehood as the fiftieth state in 1959 and is home to a preponderance of people of color.

Pamela Yamaguchi cited a Buddhist summer festival in her home-town in eastern Oregon that exhibits Japanese food, dancing, and arts and crafts as evidence of American as multiracial and multireligious. Articulating multiculturalism as an additive, Pamela says: "I think how much that adds to America. Because I don't like this idea of America as only being . . . White-bred and Presbyterians. . . . This is great stuff we're adding to . . . the whole American cloth." Pamela draws on a cultural contribution rhetoric to position her racial group as positive additions to an overly narrow racial and religious definition of American.

For mixed-race (Native American, Pacific Islander, Caucasian) Quincey Bernabe, opening the parameters of "American" could be initi-ated by a bureaucratic change such as how forms collect racial data. She wants multiracials to be able to honor their multiple racial lineages and fully count as American:

Whenever I see on a form "select your race" . . . I think that you should be able to pick as many races as you want. It just bothers me when I can only pick one or two. . . . It's like, "Do you want apple pie or ice cream?" . . . You [want] both. [It] makes it feel like one is more important than the other when [it] may not be. . . . It makes me feel like I have to discount [an] identity.

Multiracial individuals tend to affirm an "integrative identity" that uses multiple communities as reference groups and hold a "pluralistic identity" that blends aspects of contributing racial/ethnic communi-ties but is not identical to any one.[94] Even this modest change could chip away at the conception of American as fused with Whiteness by opening the bureaucratic door for more people to claim their racial mixedness as a legitimate, recognizable manifestation of American.

Even if racialization continues to set mixed-race people apart from "undisputed American" placement, shifts in how demographics are collected unlock potential for multiraciality to broaden the embrace of the title "American."

Cultural change that incorporates "subjugated knowledge"[95] from communities of color can shift understandings of who comprises US society's membership base and cultural tableau. Beau Landon (Native American) speaks to how inclusion of Native practices would benefit everyone. Beau pitches Native values as ascendant, saying, "Bringing tribal values to the American government would be ideal. If we could get our . . . [US] government to give healthcare to everyone and education to people . . . it does make for a better . . . community." Having been well provided for through his tribe (including college tuition), Beau advocates for injecting Native governmental practices into US governmental structures. He desires greater synergy between Native perspectives and US society: "Ideally . . . me being more Native . . . can go hand in hand with me being American." Making that "ideal" a reality, however, is contingent upon mainstream society being receptive to lessons taught by Natives. The probability of the federal government instituting tribal practices likely rests on "interest convergence," the notion that change will only happen if it would advance the interests of White people too.[96] The power inversion of positioning Natives as knowledge-holders and authority figures would empower Native Americans but may fan anxiety among White people who fear non-White diversity as an incursion into White cultural dominance.

Global and Decolonial Perspectives: Decentering "American" as the Epitome of Belonging

Inclusion in US society is not always the ultimate goal. Some respondents of color overturned the idea of inclusion as desirable and argued instead for human dignity measured by a different yardstick. Desirée Robinson (Black) and Ross Reece (Native American) best illustrate the use of global and decolonial perspectives that question the appeal of inclusion in a nation founded on the oppression of their groups. White respondents with at least one marginalized identity, such as gender, class, or sexual orientation, also articulated this theme.

A global perspective that sees the history of African-descent people as originating in Africa, rather than American-brand slavery, is a salve for racial wounds. Desirée schooled me. I asked a question with a limited focus on the United States and she broadened the scope of the question, a move that boosted her esteem because it reached back to a civilization prior to antebellum slavery. I had asked, "I'm wondering if the history of your racial group in the United States impacts the degree that you feel included or not?" She leapfrogged over my question to root her racial history in African royalty. Desirée draws on natural science and world history as a foundation for her racial identity, bucking subjugation in the United States as the *only* relevant piece of Black history:

> People don't want to say it, but I mean, *science is science.* . . . People origi-nated in Africa. We were kings and queens. . . . So this little penny-ante stuff we're talking for America . . . I think that's where some of the angst and the pushback comes from. . . . Our history is not being American . . . our history is more rooted in being from Africa.

The African slave trade kidnapped, stole, and uprooted African people, forcibly removing them from their lands, communities, and cultures. Desirée offers a global perspective which establishes that African Americans are not limited to slavery or slave descendancy:

> Like slavery . . . my people, we were only given scraps to cook with so we just did with what we had. . . . Those scraps have become staples and soul food. . . . We've *turned it into culture*, but our actual culture of food and music . . . that's *Africa stuff* that we don't really even get to touch on. . . . I think people try to make our culture rap music and food and playing sports. That's bullshit! That's not our history, that's not our culture. And *slavery is not our history.* Yes, it is part of our history, but *that is not what makes us*, you know? But it's hard to articulate that when we have not been face to face with *our actual ancestors who are from Africa.* . . . That's the real history, but hell, we haven't been there, we don't know. So, this stuff . . . that . . . gets taught in school . . . that's silliness . . . in comparison.

Opening up an elongated view of Black history allows Desirée to har-ness pride in deep historical origins that antedate slavery. Like other

African American respondents, she honors her enslaved ancestors and contends that constricting African American history to *only* slavery and oppression is unfairly limiting and a lever of oppression in the present. Perseverating on slavery as the official version of African American history taught in schools short-circuits dynamism of the past and risks truncating visions of African American futures. Desirée indicts the educational system as perpetuating "silliness," like an official curriculum that sidelines marginalized communities, as discussed in chapter 4. A global perspective that embraces world history eases a burden of belonging by broadening the field of vision and offering a more inclusive buffet of elements from which to construct a rich racial identity not beholden to the United States.

Ross Reece (Native American) takes a decolonial perspective: He is less concerned with diversifying "American" than with decolonizing his tribe from vestiges of conquest. Having grown up in a small rural community of mostly tribal members, Ross identifies with his tribe and not with American. With a Native cultural core, Ross is concerned not with making the term "American" more inclusive but in divesting his tribe of colonial interference. Ross mourns the grave losses that colonization sparked and aspires to return to the nourishing land, animal, and spiritual practices that predated colonization. Ross muses: "There's a term called decolonization. . . . There's no such thing as being decolonized just because it's always going to be there and it's always going to be part of your history now. . . . I think that concept of *fighting to be decolonized* is the perfect way to interpret where I'm going to be." Ross strives to excavate Native American tribal cultures from the hard-handed imposition of "American." Because of the intractability of history and the continuing project of settler colonialism,[97] Ross considers his decolonization aspiration as ongoing and never complete. As a US-born citizen who is a member of a sovereign tribal nation, Ross's critique of American comes from a deep-seated place of decolonial feelings and efforts.

Select White respondents expressed anti-racist and decolonial sympathies by challenging Whiteness as tantamount to belonging. Survey research has found that White sexual minorities (LGBTQ) express less racism than White heterosexuals, likely because of their greater awareness of homophobic discrimination.[98] In alignment with that finding, Chance Green, a White transgender/genderqueer man, issues a counternarrative about people of color that upends the dominant schema of White people as the preeminent Americans:

> I think a lot about Indigenous people who have cared for this land for a long time. And I think about what does it mean to have been a descendant of a chattel-person and then call yourself an African American? Right, like, what a mind-fuck that is. . . . I do think about migratory patterns . . . as being part of what it means to be American . . . that most people who came to settle here were fleeing some other bad situation.

Chance stretches and recalibrates meanings of being American by being mindful of the global histories of subordinated people. By historicizing the plights of communities of color and implicating settler colonialism, systemic racism, and global migration, Chance deftly decenters Whiteness as the epitome of belonging in the United States.

Conclusion

Irrespective of racial background, respondents viewed the prototypical "ideal" American as White. Not without critique, all respondents see Whiteness as a precondition for unquestioned Americanness. This conception of Whiteness as requite for "ideal" Americanness facilitates belonging for White people and marginality for people of color.

Because Whiteness is baked into Americanness, White respondents easily (and often with laughter) pronounced themselves American. As undisputed Americans, White respondents find that their race aligns with expectations of Americanness codified in culture and media. Needing to legitimate their status as American despite a racial mismatch, most US-born respondents of color, as "fact-of-the-matter Americans," pointed to their birthplace and citizenship as documented proof of their belonging. Even as Whiteness and non-Whiteness is a dividing line, it is contested. People of color are challenging the linkage between Whiteness and Americanness by calling on the deep ties racially diverse populations have to land and nation-making.

Barriers to belonging include: a majority-White racial landscape that makes Whiteness appear natural, normal, and a precondition for acceptance; the anti-Black and anti-Indigenous structure of society that stems from the White supremacist institutions of slavery and settler colonialism; legal status; and White actors who symbolically mark territory in interaction with people of color. I have also illustrated that racial formation is a multi-pronged process. Groups are "made" into categories by racial formation processes that occur on dual collective levels (shaping "people of color" and specific racial groups) as well as marshal meanings that are consolidated in relationship to multiple racial groups and subgroups.

Even in the face of barriers, respondents of color establish belonging in three chief ways. "Concentric circles of belonging" is a claim to group membership that is rooted in smaller circles of daily life and less connected to larger, more abstract communities. Efforts to diversify conceptions of American aim to detach American from Whiteness-only, allowing room for a rainbow of Americans. In tandem with that effort, some respondents of color either staked a claim to Americanness by hitching their belonging to a *global* (not US-based) barometer or eschewed inclusion as a goal and strove instead for decolonization. Evidence of tenuous belonging, respondents of color are the foot soldiers in establishing belonging because they have the most to gain by arguing for their cause. A thread connecting this chapter and the next is the primacy of Whiteness in the United States that pervades institutions. I argue next that the US educational system is predicated upon and perpetuates Whiteness, protects White comfort, and generates discomfort for people of color.

4

White Comfort and Non-White Discomfort

Education's Multi-Level Messages

In September 2016, in response to demands from the Black Student Task Force, the University of Oregon changed the name of a campus dormitory that had been named for Frederic Dunn, a former faculty member and Exalted Cyclops of the Ku Klux Klan.[1] After years of student activism, the University Board of Trustees also renamed the school's oldest building, Deady Hall. The building's namesake, Matthew Deady, was president of Oregon's constitutional convention in 1857, a federal judge, campus "founding father," and university leader. The Oregon constitution (approved in 1857), which Deady had a hand in drafting, included a legislative restriction on the number of free Black people to be admitted to the state in the event an outright ban on the presence of free Black people did not pass. In fact, the anti-Black prohibition did pass in an 8-to-1 vote in favor of making it illegal for Black people to live in Oregon. In advocating for a name change, the University of Oregon student government president cited the murder-by-car of Black teenager Larnell Bruce in a Portland suburb by a member of a White supremacist prison gang in 2016 as evidence of contemporary White supremacy.[2] Oregon State University began a similar process of evaluating building namesakes in 2016, with five buildings under consideration for renaming, some named in honor of university leaders with ties to slavery, proslavery advocacy, and service in the Confederate army.[3] Indeed, "a politics of belonging is materialized and negotiated through the geographies of university social life."[4] This chapter argues that the school systems that respondents encountered (from elementary school through university) prioritize the comfort of White people and produce the antonym—discomfort—for people of color.

White comfort is a socially constructed emotion that is designed to preserve White normativity.[5] Much of the literature on White comfort is dedicated to educational systems, this focus implicating education as a "racialized organization"[6] that ensures White satisfaction and equanimity.[7] However, the topic of how White comfort fosters its inverse of discomfort for people of color remains relatively unexamined, a missing link this chapter adds. Operating in relationship, White comfort constitutes "a symbolic form of violence experienced by people of color."[8] When institutions, spaces, or societies satisfy White people's expectation for comfort, these racialized emotions "reinforce the normativity of experiences of relative power and efficacy to which White people are accustomed."[9] Racialized emotions indicate structural positions in a racial hierarchy, "emotional subjectivity generally fitting of [its] location in the racial order."[10] Emotions indicate power relations.

White comfort, rooted in settler colonialism, systemic racism, and White educational spaces, perpetuates emotional and experiential inequality by race. Education scholar Zeus Leonardo calls for "a critical pedagogy of white racial supremacy [that] revolves less around the issue of unearned advantages, or the *state* of being dominant, and more around direct processes that secure domination and the privileges associated with it."[11] Answering that call, this chapter examines how the educational system performs the "constant ideological maintenance" that racial inequality requires in what schools teach, how they are organized, and whom they serve.[12] A goal of this chapter is to re-insert organizations and agents into the process of domination, to make abstract concepts like "White privilege" real by conceiving of White privilege as an outcome generated by organizational structures, policies, actions, and people. White comfort and non-White discomfort do not materialize spontaneously; they are manifestations of deeply rooted historical processes that index the racial hierarchy in a routinized yet intensely felt fashion.

Organizations are not race-neutral bureaucratic structures. Rather, "organizations are key to understanding racialization processes spanning macro-, meso-, and microsocial levels."[13] Colonization is the "hidden backbone" of the educational system[14] and racial discrimination is best seen as a "system" where "feedback loops" reinforce component parts that exacerbate disparities.[15] This chapter takes a system-based approach, meaning that racial domination constitutes a whole *system* that is larger than the sum of its parts.[16] Viewing domination as an ongoing, dynamic process (rather than "dominance" or the "state of being domi-nant" which is a static outcome)[17] opens the door to examining pro-cesses operating at the macro (institutional), meso (community), and micro (interactional) levels.

Institutions broker belonging.[18] Settler-colonial and racist ideology wends its way through the educational system and produces White comfort and non-White discomfort, indices of privileged and burdened belonging, respectively. As a generator of multi-level messages, schools actively construct non-White people as a social problem—a label and mandate that produce discomfort. The inverse of *discomfort* for people of color is White *comfort*. White spaces, which characterize the field sites for this book, privilege "tastes, preferences, and experiences . . . that creates . . . a White 'vibe,' that 'makes sense' and 'feels right' to those who have been socialized in the White habitus. These spaces socially and culturally craft 'comfort' and safety for Whites."[19] In this "affective apartheid,"[20] White comfort is "institutionally protected."[21] With White comfort prioritized in White spaces,[22] the cumulative multi-level mes-sage is that society is built to privilege and protect White people, to the detriment of people of color who are excluded, overlooked, tokenized, disparaged, and made uncomfortable. The educational system, char-acterized by settler colonialism and systemic racism, promotes White comfort and non-White discomfort.

Institutional Level: Fostering Comfort for White Students and Discomfort for Students of Color

In 1920, W.E.B. Du Bois acerbically decried lack of access to information that deprives learners of the beauty, knowledge sets, cosmologies, cul-tures, and contributions of communities of people of color. In his work, *Darkwater*, Du Bois castigated the educational system for perpetuating knowledge inequality which shapes what people know of the world and handicaps how they think about racialized people across the globe:

> Europe has never produced and never will in our day bring forth a single human soul who cannot be matched and over-matched in every line of human endeavor by Asia and Africa. Run the gamut, if you will, and let us have the Europeans who in sober truth over-match Nefertari, Moham-

med, Rameses and Askia, Confucius, Buddha, and Jesus Christ. If we can scan the calendar of thousands of lesser men, in like comparison, the result would be the same; but we cannot do this because of *the deliberately educated ignorance of white schools by which they remember Napoleon and forget Sonni Ali.*[23]

Education is an exercise in knowledge construction: it "deliberately educates." With the authority to install ignorance or awareness, education is a display of power that erects hierarchies. Education scholar Michael Apple opined, "The curriculum is never simply a neutral assemblage of knowledge, somehow appearing in the texts and classrooms of a nation. It is always part of a *selective tradition*[.]"[24] The process of selection that canonizes certain groups' knowledge issues from and reinforces the racial hierarchy. This "selective tradition" that sanctifies some groups' knowledge and pushes others to the shadows is a knowledge production process that socially constructs reality. Education trains people to know and see. It also does the converse, training people in opacity and naiveté. The dividing line between official curricula and subordinated knowledge is racial and colonial status: Visibility is reserved for White people, whereas people of color are obfuscated. The educational system is a key site where knowledge construction works in tandem with the construction of everyday life.

Curricula: Overwriting People of Color

"Education has the potential to oppress or liberate."[25] Oppression takes many forms in the educational system. White-centric curricula overwrite histories of communities of color who recount past events from different vantage points than the "victors" who write the history canonized in mainstream textbooks. As education and Native scholar Leilani Sabzalian writes, "settler colonialism manifests in curricular silences, what is not taught and not said in classrooms."[26] Euro-centric schools set up a warped mirror in front of students of color that casts a distorted and unfavorable reflection. The nation-state outsources settler colonialism and racism to institutions that do the dirty work of White supremacy.[27]

While there is variation in curricula and educational organizations across the nation, the vast majority of respondents of color volunteered that their schooling belittled their racial background. With K-12 education compulsory in the United States, youth are exposed to institutions that may not value the groups to which they belong or offer culturally competent pedagogy. Education is commonly viewed as "the great equalizer" for intergenerational socioeconomic mobility,[28] yet what a focus on socioeconomic mobility misses is that White spaces, such as historically White colleges and universities, subordinate non-White people.[29] The opportunity for higher prestige and income often comes at a cost for students of color. Absent programming, cultural centers, and structural diversity that supports students of color and their learning,[30] education can constitute a burden of belonging in a nation that prizes Whiteness. Notably, middle-class status is not a never-failing protectant against systemic racism seeping out of schools: Nearly all the respondents of color, including those from middle-class families, narrated examples of being subjected to institutional or interpersonal racism in schools.

Shayla Pierre, an African American college student, complains that the content taught in the overwhelmingly White schools she has attended is White-centric and does not empower Black people. Curriculum is political. A racial hierarchy is substantiated by virtue of whose history and knowledge is taught and whose is not. Shayla criticizes these curricular choices:

> History classes do a poor job on educating everyone [on] Black history especially. . . . I understand why—because I live in a super-White town. A lot of White people don't really care about that. . . . But I wish, personally, that I learned more about my Black history because until a few years ago, I had honestly thought that the only thing about Black history was just slavery. . . . You learn slavery, and then you learn Martin Luther King, but that's about it. I didn't really know about the Black Panther Party and all those activism groups.

Slavery is not the singular truth of Black history. Shayla learned in college, but not before, that Rosa Parks of Montgomery Bus Boycott fame was secretary of her local National Association for the Advancement of Colored People chapter and had *planned* her act of civil disobedience. Forty-two years old at the time, Rosa Parks was not too old and tired to move to the back of the bus. Indeed, Black Studies courses provide routes to psychological empowerment, self-determination, and counter-spaces for Black students attending predominantly White institutions.[31]

Shayla argues for educational reparations. As knowledge repair work, educational reparations would advance multiracial curricula that White-centric curricula have elbowed off-stage. Shayla contends, "I feel like it's . . . *owed* to us, to learn [multidimensional Black history]. . . . I learned about slavery. . . . It's like they only bring up stuff to make us feel uncomfortable in class. They never bring up stuff that will make us feel empowered." I asked Shayla what she would want to be taught that is currently missing. She replied:

> The activism stuff. . . . Not only the challenges that they face but how Black people overcame that and still continue to fight. . . . I honestly think everything is planned because they *plan* to only teach us about slavery and the stuff . . . that made us seem weak and helpless. . . . They think, "We did it to you once, we could do it again." They don't want to teach us, "Hey, you guys are actually capable of standing up and fighting against injustice. Because then you're going to teach future generations, 'If they did it, we can too. And so we have the ability to actually stand up and change the system.'"

Representation matters. The absence of powerful role models who counterbalance the representation of Black people as *only* enslaved is systemic racism. Since the colonial era, educational institutions have been, and continue to be, critical sites for the transmission of anti-Black messages.[32]

Like African American respondents, Latino respondents saw their group histories omitted from or skewed in official curricula. Candi Perez, a twenty-three-year-old Mexican-born woman who arrived in the United States as a baby, does not see herself reflected in standard curricula. Being from a country that was at war with the United States (1846–1848) positions Candi's ancestral community as a (vanquished) problem, one that can be disregarded. This lack of academic attention is a notable omission in light of the fact that Mexican-origin people constitute the largest national origin group within the Latino category in the United States.[33] Candi reports:

It wasn't until . . . college when I started to learn about [racial issues], because they don't teach you this kind of stuff in high school. They avoid it. Big time.

JVT: Why do you think they're avoiding it?

CANDI: I think they're just avoiding . . . the truth. They don't want to make themselves, the United States, look bad even though . . . they have done a lot of wrong. And I became very curious. That's why I started taking Spanish classes . . . [and] history of Latin America. . . . In high school they don't talk about the bad . . . the United States did. They talk about "Oh, we won the [Mexican-American] war." But when I started taking these other classes about what really happened on the other side, then I was just like, "Why did they keep so many things out?" I guess they just don't want . . . to . . . make themselves look bad? 'Cause they don't have anything in the textbooks . . . about the Mexico side, their side of the story. . . . So, it's one-sided in favor of the United States.

In Candi's telling, the US educational system is a marionette whose strings are pulled by a governing White cultural core that is devoted to propping up the White racial state and excusing harms inflicted on other countries. "One-sided" renderings of international conflicts dismiss competing narratives. Master narratives subsume alternative histories and constitute hidden curricula ("unspoken lessons transmitted at schools"[34]) that reflect the hegemony of the dominant class and multiply inequalities.[35]

Education systems founded on settler colonialism and systemic racism churn out students who are fed incomplete, one-sided histories. Such a lopsided storyline casts White settlers as establishers of the nation (omitting the sovereignty of Native nations) and non-White people as problems, conquered, or invisible. A study of K-12 US history standards found that the textbook presentations of Indigenous people were overwhelmingly restricted to the pre-1900 context, which continues a colonial mindset and erases Indigenous resistance, survivance, and presence.[36] This whitewashed rendition of history that is the master narrative of the nation taught in schools generates discomfort for people of color alongside White comfort. Native American Evelyn Xus speaks to the complementary dynamic of non-White discomfort and White comfort:

For people to understand what treaties mean [you would have to say],
"For the survival of your [Native] community, they handed over large
pieces of land, basically, and endured the early reservation systems and
the boarding schools. . . ." *None of this would exist without that*. . . . [Non-
Native] people don't like to think about it because then they have to think
about all the stuff that comes with it. . . . [For example,] the Willamette
Valley Treaty . . . relocated the Kalapuya people . . . so we could be here
sitting in this building [on a public university campus] [laughter]. . . . *It
makes people uncomfortable* and they don't like thinking about that.

In this scenario, topics that are uncomfortable for White people are
submerged for the sake of maintaining White comfort vis-à-vis "White
ignorance" or silence around racial and colonial topics even in the face
of facts.[37] Yet Native Americans "on the other side of history," as another
Native respondent put it, must manage discomfort that comes with
educational institutions that sit on stolen Indigenous land and jettison
Native knowledge.

Logics protecting White comfort and producing non-White discomfort extend beyond Oregon. As of early 2023, seven states had banned
critical race theory (race-conscious teaching and workplace training) and
sixteen more states had restrictive bills moving through the state legislature (or schools with bans).[38] A widely publicized case, Florida passed
the "Individual Freedom" bill in April 2022 (which in August 2022 was
ruled as violating the Due Process Clause of the Fourteenth Amendment
in *Honeyfund.com, Inc. v. Desantis*). Florida's Governor DeSantis invoked
critical race theory when proposing the "Individual Freedom" bill. The
legislation intended to outlaw rhetoric and practices that would make
people "feel discomfort, guilt, anguish, or any other form of psychological distress on account of his or her race, color, sex, or national origin."[39]
But this concern for emotional equanimity is circumscribed by race. Opposing the bill, Democratic State Senator Shevrin Jones (Black), criticized
the bill as legal protection against White people feeling uncomfortable:
"They are talking about not wanting White people to feel uncomfortable?
Let's talk about being uncomfortable. My ancestors were uncomfortable
when they were stripped away from their children."[40]

Institutions and popular consciousness, laced with settler-colonial
and racist logics, produce varying levels of comfort and discomfort

that are calibrated by racial and colonial status. Continued racial sub-ordination for people of color is achieved through educational systems that traffic in racial messaging that benefits the White category and dis-empowers other groups. Educational reparations, such as overhauling educational systems to present people of color as complex, multidimensional, and agentic, would disrupt the inertia of White comfort and non-White discomfort.

Centering Whiteness through Mascots, Policies, and Language Bias

Institutional emblems, policies, and practices enshrine Whiteness and trivialize and marginalize groups that do not fall in line with the White cultural core. Laws, regulations, gatekeeping, and invisibility all protect White space.[41] Through bureaucratic policies that may appear race-neutral, schools protect and reproduce Whiteness, to the detriment of students of color who did not fit the mold of Whiteness.

Dehumanization can result from overt racism, as happens when "horribly distorted depictions" of Natives are used as team mascots.[42] Racism against Native Americans has been "normalized and institutionally legitimized," actors inured to the symbolic racial violence they witness, authorize, or reproduce.[43] During her high school years in Oregon in the 2000s, Evelyn Xus was a student activist who decried the use of Native American mascots. Centering her critique on "who gets to represent who Native people are and what that means," Evelyn underscores that much Native misrepresentation has been done by non-Natives. Self-definition is a core tenet of racial freedom.[44] If groups lack power of self-definition, they are vulnerable to domination and manipulation. Evelyn quips, "the whole idea of mascots is really gross . . . and dehumanizing." To be reduced to a stereotyped caricature flattens vibrancy, personhood, and intra-group diversity. Evelyn condemns the cooptation of Native people by non-Native people for sport, saying: "For [non-Native high schools] to be like, 'We're the Indians. We're the Molalla Indians'—that's the name of one of the recognized tribes . . . in Oregon . . . Molalla people. To . . . wear that on their shirts . . . is a really grody way of also claiming land." Using Native people as a mascot does settler-colonial work. The United States operates as a settler-colonial nation-state and empire by displacing and exploiting colonial subjects through colonization, occupation, and settlement of Indigenous lands.[45] Schools with Native American mascots engage settler-colonial maneuvers: "Since many Euro-Americans encounter Native Americans only as mascots and moving images, these unreal Indians materialize the most base images of Native Americans, presenting them as warriors battling settlers and soldiers, noble savages in touch with nature, uncivilized barbarians opposing the civilized and ultimately triumphant advance of Euro-America."[46] American Indian mascots are harmful to American Indians, research finding that greater exposure to American Indian mascots is associated with more prejudice toward and less support for American Indian rights.[47] Even so, Native people hold varying opinions on Native American mascots.[48] In the case of the "Molalla Indian" high school mascot, the Confederated Tribes of Grand Ronde Tribal Council granted the use of the mascot in 2017 provided that the mascot design move away from a literal representation of an Indian toward a more culturally appropriate symbolic representation. The new logo pictures a bear, a coyote, and trees.[49]

The institutionalization of Whiteness that promotes White comfort and the degradation of people of color that engenders discomfort can turn on seemingly "race-neutral" policies. Maggie Rose (Chicana) works at a university where she is enrolled and has an insider viewpoint on how the racialized bureaucracy that defends White ways of being can harm people of color. She ruminates about how the university constructs people of color as problems even as it professes diversity, equity, and inclusion. Maggie offers examples of university-led violence against people of color:

> When I say violence, I think about everything from the fact that every institution of higher education exists on land that belonged to somebody else. [The land] was violently taken from Indigenous folks, first and foremost. And then I think about how [higher education] was used actively to be exclusionary—it was meant for White people. So [from there] . . . to . . . not knowing how to hold faculty accountable [for] racism that they . . . perpetuated in the classroom, whether it's through curriculum or . . . teaching styles. . . . Those kinds of things . . . are inherently violent. All the way down to certain policies that we don't see as racist, but can be—[like rules] in the dorms around sound or volume or smell . . .

that somehow always end up picking students of color as the people who break those policies. . . . It's just subtly racist. . . . It feels absolutely like an institution of violence against people of color.

Eviscerating the supposed fairness of "colorblind" policies that end up punishing people of color, Maggie exposes how universities' establishment, culture, and rules harm people of color.

In addition to mascots and policies, institutionalized White privilege can manifest in the dismissal of non-English languages. Consuelo Nodal is a Mexican American speech language pathologist whose experience as a bilingual student inspired her career. Stratification is visible in the treatment of languages. Social theorist Gloria Anzaldúa used the term "linguistic terrorism" to refer to "repeated attacks on our native tongue [that] diminish our sense of self."[50] Consuelo criticizes schools enacting linguistic terrorism:

When there is a dialectal difference, [children are] often placed in special education because no one knows what to do with them. And it's not the educators' problem. And, it's not only the child's problem, but it's the parent's fault. Because . . . "they're uneducated, because they don't speak English well enough. Because they don't value education. Because they don't do their homework with them." So, they're seen as the problem.

Rejecting the idea that immigrant, non-English speakers and their families are "the problem," Consuelo wants "to build a bridge . . . to include these families." English-only referenda that periodically pop up send the symbolic message that English should be revered as the official language. When educational systems require linguistic and cultural assimilation, people of color are stripped of cultural resources. English-only instruction and dearth of bilingual programming and instructors activates discomfort for parents conversant in non-English languages. Consuelo speaks to the symbolic and practical exclusion felt by parents learning English: "Why would you go somewhere where you don't feel welcomed, or you don't feel like you could connect?" Immigrant families who do not have English proficiency nevertheless possess "community cultural wealth," that is, an array of knowledge and non-dominant forms of "capital" that often go unrecognized.[51]

White comfort and discomfort for people of color is structured into schools. With education as both a "racialized" and "racializing" institution,[52] the socialization of students is a lynchpin for the maintenance of the status quo. Schools are organizational settings that impart lessons about the racial hierarchy—and students' place in it—this hidden curriculum a "latent function" of educational systems.[53] In reaction to a host of campus stimuli, respondents of color discussed their experiences with White-centric education negatively. Yet many still see education as a place where they hope to intervene as a mentor or teacher so they can re-construct whose knowledge is included, who has access, and who receives support to achieve academic success.

Community Level: Racial Misfitting

Most respondents of color were transplants from more diverse locales, and their presence on predominately White Oregon university campuses where they were numerical minorities jarred their sense of comfort. Place is central to racialization because racial meaning-making occurs within a local context. Spaces are not race-neutral but are sites where racial inequalities and relations are embedded and reproduced. American studies scholar George Lipsitz connects race and space: "The lived experience of race has a spatial dimension and the lived experience of space has a racial dimension."[54] Place is important in the predominately White Oregon context where people of color are viewed as aberrant, unfamiliar, and "out of place."[55] To this point, Adam Selam (Black), US-born son of two Ethiopian immigrants, remarks that in "extraordinarily White" Oregon, people "hard-core notice your race." This "racial politics of belonging" marks people of color as outsiders, especially in predominately White spaces where their right to be present is questioned.[56]

When outnumbered by White people on campus as well as outranked by Whiteness in the curricular content, rules, and predominating culture, students of color are hyperaware of their non-Whiteness. Most students of color view being a numerical minority on campus as indicative of an institution not intended to serve or benefit them, but to serve and benefit White people instead. Many students of color in Oregon painfully felt their "invisibility" and "hypervisibility" on campus.[57] The burden of belonging on a majority-White campus falls on the shoulders of students of color who must reckon with the Whiteness of their surroundings and the discomfort of navigating institutions that do not represent or include them well.

Attending a predominately White public university where she estimates with a laugh that 1.9% of the student population is Black, Shayla Pierre wonders what it would be like had she chosen to attend a historically Black college or university [HBCU]. As an African American, she suspects she would not feel like an "outcast" like she does now: "I didn't realize how . . . alone I would feel." Shayla contrasts her college environment with that of a HBCU: "I am friends with some Black people on campus . . . [but] it's kind of like a scavenger hunt to find those people." Another phenotypically Black woman on the same campus, Patrice Park, concurred: "I won't see anyone like me for three or four minutes—or maybe ten minutes—walking on campus, and . . . that's just crazy." In a report conducted by the Higher Education Coordinating Commission (HECC) for the year this interview took place, the University of Oregon had grown its underrepresented minority student population to 5.12% of the nearly 23,000 students.[58] While this represents an increase (up 70% since 2011), sheer numbers remain small, with Black non-Hispanic students hovering around 500 in 2018 (and dropping to 400 Black undergraduate students in Spring 2022).[59] Given these numbers, Patrice's "scavenger hunt" reference is apt.

As obvious visual subjects, Black respondents are hypervisible in predominately White contexts. Being one of few Black students can be "psychologically distressing" and lead Black students "to feel pressure to dispel negative stereotypes and represent all Black people."[60] This hypervisibility unfairly tasks students of color with representing their group. For Adam Selam, his Blackness was so germane to his student life in Oregon that he joked he may as well be known as "Black Adam" because his Blackness is noticed first. Shayla Pierre agrees that her Blackness is the first identity feature people notice: "I'm always going to be the first person seen. . . . Everyone notices my Blackness the second I walk in." In White-dominated spaces, Black people are viewed as racial "misfits" that are "visually indiscreet."[61]

"Misfitting" a local environment creates discomfort and problems for people of color. Shayla Pierre (Black) says that "it sucks" to feel devalued on campus. She wrestles with anti-Black stereotypes and wants to "detach" from the racist lens that disallows her individuality. She shies away from being noticed. Shayla alters her clothing, hairstyle, speech, and behavior to curb her hypervisibility:

> I don't talk much. When I sit in class, I . . . sit up and off to myself. . . . I always have my hair in braids . . . I wore an afro to school and . . . the person with the afro is always noticed. I had silver braids these past few weeks but . . . I felt more of a presence on me with them, [so I] took them down. . . . I hate being super-noticed . . . and so I just try and blend.

Staring is an "interrogative gesture of interest" that "at once provokes and paralyzes its object, eliciting both anger and anxiety."[62] Being stared at also increases one's heart rate, an indicator of physiological unrest.[63] Shayla submerges her identity in an effort to minimize attention cast in her direction; in a place characterized by Whiteness, her Black body is read as "out of place."[64] To ward off the "presence" on her body (what others have called the "White gaze"[65]), Shayla tries to "blend," a cost to her natural appearance. Shayla's predicament and strategies echo early African American studies theorist Franz Fanon who wrote: "I slip into corners, I remain silent, I strive for anonymity, for invisibility."[66]

Not exclusive to African American students, non-Black students of color also reported feeling a "White gaze" on them which suggested they were out of place. "Controlling images" that override the student status of respondents of color risk reducing their presence to token representation.[67] Undergraduate Perez Ochoa (Latinx) remarks on the collision of racial status and underrepresentation in the classroom that make them hypervisible: "I took an anthropology class and we were talking about immigration and . . . I was one of the only people of color in that class and one of the only Hispanic or Latinx people. . . . People were looking at me. . . . I'm just very conscious of it."

Sefina Sosene, Pacific Islander, was "culture shocked" when she arrived at her predominately White university and felt "not welcome." She was told the campus was "diverse," but given that her frame of reference was the San Francisco Bay Area, that word was misleading: "They said [the university] was really diverse and I was . . . excited for that. . . . It may be diverse for Oregon but from where I'm from, it's not as diverse." This shortfall in diversity was a basis for Sefina's discomfort. She struggled with making friends; White students she met lacked similar experiences. Coethnic friendships were a solace: "Once I found people who identify as Pacific Islander it was really relieving that I could talk about something and they'll get it. They won't look at me confused or I have to explain it." Lack of group size, cultural representation, and power make students of color feel "out of place." Sefina's resonance with students from similar backgrounds illustrates a self-conscious desire to find a haven where race, racism, and racialized experience are seen as true accounts rather than exaggerations or misinterpretations.[68]

Anna Hernan, a Mexican American computer science major, observes about her university, "most of the campus and most of my classes were White males." White men earned the highest number of bachelor's degrees in computer science in 2019 (40%), far outpacing every other combination of race/ethnicity and gender.[69] A dearth of people of color and women in Anna's classes is off-putting to her. By virtue of the White setting that is "instilled with racial meanings" and "reinforced institutionally,"[70] Anna feels as if she is expected to shelve her ethnic accessories. She muses:

> Going to a computer science class [for my major] . . . I feel a little bit apprehensive walking in if I'm wearing a traditional piece. Because then, I'm like, "These people are probably like, 'What is she doing?'" I know most of them aren't probably thinking that. But it's just a little bit more pressure. . . . I feel like there is [an] expectation to bring down my race or . . . tone it down so that they feel more comfortable. . . . I feel like a lot of White classmates . . . feel more uncomfortable talking about race, so they don't want to see it.

The "racial politics of visibility" are operating here,[71] both invisibility and hypervisibility signaled by an expectation to leave racial/ethnic identity at the door to meet the racial standards of a White space. White comfort is encoded in the standards set for academic space, including concessions people of color are expected to make so that "*they* [White people] feel more comfortable." Anna says that her White peers are "uncomfortable" with race, an orientation that alienates people of color and leaves Whiteness as a normative, unmarked category.[72] White space demands that Anna sacrifice her comfort and submit to discomfort, forgoing traditional clothing that she would like to wear but would mark her as aberrant. Observing that White people "don't want to see" race, this willful ignorance about race burdens Anna with decisions about how to navigate conflicting priorities, such as *her comfort* that is at odds with White comfort and her potential success in that environment.

Anna speaks to the stress of being a numerical minority:

> I do feel excluded if I'm in the big class and I'm the only Latino. . . . That . . . feels frustrating. . . . "Why aren't there more Latinos?" Like, "Is there . . . something against being in computer science and being Latino?" . . . I sometimes . . . wonder. . . . A lot of Latinos don't feel like they can be part of this and so that does feel . . . exclusive.

Black and Latino people remain underrepresented in the science, technology, engineering, and math (STEM) workforce.[73] Without role models, Anna struggles against a narrow vision of racialized career tracks that leave Latinos out of computer science. "I sometimes wonder" hints that it takes effort not to internalize racism, a self-defeating phenomenon to which people of color can fall prey.[74] Additionally, to be faced with continual assaults by institutionally supported racial microaggressions can lead to "racial battle fatigue" (emotional, psychological, and physiological distress).[75]

Ironically, Anna's efforts to integrate have the opposite effect of reminding her of her racial nonconformity. Anna explains the unintended exclusionary effects of networking:

> When I go to more professional events, I do feel a little bit excluded. . . . I feel like being a Hispanic and a woman, I have to . . . be way more outgoing . . . because I [have] something to prove. . . . So . . . that can sometimes feel like I'm being excluded even though I'm trying to be included. . . . Because of who I am and what I look like, I feel like I need to make up for something, [though] I'm not sure what I'm making up for. [laughter]

Mismatching racially, Anna's efforts to be "more outgoing" and "make up for something" only exacerbates her sense of exclusion *despite* her attempts to belong. The phrase "I'm not sure what I'm making up for" intimates that the racialized barrier is not personal per se, but is a group-based burden with which she is saddled nonetheless.

The double burden of being a woman of color exposes a paradox: To possess burdened belonging means that *marginality is a condition of belonging.* In her large science and engineering classes, most of Anna's peers are White men, which compounds her sense of being a "misfit"[76] and multiply disadvantaged as a Hispanic woman. The imposition that Anna be "outgoing" (not her natural personality, which she describes as "passive") is a behavioral response to the racialized feeling that she must "prove" herself. Adopting an "outgoing" persona is a form of "emotion work."[77] Scholarship on emotion work and "feeling rules" emphasizes that feeling rules are not universal but are contoured by gender and race. For example, Black people are held to different emotional standards than White people in workplaces, the result being *constraints* on Black people's emotional expression.[78] Anna's insight puts a twist on racial-ized feeling rules: She uncovers an added component of how gender and race not only constrain but *facilitate* emotion work or outward display of emotions to maneuver particular settings. Anna explains how racialized emotion work puts her on display:

> It feels like I'm trying to show the world, "Oh, I'm Latino but . . . I'm still smart and I can still make good conversation, I can still do this or that." So it kind of feels like I'm putting on a face for the sake of trying to show people [older White adults at networking events] that I can fit in with them. To show them, "Oh, I can work really well on your team."

Racialized institutions and social settings compel behaviors and emo-tional displays that require discernment and labor from people of color. To diminish one's race for the sake of success in an institution is a fail-ure of diversity initiatives and emblematic of burdened belonging. Anna challenges the notion of a college student as a *White* student, and a computer scientist as *not* Latina. Such narrow, ingrained ideas presume racial groups are predestined for certain occupations. If White students occupy most college classroom slots, students of color are squeezed out from imagining their own futures as degree-holding professionals. As a recipient of mentorship in high school, Anna aims to mentor first-generation college-bound youth, a topic covered in chapter 6.

Ensconced in largely White institutions, respondents of color were race-conscious in their critiques of educational systems, including the bankruptcy of racial awareness. Colorblindness (non-recognition of race) only serves to minimize racism, pathologize people of color who call out racism, and keep racial inequality embedded in institutions intact.[79] As much as this section centers respondents of color who are students or employees at Oregon universities, White respondents' viewpoints can also be instructive. Chance Green, a White employee at a large public Oregon university, describes how an "Oregon nice" ethos submerges race and racism. Chance wants to shine a light on settler colonialism and racism in Oregon because it is rarely discussed, observing:

> I think there is this sleepiness [in] Oregon . . . about race. There's a real sleepiness here where people are . . . just not super-present with the history. . . . We've got a real mass of White liberals who really need to be awakened. . . . Like . . . "No, really, even you, White liberal from Oregon who had two dads. . . ." People have all kinds of excuses for . . . "I'm not a racist." I'm like, "No, really. No, really, *you too*. All of us, together [are] in this." [laughter]

Calling themselves an "aspiring ally" (implying that the work is never done) and an "accomplice," Chance works to move the needle on conversation about racial issues that affect their town and university.

Luna Espinoza, a mixed-race woman (Asian/Latinx) who works at the same university as Chance, describes the prevailing attitude about race in Oregon as one of "vacancy." When she lived in California, Luna found that the "'what are you' question . . . stemmed from sheer curiosity." In contrast, Luna observes:

> There's . . . a vacancy in Oregon of even asking any questions and I think that has everything to do with Oregon not wanting to talk about race because of its historical legacies in White supremacy. . . . I don't think people want to ask about your identity or culture or where you grew up. . . . They don't want to touch it with a 10-foot pole.

The climate of racial "vacancy" that denies her racialized experience and augers discomfort has led Luna to consider relocating to a more racially diverse state. Colorblindness, claims to ignorance,[80] and protection of White comfort are made easier when a community shelves discussions aimed at seeing and dismantling systemic racism and settler colonialism.

Educational systems can be inviting or off-putting, depending on the racial communities that are overrepresented, underrepresented, and misrepresented. When systemic racism and settler colonialism combine to produce majority-White faculty, staff, and student populations in addition to White-centric curricula and policies, White comfort and non-White discomfort result. When people of color are pushed to the periphery, burdened belonging—or marginality as a condition of belonging—emerges.

Interactional Level: Marginalizing Students of Color

Erasure

Interactions in schools deliver the consonant message that groups are unequally valued. Symbolic interactionism holds that we learn social meanings "through the indications of others," such as the way people interact with and talk about objects or subjects.[81] Interactions (words and actions) are conduits that carry meaning. Positive attention, negative attention, and lack of attention all build meaning.

In her Oregon elementary school where she and her brother were the "darkest kids in school," Evelyn Xus (Coastal Chumash) was removed from her classroom daily for her decision not to stand for the Pledge of Allegiance. The school administration's choice to pull her from class during rituals she protested *literally* extracted her from her peers because of her critical colonial consciousness that found fault in the Pledge of Allegiance. Evelyn recalls:

> When I was little I didn't agree with the Pledge of Allegiance and I actually still don't. And I've never stood up for it because my whole philosophy around that is that *we're not all free,* and so how can you stand for something that's not true? . . . That's when they used to have all the kids say the Pledge of Allegiance in the beginning of the day. . . . So what they used to do is have me sit outside [laughter] until they are done, which I now know is totally illegal. . . . They would have me sit outside, no matter what the weather was like, until they did the Pledge of Allegiance because

they didn't want the other students to see me sit. Now that I'm older . . . [I] understand . . . that's so messed up. . . . That institutionalized treatment around the flag was pretty intense.

A school mandate for classrooms to perform a symbol of "national unity" is obtuse to how this semiotic act is discordant for a Native American student. Then school authorities literally exclude her because she disagrees and refuses to conform. Settler-colonial theory reminds that colonialism continues in the present moment.[82] Educational practices enforced by school leadership can function as an arm of settler colonialism. At the interactional level, schoolteachers and administrators advanced White-centered teaching and discipline that engineer Native invisibility. Erasure does not happen by accident—it requires foot soldiers to carry out the mission.

Evelyn's removal from the classroom echoes the nation's prior forced removal of Native Americans. "Indian removal" formally refers to the passage and consequences of the Indian Removal Act (1830) when US President Jackson enforced the physical removal of Native Americans "under the guns and bayonets of the US Army."[83] Fast-forward and, like her predecessors, Evelyn is judged to be a problem by the White power structure and is forcibly removed. History repeats itself.

Evelyn's "feeling of invisibility as a Native person" typifying her "whole life in schools" was conjured through repeated interactions. Partially homeschooled and attending public school three days a week, Evelyn encountered lessons in those two settings that were diametrically opposed. She was socialized in "'seeing' double," that is "seeing from two or more perspectives simultaneously."[84] Public school curricula, she says, "was always a challenge because we were taught something different at home [chuckles]." Teaching around Thanksgiving and Christopher Columbus illustrates the disjuncture. Evelyn recollects being reprimanded after arguing against a teacher's pro-Columbus "discovery" narrative:

I remember . . . getting sent to the principal's office often . . . for saying stuff that [was] questioning the teachers [laughter]. . . . I remember very specifically . . . one of [my fifth-grade teacher's] heroes [was Columbus]. . . . [chuckles] And he didn't like that I called him a rapist and a murderer in school and so he made me leave class and go to the principal's office. . . . [chuckles]

From the perspective of a Native woman whose distant ancestors were likely raped and murdered during conquest, the praising of Columbus and erasure of her forebearers was intolerable. This construction of Evelyn as a problem in the classroom who deserved ejection fits with, as she phrased it, "the romanticized notion of us [Natives] being a people of the past . . . barely . . . blips . . . in history books." If White-saturated educational curriculum eclipses Native history from their points of view, how can students and teachers know they exist and see them with equal humanity? Upon questioning curricula that supported White comfort, exclusion and punishment fomented Evelyn's discomfort. Interactional sanctions aim to silence, disempower, and make ill-at-ease people of color who articulate counternarratives at odds with master narratives that uphold White supremacy.

Interactions that provoke discomfort for people of color can be entangled with bureaucratic policy. Interactions encompass peer-to-peer and school personnel-to-student exchanges, where power flows horizontally or vertically, respectively. Quincey Bernabe is a twenty-year-old who identifies as Native American/Pacific Islander/Caucasian, though she has "never been attached to" her Caucasian side. Filipina on her mother's side, Quincey's mother came to the United States as a young adult migrant farmworker. Interactions in schools influenced Quincey's mother's decision not to teach her Tagalog, the Filipino language. According to Quincey, her mother learned that teachers forbade Tagalog by watching her siblings: "Teachers got mad at them for speaking Tagalog in class. . . . [The teachers] had the principal tell my aunts and uncles to stop teaching them Tagalog. . . . And so, yeah, my mom didn't teach us anything." Teachers bringing in higher-level authority (the principal) to authenticate their message doubles down on the prohibition against Tagalog. Teacher-student interactions are enough to snuff out culture.

School policy that emboldens interaction shows the intermingling of levels of an organization that cooperate to send uniform messages. Policy decisions set the stage for micro-level interaction. Quincey's high school had promised Native students that they could organize a "Natives Day." The commitment was reduced to half a day. Then it was downsized to drumming in a hallway after school. Suffering a trimmed-down time allotment and set after school, the Native event was sidelined. One can argue that the administrators' relegation of the Native event to an unofficial time and place allowed for ridicule. Quincey recalls the incident with dismay and discomfort:

> It was not very fun. . . . My group was drumming in the hallway and [it] was freezing outside raining . . . and these [White] kids were making fun of us. They were circling, dancing around like idiots. . . . It was really rude: The vice principal's standing right there. He didn't even do anything to stop [it]. . . . So we went from a whole school day that we were promised to drumming in the hallway in the freezing cold rain and being made fun of.

This insouciance from a school administrator, a maker and enforcer of school policy, sent the top-down message that respect need not apply to Native American students. The incident opened Quincey's eyes to "not being respected." Here, the "tick box approach to diversity" (as in, holding the event) backfires and works against effectuating an inclusive environment.[85] From event-planning (structural level) to the non-interventionist inaction of the vice principal (structural and interactional) to peer mockery (community and interactional), this episode shows how power dynamics cut across multiple levels. Power-inflected situations that produce discomfort for students of color, as well as comfort for White students, consolidate messages about belonging.

Peer-to-peer interaction that marginalizes non-White racial group knowledge and culture occurs in classroom dynamics too. A Latina graduate student, Maggie Rose, was overjoyed when she read an assigned book authored by a Latina scholar for a seminar. She was validated by the text, which honored her racialized experience, a refreshing break from scholarship authored by White scholars read earlier.[86] When she expressed resonance with the reading in class, the other (all White) graduate students looked at her oddly, indicating that she was alone in this sentiment. To Maggie's consternation, the authentication she felt when reading the book devolved into being "othered" by her White classmates. Perversely, a feeling of racial resonance transmogrified into loneliness in the context of an otherwise White classroom. Interactions, even non-verbal cues such as facial expressions or staring, deliver laden messages. These silent interactions generated discomfort for Maggie, a student of color, and created a bulwark of Whiteness behind which the White students retreated to regain their comfort.

Labeling

Racial stereotypes and labeling can "misframe" youth.[87] Victor Rios, a sociologist who studies the criminalization of Black and Brown youth, defines "cultural misframing" as "the process by which institutions construct, define, and impose simplistic, fixed, negative identities on individuals based on misunderstandings of their symbols, language, expressions, and actions."[88] The lenses through which school staff read or "frame" youth with different racial backgrounds and cultural styles can boost or damn their futures when staff, in turn, provide or withhold resources and support. Schooling rooted in a White-centric foundation can lead to "subtractive schooling" for students of color where an assimilationist agenda divests them of culture and language.[89] Cultural misframing and subtractive schooling are useful tools to better comprehend how students of color are misunderstood and improperly served by a school system structured to protect White comfort.

Adam Selam's middle school experience is emblematic of the phenomenon of Black boys being targeted by teachers and school leadership for extra doses of surveillance and punishment.[90] Adam faced racially stereotypical labels in school about Black families as poor and about Black boys as disruptive. He explains how administrators concocted racial meanings concerning his Black masculinity which shaped their interactions with him:

> When I was in middle school I would get in trouble a lot. And I was never a bad kid. . . . I was just high-energy. That was it. It just starts and ends there. . . . I was never aggressive. I've never punched a hole in the wall or anything like that. . . . But for whatever reason I'm getting in trouble all the time at school, right? And so, I personally think that my teachers and the administration of the middle school . . . [were] accidentally more stringent on me because they noticed more of the things I did. And . . . I was automatically labelled as food insecure. . . . I grew really quickly and I was skinny. . . . Sometimes I wouldn't have a lunch with me at school

because I may have eaten it before lunch even happened. But, I was never . . . food insecure in middle school.

What Adam calls "accidental stringency" and "noticing [him] more" is indicative of school employees "misframing" or misunderstanding students. Instead of asking level-headed questions to arrive at answers, in misframing, school authorities make incorrect racialized judgments about students. This is not a one-off interaction; it is important to view the actions of teachers and administrators as institutional agents because this signals alignment between organizational levels. As sociologist Victor Ray explains, "In isolation, individual prejudice and racial animus may matter little; but when these are put into practice in connection to organizational processes such as racialized tracking . . . or exclusion, they help shape the larger racial order."[91]

In his own words, Adam lays out the premise of stereotype threat which argues that negative group assumptions about a person will add stress which, in turn, depresses performance.[92] Adam imagines himself a teacher as he provides a textbook example based on his experience as a student:

> Let's say I believe that Black students are more aggressive and they don't do as well on tests, right? If a Black student in my class now scores poor on a test, it just reinforces what I already believed before, and I think that cycle is what causes a lot of students to do poorly in school. I don't think they're just inherently stupid or inherently less capable. I think a lot of it is people automatically assuming the worst in their Black students.

Educators can boost or break students. Not wholly individual, implicit bias is an outgrowth of institutionalized racism that arms administrators with damaging meanings of, and low expectations for, students of color. Implicit bias is a key mechanism of multilevel racial messaging because it operates at the structural, organizational, and individual levels simultaneously and links these domains. Once societal racism is inculcated into the minds of educators, it then infiltrates their actions such as funneling resources (teachers' time and attention) toward groups with positive preassessments and away from those with negative ones. Systemic racism, in the cloak of individual-level implicit bias, can also breed confirmation bias (looking for data that validate a preconceived notion). Confirmation bias inflates the misdeeds of students of color while forgiving those same actions for privileged students.[93]

Pacific Islander Sefina Sosene says being typecast as an athlete rather than a student "hurt her." The duality of "brain or brawn" pits intellectual pursuits against athletic ones, deleting the possibility of "student-athletes" who occupy both identities. Because of her Pacific Islander identity, Sefina finds that people typecast her only as an athlete, their vision of her success limited to sports fields. This stereotyping of people of color as bodies without brains is not limited to Pacific Islanders but also affects African Americans and Latinos.[94] Stereotypes of people of color as athletes-only assist in producing the outcome they predetermine. By typecasting people of color only as athletes, their trajectories are routed toward sports and away from academics and other opportunities by teachers, administrators, and even their imaginations that have been shaped by racial socialization. Sefina explains: "A lot of people would ask me if I was an athlete. . . . That . . . hurt me that people would think . . . that's all I'm good for. And they don't see my creative side or my academics. It was just my physical abilities." Butting against these messages that label and confine, Sefina "embraced all sides" of herself. Sefina's resistance to being boxed in aligns with Pacific Islander scholar-activists who insist on their own knowledge approaches, self-determination, and dynamic identities.[95]

White Respondents: Racial Fit in Education Produces White Comfort

The burdens or privileges born by education vary by race. Respondents of color spoke about how school was difficult, whereas White respondents talked about their education with ease. First, with the rare exception of racially heterogenous schools, Whiteness is baked into education and thus normalizes Whiteness. White respondents were implicitly taught that they can rely on a White power structure to benefit them. Second, White respondents *intellectualize* racial inequality and their anti-racist efforts. This ability to intellectualize racial status is a consequence of White people's structural location of privilege that releases them from the knee-jerk emotional response people of color experience. This "intellectualization of racism" is a form of violence: White people can step away from racism and reduce it to cognition, whereas people of color must live it out.[96] Third, college courses centered on subordinated knowledge (e.g., communities of color) were turning points in White respondents' awareness of racism and settler colonialism. But, because multicultural education classes are not nationally required curricula at elementary or secondary school,[97] only college students who elect to take race-conscious classes benefit from them.

A White cultural core as the basis of the US educational system directly benefits White students. Olivia Renee does not mince words: "The messages that we get . . . through the . . . education system . . . the media. . . . the legal system . . . every institution, is racist. [chuckles]" Olivia explains how White supremacy translates to unearned advantage: "The laws and policies that come out [of] the education system—all the institutions—I know they're all going to work in my favor." Connecting to settler colonialism, Olivia says that as a "settler" they are not "entitled to be here at all" and yet they gain advantages through White privilege endorsed by society's institutions, including education. Tess Smith attended an elementary school where Whiteness was ubiquitous. In school, the word "race" referred to non-White groups, a technique that universalizes Whiteness and constructs non-White groups as exceptional: "I think that race was . . . a neutral issue aside from [when it was] studied or reflected on . . . [such as] the civil rights movement." In contrast to respondents of color who learned in school that their racial background can have detrimental effects, Tess learned the opposite: "[My Whiteness was not] something that was going to affect me or threaten me or jeopardize my life choices in any way."

The inverse of *discomfort* for people of color is White *comfort*. Nellie speaks to the ease of making new (White) friends in her majority-White university setting: "I don't feel like I don't belong here—going to school and . . . making friends. . . . I never felt anxious to be here." Her White racial heritage facilitates inclusion on a predominately White college campus. She instantly "identified with a lot of people," including her roommates, who were all White. I asked whether seeing mostly White people on a daily basis makes her feel like she belongs in her college setting. She responded the same as her peers of color: Seeing people who race-match her is important to feeling at ease in an environment. But, in contrast to respondents of color on a majority-White campus, Nellie *does* see an abundance of White people: "I think for any race it's nice to see yourself represented on campus."

Whereas respondents of color volunteered that White-centric curricula do not reflect their racial history, White respondents were reticent in their comments about curricula. The discordance here is because the course content was aligned for White students and misaligned for students of color. Yet some White respondents are race-conscious, such as Jubilee Thompson, who said: "White people . . . don't own America, you know what I mean? What happened to the people who were already here . . . was really awful." Jubilee credits her family for her anti-colonial views that question the White savior mythology of the founding of the United States. Pinpointing racial socialization that would "happen around the dinner table," Jubilee summarizes: "My family really emphasizes . . . that colonization was actually really awful. [That message] would have slipped by me if it was only in school."

Whiteness also figured into school choice for White respondents' families. In watching parents navigate neighborhood and school choice, White children learn that homogenous White contexts are associated with higher class status and "better schools."[98] For some parents, White racial identity becomes salient in accessing a "good" public school—one that is predominately White. This demographic makeup fosters a "white racial habitus"[99] that constrains exposure to racially diverse settings and limits opportunities for interracial friendships and progressive racial attitudes.[100] Chance Green, who grew up in Cleveland, Ohio, says that their parents were part of "White flight," moving from the racially heterogeneous city to a White suburb to secure "good schools." Piercing through the colorblind veil of school choice, Chance sees the racial connection: "[My parents] wanted to live out of the city. . . . I think of that as a way of structuring proximity to Whiteness and reducing proximity to Blackness. . . . I think if I were to [ask] them [about their residential choice] . . . it would get coated as, 'Oh, but we wanted to put you in good schools.' Well . . . there are lots of good schools, right? [laughter]." School choice is a way to preserve or gain White privilege that is wrapped in non-racial language, even as the motivations and consequences are racial.

Whiteness permeating US culture and institutions makes White respondents' assurance about their social membership effortless. Nellie

Locke addresses society-wide White privilege: "[Race] was never an issue for me. I never had a moment where I was like, 'Oh, I'm White,' because it never held me back." When I asked if she "thinks that it might be easier to be successful because of Whiteness," Nellie says "yes." She blames White school administrators' inclination for homophily (racial sameness) for lack of racial diversity in schools: "In school systems, there's a lot of White administration, and . . . I think that's a psychological thing where you prefer people that are your same race. So, I think that's what makes it easier for White people, and that shouldn't be the case, but sadly it is."

College-level multicultural education courses signified turning points in some White respondents' awareness of race and settler colonialism. Since higher education is not accessible to (or desired by) all, there is selection bias in who takes and learns from elective higher-education multicultural courses—namely, those who can afford college and want to learn about these topics. Lizzie Rhodes reports that college education taught her global history in a way that decentered dominant US tropes. In offering history classes from alternative, non-US-centric perspectives, college undid some of the racial socialization built into public school K-12 curricula: "It wasn't until college that I really started learning about US history and our impacts on other groups. . . . In our school system . . . you're taught that your country is just so amazing. When in reality the reason that they were so successful is because they were stepping on other groups." Similarly, Olivia Renee learned of settler colonialism in a college class: "The first time I learned about that word [settler] was in history classes [in college] talking about Columbus. But it wasn't . . . the typical . . . Columbus 'discovery' language. . . . [One college professor] talked about settlers not as a past thing, but as present day: 'we are settlers.'" Race and coloniality are foundational to US nation-building,[101] yet this lesson is omitted from mandatory K-12 education, this "selective tradition"[102] of curricula one way of installing comfort for White students.

Conclusion

The formal education system in the United States, which stems from systemic racism and settler colonialism, is *productive*—it produces effects.

School buildings, classrooms, lessons, administrations, and interactions are emblazoned with racial and colonial dynamics. White knowledge and history that are authenticated and disseminated above the knowledge and histories of communities of color perpetuate differential group valuation. In a largely White context with a historic "spatial identity" committed to Whiteness, the prospect of "homemaking" for people of color is a challenge.[103] An educational system that bears the trappings of racism and settler colonialism (in architecture, curricula, policies, and lack of structural diversity in historically White schools) perpetuates a hierarchy and yields an imbalance of comfort and discomfort. In sum, the workings of educational systems make clear how the level of comfort or discomfort people experience corresponds to, and reinscribes, their racial and colonial status.

The educational system operates via "multi-level messaging": Students receive information about the extant racial-colonial hierarchy, and their placement in it, from multiple origin points within the institution. These messages snowball to effectuate White comfort and non-White discomfort. Most respondents reported that educational systems taught, valorized, and normalized Whiteness, crucial ingredients that amount to White comfort. In corollary fashion, schools tend to discredit, omit, or sideline groups of color, which generates discomfort. Education contributes to racialized emotions, self-concept, and perspectives on other groups. Education bespeaks valuation: What is taught is honored and what is neglected is devalued. Reinforcing differential valuation of groups at all organizational levels, educational systems produce racial fitting and comfort for White people and misfitting and discomfort for people of color.

Educational systems construct degrees of belonging, as indexed by comfort and discomfort. Indicative of system-wide racism and coloniality, multi-level messaging operates at all layers of an organization, protecting White comfort and evincing non-White discomfort. There are three levels at which multi-level messaging occurs: (1) the institutional level, which encapsulates curricula, organizational structure, policies, and rules; (2) the community level, which refers to how racial demographics and group-level relations play out; and (3) the interactional level, which concerns interpersonal dynamics. The "hidden curriculum" embedded in these multi-level messages that constructs comfort and belonging for White people and discomfort and non-belonging or marginalized belonging for people of color reinscribes racial inequality.

When students of color are regarded as problematic or peripheral to the educational system, the educational institution *becomes a problem* for them. When treated as racially non-conforming in schools, students of color bear the brunt of misunderstanding, misframing, and exclusion. When people of color *are seen as problems* in schools, this produces *problems for them.* These problems carried by students of color are consequential, ranging from barriers to academic success to alienation to racial stress.

Educational reparations, or re-fashioning schools to fully embrace people of color, represent a liberatory disruption of systemic racism and settler colonialism. If such emancipatory change is to happen, institutions should take a cue from literature that is critical of organizations boasting "diversity ideology," noting that diversity ideology is superficial, does not shift power dynamics, and only commodifies people of color and their cultures.[104] Instead, schools should pay heed to the people who inhabit the institution but are on the periphery or wish to enter but are left behind.

Structural diversity is a partial antidote to the comfort imbalance in educational institutions. Including more people of color at all ranks of an institution and ensuring their voices are listened to can shift the balance of power. Mentoring students and faculty/staff of color is key to their success, retention, and satisfaction.[105] Recruiting and retaining people of color, ethnic organizations, and mentorship all support a minority culture of mobility where ethnic culture is a resource (rather than detriment) for upward mobility.[106] Students of color benefit from institutional agents that ensure access to resources and can advocate for them as well as peer support networks and on-campus involvement that foster belonging.[107] Race consciousness is a step toward balancing out comfort inequality (e.g., racial inequality) in education. This is because the alternative of neglecting race in colorblind classrooms and campuses preserves Whiteness as an undeclared privileged position and norm.[108] The validation of racial experience is consequential; it honors a person's entire life experience rather than dismissing a central component. Since predominantly White institutions house race-related stressors for students of color, institutions should invest in reducing these stressors and create an inclusive environment for the sake of student health and well-being.[109]

Community and interactional level shifts can stem from institutional changes, but they also require focused support. Recommendations include intentional messaging of value and supportive practices for all constituencies involved in schools. Building role models by promoting leaders from a variety of backgrounds is important for everyone. Flipping racial power dynamics is also instructive for all: For example, hiring and retaining inspiring Black teachers means that all students see those teachers as knowledge-holders, Black students have role models, and non-Black (especially White) students expand their scope of authority figures. Culturally responsive pedagogy is also needed so that students see themselves, their histories, and their possible futures in the curricula. Multiracial, race-conscious curricula would also potentially re-shape how people interact, encouraging greater sensitivity, knowledge, and understanding unhinged from misconceptions. As reported to me, however, schools house and disseminate multi-level messages which collude to generate White comfort and non-White discomfort. The next chapter picks up the baton from here to examine "embodied burdens," that is, physical, mental, and emotional manifestations of racial and colonial subjugation that interfere with the health and wellness of respondents of color and remind them that they are living out racial inequality.

5

Embodied Burdens

Trauma, Health, and Safety

Picking up the theme of Whiteness as an unspoken prerequisite to American identity and warm reception in US institutions, Mexican American Maggie Rose ties her anxiety to challenges in being perceived as American:

> [I do not feel like] I had a lot of room to *not* be perfect, which . . . [goes] into conversations about . . . being American. Like, you have to be perfect in all of these other ways when you're a person of color in order to balance those things out to be seen as American. . . . I think . . . my anxiety comes from . . . needing to *be* a particular way to be *received* a particular way.

Racial distance from Whiteness is what Maggie suggests needs to be "balanced out" to be viewed as American, being "perfect" in "other" (non-racial) ways as the only option to elevate her. Being non-White in a society that privileges Whiteness provokes anxiety. A reaction to a racial deficit model that pictures communities of color as deficient in important elements compared to the dominant White group, anxiety is an embodied consequence that is a physically, mentally, and emotionally *felt* burden of belonging.

The materiality of the body is central to colonial and racialized experience. Colonialism is a social determinant of health: Colonial social processes such as extractive economies, unequal citizenship, and labor exploitation damage public health.[1] Relatedly, as racial formation theorists Michael Omi and Howard Winant write, "*The body is the person.* . . . [D]espotism operates on the racial body, assaulting it, confining it, and profiling it."[2] Power dynamics of colonialism and racial domination can be read through bodies. Trauma, health, and safety are roads this chapter travels to access the patterned experiences of differently racialized bodies.

Social epidemiology research informs that health outcomes vary by race as a result of social experiences that are steered by racism and colonialism (as opposed to biological predisposition).[3] Such an ecosocial approach holds that discrimination "becomes embodied inequality and is manifested as health inequities."[4] Sociology of health research is clear that individual behaviors only go so far to foster physical health. Instead, health researchers advance a "social determinants of health" model that underscores the crucial role of factors such as race, class status, migration history, and neighborhood context on health.[5] This chapter takes up the call to "think about the social context that produces racial disparities."[6] Exposure to—or protection from—systemic racism and colonization produce disparate illness and wellness experiences. Intergenerational trauma, stress, and ability to feel safe are contingent upon racial and colonial status, and I argue that these embodied vulnerabilities are simultaneously *symptoms* and *reminders* of racial subjugation.

This chapter centers the material reality of the body in three senses. First, despite race being a social construct, physical appearance is "raw material" which triggers racial categorization and treatment. Second, the body holds racial and colonial memory, such as historical trauma that is experienced at individual and collective levels.[7] Third, trauma, health, and safety are experienced not only *due to* but also *in* the body. While it is increasingly common knowledge that not everyone has an equal shot at living a healthy life, class status tends to be the headline news in this arena, as exemplified by the phrase "wealth equals health." That colonial and racialized experiences influence health is an important social problem that this chapter illuminates with qualitative research, filling in gaps regarding the ways in which people understand how colonialism and racism lodge in their bodies.

Embodiment literature discusses how cultural constructions of the body, objectification of bodies, and varied meanings attached to bodies do cultural and nation-making work.[8] Bodies are rich terrain on which to etch and send symbolic messages about race, gender, and nation. In light of embodiment literature, it is telling that respondents of color reported an abundance of race-related trauma, health, and safety concerns. Vulnerability to trauma, health, and safety harms is central to the lives of respondents of color and indicates the embodied gravity of racial stratification. Trauma and differential access to health and safety are effects of systemic racism and colonialism that are experienced in body, mind, and spirit. Exposure to (and the need to manage) trauma, health, and safety issues constitute burdens of belonging for people of color in the United States.

This chapter argues that overexposure to trauma, health stressors, and safety violations for respondents of color are simultaneously *symptoms* and *reminders* of racial subordination. The material is subdivided into two main sections: "trauma and health" and "safety concerns." These embodied issues are burdens of belonging shouldered by respondents of color. It is not that White people do not experience health and safety difficulties but, in aggregate, people of color are overexposed to health and safety violations by virtue of racial domination and colonized histories. Trauma, health, and safety precarity are physiological and psychological signals and ramifications of "unfreedom"[9] and constitute embodied burdens of belonging.

Trauma and Health: "We End Up Somaticizing All These Things"

Research amply testifies that perceived racial discrimination, persistent fear, and safety concerns manifest in depressed health outcomes.[10] Stress, fear, and trauma, as by-products of systemic racism and settler colonialism, indelibly mark the health of people of color and colonized people. Since social conditions are a "fundamental cause of disease," a key question becomes "what puts people *at risk of risks*"?[11] This section argues that persistent stress, fear, and trauma stemming from a racialized social system that works in tandem with settler colonialism negatively affects people of color in the United States and is a burden on their bodies.

Racial Stress as a Symptom and Reminder of Racial Oppression

Living on the underside of oppression means having exposure to negative stereotyping and treatment. For example, African Americans, Latinos, Asian Americans, Pacific Islanders, and Native Americans have higher rates of depression than White people, which co-occurs with other mental health disorders and physical ailments such a chronic pain, high blood pressure, and cigarette smoking and alcohol use.[12] The World Health Organization (WHO) cites depression as the leading cause of disability in the general population, damaging the quality of life of sufferers. People of color are also less likely to receive appropriate treatment compared to White people.[13] Harkening back to the social determinants of health model, there are damaging body, mind, and spirit consequences to living in, and coping with, a society stratified by coloniality and race.

Racial stress (which I define as cognitive, emotional, and physical tension directly related to one's perceived race) is a symptom and reminder of racial subjugation. In addition to race, class, gender, sexuality, and legal status are social identities embedded in systems of oppression that also influence trauma, health, and safety. "Racialized legal status" is a social determinant of health: Holding a discredited legal status entails negative mental and physical health consequences.[14] For Latina Graciela Pinela, the multiple stressors of racism, sexism, queer-phobia, legal status, and anti-immigrant sentiment intersect and are evident in her health. Graciela coped with extreme duress by turning to alcoholism and cigarette addiction. After we covered one painful topic after another, I asked how she was feeling. Significantly, this is when health cropped up. Graciela said these stressful topics were "hard but important" and that she felt "unease." Here she abruptly stated, "I really need a cigarette!" We left the coffee shop and went for a walk, Graciela's phone mapping us to a local corner store that sold cigarettes. After her cigarette purchase we landed at a park bench where Graciela's narrative flowed into the health consequences of sitting on the lower rungs of multiple hierarchies:

> As far as what is considered valuable in this particular society . . . I'm *way* down. [laughter]. . . . I'm an immigrant and I didn't grow up here—I immigrated as an adult—so that's . . . a few less points. . . . I am a single parent. My first child died. . . . I do suffer with mental health issues: depression, anxiety and . . . PTSD [post-traumatic stress disorder]. . . . So, yeah, add that to the stack. [I'm] definitely somebody that our society does consider to have less value . . . a pariah. I'm queer as well. I'm currently unemployed. . . . I don't have much of a college education. . . . Soci-

ety values more people who have had less suffering in their lives: people who are straight, people who are White.

In her final sentence, Graciela hits on the point that "society values people who have had less suffering," yet it is precisely because society "values" classes of people differently that they are exposed to more or less "suffering" because of how society treats them. Immigration status, marital status, sexual orientation, race, and class all combine to render Graciela "way down" the value hierarchy, numerous social conditions combining to put her "at risk of risks."[15]

Social determinants of health literature emphasizes that living conditions (such as racism, class status, anti-immigrant bias, violence, and trauma) supersede individual genetics or behavior to influence health outcomes. Graciela faced domestic abuse and legal status domination in her first marriage and queer-phobic, racist heterosexism in her second marriage. Both intimate relationships exploited her vulnerabilities and imperiled her health and safety. A domestic abuser, Graciela's first husband was a US citizen and he flexed his legal privilege over Graciela (who was undocumented at the time) as a form of domination. People without documentation are less likely to call authorities for protection out of fear of deportation. Illegality can keep undocumented migrants in abusive relationships because partners with legal status may use their status to control their dependent partner.[16] This is true for Graciela, whose undocumented status facilitated sexual violence, bodily harm, and threats of deportation in her first marriage:

> He had threatened me so many times with getting me deported. . . .
> That's a really common threat. . . . It was absolutely terrifying. It defi-
> nitely pushed me to that point where I just could not eat because I was
> just so, so nervous all the time . . . just the thought of "What if?" . . .
> For a while we were just waiting for my son to die . . . he was on hos-
> pice. . . . I'm like, "What if . . . I get deported in the middle of this?
> How horrible would that be, you know?" It was . . . an additional stress
> that . . . almost broke me.

Graciela's health and well-being were sucker-punched by her unique life circumstances that were exacerbated by her race, gender, class, and legal status.

Graciela's second husband, Tony, was a heterosexual White man who wanted to "save" her from her Latina heritage and queer identity. Marriage is no antidote to racism.[17] Instead, marriage can house racism. Tony positioned himself as a "White savior" whose efforts to "save" Graciela reproduced a heteropatriarchal and racial hierarchy. Graciela describes the racism that festered in her second marriage: "[My in-laws] were all agreeing with Trump . . . this anti-immigrants stuff. . . . It was just like: 'They [immigrants] want to breed us out; we'll breed them out first.' . . . He was trying to save me. . . . I really feel that he thought that [marrying me] . . . was doing me a favor. Yeah." The idea of "breeding out" non-White people harkens back to eugenic notions of who is deemed "fit" (in terms of race, class, and ability/disability) to reproduce.[18] Graciela says of her high-conflict second marriage: "When race has been politicized, when immigration has been politicized . . . *my whole existence has been politicized.*" Living with an inheritance of White supremacy, settler colonialism, sexism, heteropatriarchy, and classism squelched Graciela's health and happiness. Portraying the marriage as "killing [her] soul," Graciela and Tony divorced after four years.

"We end up somaticizing all of those things," Graciela concludes. She survived two violent marriages that involved intimate partner violence, threats of deportation, and attempts to "fix" her non-White race and queer identity. These individual troubles are linked to society-wide stratification systems of race, class, sexual orientation, and immigration status, all of which influence health. Graciela responds decisively to my question, "Winding back to health, [has] all this manifested in . . . your health?":

Definitely. Definitely it's taken a toll on my body. . . . The other issue with depression: it's not having the energy or motivation to eat healthy foods. . . . That's a huge one. The amount of energy that it takes to even get out of the house and grab some fast-food. . . . You think that it's easy, but. . . . We're making healthier choices [now] instead of just like, "Yeah, I'm just going to have cake."

Graciela smoked two cigarettes during our conversation and remarked that she was trying to limit herself to five-a-day, a limit she was not keeping. In her interpretation, Graciela is somaticizing life on the underside of multiple oppressions, her addiction and ailments embodied signs of her devalued placement in society.

Depression and addiction are somaticized outcomes of racial stress and multiple marginality. Xavier Bow is a working-class Black transgender and queer person whose refrain was: "There is so much garbage" in society. Like Graciela, Xavier smoked a cigarette during a difficult portion of the interview. Xavier's daily subjection to racism and transphobia cancels out Oregon's reputation as a socially progressive state. Xavier remarks, "I'm just calloused. . . . I sometimes will walk around and hear people say the 'N word' about me." Xavier describes their daily encounters with White supremacy:

> I *know* [the racial epithet is] for me, you know? I know they're not just saying [it] randomly. . . . It's pretty disgusting. . . . [And,] we don't get jobs because our names are on the resume. . . . There's so much garbage. . . . There's . . . this low-level anger that's just always there.

Xavier touches on multiple levels of racism: the interactional level (being called a racial epithet) and the institutional level (being passed over for a job). There is emotional wear to being enraged all the time. The "low-level anger that's just always there" has a damaging influence on physical, emotional, and mental health.[19]

Anger is a transhistorical element of Black lives in the United States. Black feminist Audre Lorde wrote:

> Women of color in america [sic] have grown up within a symphony of anger, at being silenced, at being unchosen, at knowing that when we survive, it is in spite of a world that takes for granted our lack of humanness, and which hates our very existence outside of its service. And I say *symphony* rather than *cacophony* because we have had to learn to orchestrate those furies so that they do not tear us apart.[20]

Anger is an emotional reaction to racial stress that is hard on the body. Gender and sexuality regimes intersect with a racial hierarchy to compound Xavier's exposure to multifactoral discrimination.[21] After having moved seamlessly from a story of racism to one of queerphobia and transphobia, Xavier answers my question about the costs of these race and gender burdens:

> It's not like I walk out and immediately get a headache or something, but yeah . . . I just sort of have to *swallow that anger*. . . . Sometimes . . . I need to go home and have a cigarette or something . . . because [I] just need to settle myself after this *stupid* experience. . . . [I'm] trying to quit [smoking] right now but [chuckle] I haven't done it yet. . . . It's not necessarily a positive choice for me, but . . . I'm doing this just to abate . . . [the] distress [of] just trying to be myself.

Poignantly stated, cigarette smoking for Xavier is about "abating the distress" of living their life as a racialized subject in a society not structured to support queer and transgender African American people. In the midst of this outdoor conversation about racism and trans/queerphobia, Xavier lit a cigarette, this knee-jerk reaction highlighting the connection between multiple marginality and health risk.

Denise Lareaux, a Black woman, also feels disenfranchised in her largely White Oregon town and must cope with racial stress. She laments "always having to be the first or the only one [laughs] in a group . . . it gets tiring after a while." Referring to a predominately White workplace, city, and state, Denise wondered if needing to "fall in line" to "make it here" is a drain on health. This internal debate about codeswitching— adjusting demeanors to fit varying social environments—emphasizes the health strain people of color contend with as they wrestle with such decisions and adjustments. Denise felt accommodationist pressures: "I didn't feel like rocking the boat, because I've always felt like I was the only one. . . . I think if there would have been more [Black people] around me, I think it would have been a much different reaction." "Not rocking the boat" links to what Xavier referred to as "swallowing" anger and racism so that they do not end up victimized by a potentially violent altercation. This "suppressed anger expression" is a reaction to Black anger being sanctioned, a survival strategy dating back to when Black people were enslaved and continuing in the present when they are denied the liberty of anger.[22] Being held to "racialized feeling rules"[23] confines Black people's emotional lives and requires their bodies to harbor the stress of captive feelings.

Denise speculates that there is a correlation between lack of support for her racial identity and her health:

> As the years passed, I started to lose my self-esteem. So, I think [if] I would have seen more people that look like me. . . . that would have helped.
>
> JVT: Sure, sure. So that lack of self-esteem you think was related to Blackness.?
>
> DENISE: Oh, absolutely. Absolutely. [chuckles] Yeah, I mean because it's everywhere. You look at magazines, TV, everything. . . . I obviously did not fit that standard of what was beautiful or good. . . . Over time, it does affect your—at least in my case, it did affect my self-esteem. . . . Especially in my adolescence, I was really depressed. . . . As I got older, I did do some counseling and I also do take anti-depressants. [laughs] Yeah. So it helped a lot. Yeah. It's hard.

Group-level racial value that fuses "beautiful" and "good" and positions them out of reach chips away at individual-level esteem. The demerits associated with Blackness manifested as lowered self-esteem and depression, which is how Denise understands her health obstacles. Denise's semantic move to start to say that racist messaging that devalues Black people "does affect your [self-esteem]" but then stopping to specify "in my case" suggests her belief that her experience maps onto the larger group. She pulls back to specificity but her inclination was to point out that her experience is indicative of a larger social problem. Denise perceives that group-level racial valuation is adjudicated based on the body and then is embodied via health effects.

Exhaustion is a bodily manifestation of racial stress. Feeling tired or exhausted was a common reply of respondents of color when asked about navigating society's racial landscape. For Shayla Pierre, exhaustion is a harmful physical health effect of being on high alert constantly. This perennially activated "fight or flight" response system is hard on the body. Shayla ruminates: "*I feel exhausted from fighting all the time. . . . A lot of people . . . look down on me. . . . I'm constantly . . . thinking, 'Did that only happen to me because I'm Black?' . . . I feel that . . . constant . . . idea in the back of my head. . . . It's exhausting.*" Like Denise, racial stress led to depression for Shayla. A burden of racial oppression involves not only suffering devaluation, lost opportunities, and reduced resources, but dealing with that reality. "Fighting all the time," accompanied by exhaustion and depression, requires self-care techniques. Shayla explains one modality of coping: "I write poetry . . . mostly to deal with my depression."

Racial stress is ubiquitous for respondents of color in predominately White environments. Racial stress intersects with additional axes of domination, compounding stressors for people who navigate multiple fault lines. Among respondents of color, racial stress stands out as both a symptom (physical, mental, and emotional manifestation) of racial subjugation and a deeply felt reminder of racial subjugation.

Anticipatory Racial Stress: The Power of Place

Anticipatory racial stress is the state of being perpetually on alert to detect and respond to racism, particularly in environments where one's racial group is read as "out of place."[24] "Anticipatory" refers to "in advance of" racist action or institutional blockade. "Racial stress" denotes the mental, emotional, and physical toll that racism exacts on people of color. Anticipatory racial stress is place-based in that locales vary in racial demographics and racial climate. Repeated exposure to interpersonal and structural racism primes people of color to expect racial conflict and barriers. It is not because people of color hold a crystal ball that foretells the future, but because they have experienced a life delimited by race that they anticipate racial stress, an experience quelled or exacerbated by the racial climate of a place. Anticipatory racial stress is another burden people of color carry that White people are excused from holding.

Parents of color anticipate racial stress and preemptively respond to it by teaching their children about race and racism. Concern over Black and Brown people being subjected to snap judgments corroded by bias that frames them as criminals shapes parenting strategies.[25] Elle Jaye is a Mexican American/Native American mother of two who used a plethora of health-oriented terms to describe how her everyday life wears down her body and mental-emotional state. During our two-hour interview, Elle used the word "angry/anger" eighteen times, "exhausted/exhausting" ten times, "tired" nine times, "hurt" four times, "depressed" twice, and "frustrated" once. These racialized feelings direct how she rears her children. Elle is race-conscious in her parenting, alert to the ways her children may be misperceived and mistreated. Taking a "present citizen" view that says young people have a right to full participation in society,[26] Elle took her elementary school–aged children to the police station to instruct them on their rights to service. Elle recalls:

> When it became apparent to me that society was viewing my son more harshly than my daughter, based off his skin tone, I chose, after being angry about that, to funnel that anger into something positive. So I outreached to . . . the local police department to introduce both of my kids to law enforcement to say, "Hey, these guys [police] are here to be of assistance." Not to be afraid of them, how to shake their hand, how to conduct themselves so that *they're* not being misinterpreted like, "Oh, he's criminal or she's criminal." And then, to allow the police department to recognize that this little Brown boy is not what you think he is and that he's got a mother that will be right here on it and that *I'm* taking the proactive step first. . . . I wanted [my kids] to recognize: . . . [The police force's] role in society [is] supposed to be of service; you have an ability . . . to say, "Ok, you're not servicing me properly and we're gonna call you out on it."

Systemic racism woven into society's institutions makes clear White advantage and non-White disadvantage, a point W.E.B. Du Bois referenced when addressing the police system in the South: "It was not then a question of crime, but rather one of color, that settled a man's conviction on almost any charge."[27] Like African American mothers, Elle observed that police protection—as well as violence—is doled out unequally so she engineered a response to try to protect her children.[28] Elle reminds the police of their duty to serve and protect *all*. She underscores for her children and the local police the value of her Brown children. Intuiting that police brutality is an important neighborhood risk factor for illness,[29] Elle takes a "proactive step" to secure positive valuation by funneling her anticipatory racial stress into a dual-purpose educational moment.

Racial stress and anticipatory racial stress depend on place—the racial demographics, racial hierarchy, and meanings attached to race that are bound to a locality. Mixed-race (Japanese/White) Pearl Hashimoto, who was raised in Hawai'i, feels "uncomfortable" in Oregon because people make racist assumptions about her and she must strategize about how to interact. Pearl steels herself for interactions laced with racism, telling herself: "'Okay, big girl panties on, we're gonna have to do this. . . .' And it's . . . tiring. . . . You don't really want to have to do that all the time." This preparation for racial stress is place-specific: "I never felt like that at home [Hawai'i]. Never. . . . At home I feel very safe." Pearl elucidates her strategies: "[In Oregon] . . . I'm going to have to educate people. I'm going to have to say hello first. I'm going to have to . . . speak English first. . . . It's tiring." Anticipating and being on guard to deftly handle racist assumptions is a tax levied on people of color. By contrast, White people are excused from this insecurity and labor because they constitute the numerical majority and cultural reference group in White spaces.

Predominately White places shape ideas about who belongs and who does not belong. If someone does not see themselves reflected in their environment, the space feels exclusionary. Yumiko Hoshiko (Asian American) attended elementary and secondary school in a small town where she was the only non-White student. Yumiko suggests that institutions with a racially diverse staff would be more welcoming to people on the racial outskirts, like her. She refers to the loneliness of being outnumbered in a predominately White space:

Who was supposed to back me up? . . . We never had an administrator person who is a minority . . . so who was I even supposed to go to who is in power and be like: "This is what is happening." . . . They won't even know how to react. . . . How am I supposed to feel unified with anybody? [A Pacific Islander/Black friend] was the only person I knew—and we didn't even go to the same school—who could relate to the mental health effects and the physical health effects and everything else that came with being a person of color. . . . That's why I found sanctuary in her.

Worrying about a vacuum of support and needing a sanctuary bespeaks (anticipatory) racial stress. Rather than leave students of color mired in racial stress, boosting the diversity of institutions would foster community-building among subordinated groups who could find comfort and resources among same-race peers and staff. Being Asian

American in a largely White space was a hardship for Yumiko, who felt "the pain of being a minority."

Racial context can either aggravate or calm anticipatory racial stress for people of color. Anticipatory racial stress ramps up in spaces where people of color are in an overwhelmingly White space. From the racially diverse San Francisco Bay Area, Rosie Patel (Asian, White, South American, Pacific Islander) currently lives in an Oregon college town and feels anticipatory racial stress when she enters a new situation. She has had repeated experiences of racist assumptions being used to define—and confine—her. One such experience involved a "random older White gentleman" who initiated a conversation at a community event and referred to "her people" in a generalized way. He incorrectly assumed she was from Sri Lanka and, in the face of being told she is an American citizen, he refused to back down from his wrong-headed ideas: "He was *not* willing to listen. He was like, '. . . What do you eat there?' And I was like, '. . . I'm not from Sri Lanka. *I don't know.*' And he . . . just kept going." In a majority-White place where stereotypes masquerade as knowledge, Rosie feels trapped by racial strictures: "I can't feel welcome in a place where you're telling me, 'oh, no, no, no *your people.*'" After repeated encounters where she was racially boxed in and misunderstood, Rosie foretells that public ventures will entail racial stress. Anticipatory racial stress crops up in majority-White environments where run-of-the-mill interactions can go off-track and exacerbate the feeling of marginality. Anticipatory racial stress is higher in majority-White environments because lack of racial diversity makes it more likely that White people will rely on racial stereotypes rather than real-world knowledge of people with different racial heritages.[30]

Repeated exclusionary experiences that condition people of color to anticipate racial stress affect health and well-being. Rosie connects the two: "There was a point when it [racism] affected my mental health and I was feeling really angry and depressed." A requirement for people of color, she had to "cope with it better and learn strategies to . . . compartmentalize those feelings." One coping strategy for Rosie is periodic trips to a familiar racially heterogeneous area: "What helps mental health is having something to look forward to. . . . I'm gonna go to the Bay Area . . . [and] I'm gonna have safety. I'll get my dignity back." With anticipatory racial stress being dependent on context, Rosie's escape hatch is to remove herself from an environment that piques her stress, a solution that requires disposable cash but boosts her well-being and recoups her "dignity."

Racial stress is context-dependent. Respondents of color who had lived in more racially heterogenous spaces reported that they felt a greater sense of belonging in racially mixed environments because their racial group was represented rather than aberrant. Luis Waimea, Japanese American from Hawai'i, says that he can feel his blood pressure rising in instances of racial stress. He hurts. His heart beats faster. Being on the butt end of denial of service at a restaurant and unwanted staring induce bodily effects: "I can feel my heart beating faster and my blood pressure . . . getting higher." Microaggressions cause stress in their victims,[31] as Luis draws this connection:

> I'm taking medication for blood pressure and when these things [race-related stressors] happen . . . I feel like my body is just very tense and so I'm sure that doesn't help. . . . Stress contributes to that. It's . . . probably a factor of being in this environment, having to . . . walk on eggshells all the time.

The "social conditions" of an environment in which a body is immersed, like racial dynamics and racism, can jeopardize health. Structural conditions put groups "at risk of risks,"[32] making how society is organized a bigger culprit in poor health outcomes than individual behaviors that may be a response to those conditions. For Luis, high blood pressure and "walking on eggshells" are responses to a racially stressful environment.

To say that racial stress is context-dependent is to say that being read as a racial misfit[33]—someone who does not belong—is uncomfortable. When circulating in an Asian American community, Luis feels insulated from racial stress. He offers staring as an example, a social cue of racial misfitting that happens to him in Oregon but not in Hawai'i. Staring is "a tool of domination."[34] Staring enacts a colonizing power dynamic. As Rosemarie Garland-Thomson, a women's and disability studies scholar, writes, "staring functions as a form of domination, marking the staree as the exotic, outlaw, alien, or other. The colonizing gaze marks its bearer as legitimate and its object as outsider."[35] Luis "feels" being stared at in Oregon and intuits its significance: "I just want to go shopping . . . and not have an older White couple stare. . . . We're at Costco and we're just trying to shop and you can just feel—*you can feel*—you can feel the stares and feel the . . . profiling or . . . discrimination. . . . Just the feeling of that is very troubling." Luis emphasizes "feeling" here, repeating a version of the word five times. He is "feeling race."[36] The stress of "feeling the stares" is multilayered: sensing the stare, questioning the cause of the stare, deciding how to respond to the stare, and sensing the body's raised tension. Racial misfitting, racial profiling, and racial discrimination all evoke a visceral response, racialized emotions connecting to the body's nervous system. Racialized emotions trigger embodied manifestations.

In contrast to Oregon, Luis is not stared at in racially heterogeneous Hawai'i. Luis can go about his daily life: "I can go to Costco and not have anyone looking at me." He elaborates on the lack of colonizing gazes and racial stress in Hawai'i:

> Definitely when I'm in Hawai'i I don't feel . . . any profiling going on . . . or any microaggressions or anything that feels like I'm being put in the back of the bus. . . . Because we're part of the local culture, everyone respects each other. . . . I can walk down the street and not have anyone judging.

Racial stress and racial misfitting are contextual: A person can circulate in various social environments and feel varying levels of acceptance or scrutiny. Since racial meanings are sculpted by context, a person's sense of belonging or non-belonging will also vary by context.

As these respondent narratives crystallize, racial stress is somaticized: it is a heavy toll carried in the body, emotions, and minds of respondents of color. Racial stress is a phenomenon that respondents of color confront, navigate, and then ruminate on. In making the connection between sources of racial stress and embodied effects, negative health consequences take on a double meaning: They *symptomatically* convey the ill effect of racism that is born out in the body, and they *emblematically* carry the message that racial oppression exists "out there" (in society) as well as "in here" (the body).

Trauma as an Outgrowth of Colonialism: "Colonization Will Always Be There"

Trauma is the baggage of being constructed and castigated as a problem. Native American respondents referred to "intergenerational trauma" or how injury can be passed from generation to generation.[37] Social epidemiology concurs with respondent testimonies: that health inequalities resulting from oppression operate across the life course and across generations.[38] History that is pock-marked by coloniality and race carries legacies that vary by group, as Beau Landon (Native American) addressed in chapter 1 in his insistence that history matters—in particular to oppressed groups who live on "the other side of history" and whose perspectives are missing from master narratives. He argues that despite White people's interest in ignoring the past, history is "still going on" in the form of "long-lasting traumas." The White American amnesia to which Beau refers exemplifies what Ojibewe historian Jean O'Brien calls "firsting and lasting."[39] "Firsting and lasting" erases Native people through rewriting history in a way that commemorates White settlers and settlements as the "first" (denying Native occupants who preexisted European colonist arrival) and consigning Native people to being "the last" of their kind (e.g., "the last of the Mohicans"). "Forgetting" colonialism is a technique that both flows from and perpetuates "writing Indians out of existence."[40]

Beau touches on a central point of settler colonialism—the idea that colonialism is happening *now*—when he traces "intergenerational trauma" from his great-great-grandmother to his own life:

> *How close in history everything is.* . . . People don't even realize it, but it wasn't that long ago that all this happened. My great-great-grandma was just a little girl when we were forced out of the Rogue River Valley . . . up to here [Siletz, Oregon]. . . . And then my great-grandmother . . . whom I did know, grew up here on the new reservation, and was sent to Oregon schools. And all the horrors and atrocities that come with that— rape and being beaten for speaking your language and . . . trying to kill a culture. . . . It's not remembered per se by the outside world [but] that trauma was passed down to my grandpa who is still alive and I live with, and then to my mom. . . . That's . . . what I meant [about] the generational

trauma still being here. . . . I get in arguments about it all the time. [People say,] "You can't really pass trauma down." But, I disagree with that. My grandpa was a *heavy* alcoholic and drug user . . . and I think a lot of that had to do with just growing up in the situation that he did. He faced a lot of racism.

Colonial and racial histories embed themselves in bodies. Both specific trauma and cumulative trauma are significant factors in Native Americans' high rates of substance use and abuse, traumatic depression, and post-traumatic stress disorder.[41] As argued in chapter 1, Beau's story illustrates the continuing quality of settler colonialism—it does not conclude with conquest but establishes ongoing racial-colonial relations that perpetuate inequality, cultural loss, and physical and emotional injury.

Alcohol is a "weapon of war."[42] Seeing alcohol's damaging effects on physical bodies, the social body, and Indigenous cultural roots, some Indigenous leaders petitioned (unsuccessfully) for an embargo on liquor.[43] Alcohol abuse, then, is a consequence of colonialism. Euro-American colonial powers interrupted Indigenous trade routes, ensured food shortages, and increased dependency on colonizers, which included replacing Indigenous goods with European goods. Historian Roxanne Dunbar-Ortiz writes, "In these circumstances, the introduction and promotion of alcohol proved addictive and deadly, adding to the breakdown of social order and responsibility."[44] Beau inherited substance abuse as a way to grieve colonialism. Beau says of his grandfather, "He would get called a 'drunken Indian' a lot and, even to this day, if he hears anyone say those two words together he'll fight over it. He's like seventy-six." This controlling image of a "drunken Indian" is a caricature of self-soothing the wound of colonization with alcohol. Landing him in jail at least once, Beau calls his addictions a "coping mechanism" that "was passed down." Settler colonialism and racism fester in bodies as trauma and addiction, symptoms and reminders of dominated status. Yet Beau went to rehabilitation to "stop the cycle and do better than older generations." By viewing Native Americans as living out intergenerational trauma, one can trace how settler colonialism affects physical, emotional, and mental health.

Ross Reece (Native American) is a young man from a family of medicine people in northern California who grew up in a rural community comprised mostly of tribal members. He is in "almost a different world" in a predominately White college campus, a place where he is alienated by the question "What are you?" and incorrect assumptions, such as that he lives in a teepee. With both of his grandmothers removed from their homes to the same Native American boarding school, Ross is well acquainted with these federally funded assimilationist institutions. As much literature documents, boarding schools traumatized Native children separated from their families.[45] Boarding schools' forced assimilation mission led to downstream health consequences that persist for generations.

"Colonization will always be there," Ross tells me. What colonization has disrupted, displaced, and harmed becomes a cultural inheritance for successive generations. Acknowledging intergenerational trauma is a sign of decolonization.[46] Ross recognizes intergenerational transmission of knowledge and harm: "My ancestors felt . . . turmoil . . . stripping of our culture. . . . You're supposed to pass down what you have and . . . that goes with good and bad and so that stripping of our culture and that loss of identity has been also passed down." Colonization ripples into the present moment in anger and grief as well as changed environmental circumstances, foodways, and gender relations.[47] Ross adheres to an "Indigenist perspective" that acknowledges the historical trauma of genocide, forced removal, family separation, and forced sterilization suffered by Indigenous populations and advocates for empowerment and sovereignty.[48] The intergenerational trauma present in Native American lives is a topic of near-daily conversation between Ross and his father. Ross says colonial trauma is ever-present:

My dad liked to describe it as . . . "the first cup of coffee type of talks." . . . Why do we feel the way we do? . . . Without any direct conflicts . . . why do we wake up mad in the morning with no idea of why? . . . What kind of forces are being . . . pushed on against us or . . . pulled away from us? . . . Just trying to create a better understanding of . . . our history and . . . where to go from there.

Ross interprets waking up "mad in the morning with no idea of why" as a cultural inheritance of colonization. Perpetual anger affects well-being. Ross engages Indigenous cultural practice to heal: "[We] go out and do something, whether it's cutting wood or doing some . . . burns or just anything . . . on the landscape. . . . [The trauma] really is hard to deal with. . . . As long as . . . we know who we are and where we come from, then it's easier to fight or be resistant."

Ross recalls a healthier time prior to White settler takeover of Native lands: "[White colonizers] didn't really acknowledge the fact that we were happy people, that we were living healthy . . . not obese." For Ross's tribe (Karuk), the emergence of new health problems corresponds with loss of access to healthy traditional food, notably spring Chinook salmon. Heart disease and diabetes for the Karuk Tribe are three and four times higher than the national average, respectively.[49] After the usurpation of Native territory and resources that altered ecological conditions, Native people were left to salvage lifestyles and food practices. Given the trauma of colonization, Ross wants to move toward an Indigenous-defined future. I asked, "Where do you see your life, as you move forward?" Ross replies:

> As ironic as it sounds in a way: backwards. . . . To be on the landscape more than we are today. . . . Colonialism . . . set us back as people and so . . . we've got a lot of make-up to do. And so, in a way, where we were at four, five generations ago is . . . where I want to be, is where I'm working towards. . . . Just being in the landscape more, being healthier, being more spiritually connected.

Decolonization equates to health.[50] Calls for decolonization center Indigenous land rights because deterritorialization is an original sin of settler colonialism,[51] the return of land auguring the potential for a return to self-sustaining cultural practices. Hence, Ross's goal is decolonization: to go "backwards." This view aligns with an Indigenist perspective that sees identification with a minority culture, spirituality, and traditional health practices as "cultural buffers" that are useful to Native people in coping with stress and trauma.[52] Ross sees decolonization facilitating health for his Native community: "My purpose . . . is to help my people come out of poverty . . . lessen . . . rates of suicide and . . . diabetes. . . . all those . . . health aspects that we didn't have before but we have now. . . . We want to kind of roll back in time." If a chief source of Native ill health lies in colonialism, "rolling back in time" gestures in the direction of decolonization and self-determination. With a goal of pre-contact health, Ross hopes to ameliorate present-day ramifications of colonialism that impinge on Native well-being.

Leles Talbot (Native American) spoke of stress as affecting one's organs: "Stress is always something that's anti-health." Leles spoke of disrupted diets due to the devastation of a natural food supply and child removal to boarding schools:

> Our Indigenous foods were interrupted and . . . caused us to substitute our food sources. . . . Tribal people have . . . raging incidences of diabetes and heart trouble and cholesterol because of the way we don't digest . . . processed food. So that historic . . . destruction and purposeful . . . killing the bison, purposeful putting children [in] boarding schools with the wrong food sources starving them . . . that all affected our physical health.

Food and family disruption are traumatic and wreak negative health effects. Citing the average age of death in her tribe, Miluk Coos, as fifty-nine years old, compared to the national average of seventy-eight years old,[53] Leles referred to "inappropriate coping skills" like alcohol, drugs, self-harm, and suicide that people take up when they are "not accepted." Leles connects life as an Indigenous person under a regime of White supremacy to embodiment: "The stress of trying to . . . survive in a world . . . where you have to constantly explain yourself or constantly justify your religion, your culture, your language, your beliefs, your tie to the land. . . . It's stressful on your mind, it's stressful on your . . . organs." Leles's analysis is in concert with this chapter's argument that racial stress and ill health affecting communities of color are simultaneously *symptoms* and *reminders* of racial and colonial subordination.

For Native American respondents, postcolonial trauma impacts individual and collective health. Suffering histories of trauma that forcibly stripped Native Americans of land, resources, and ways of life have resulted in emotional, mental, and physical tolls on people who carry those memories and losses in their bodies. To be robbed of the equipment to live one's best life (such as traditional land-based food) is a postcolonial burden of belonging affecting Native Americans' health outcomes today. Damaging health consequences are somaticized results of coloniality and everyday reminders of racial and colonial oppression.

Safety

Racial status informs a person's sense of safety. Impediments to safety are daily reminders for respondents of color that their physical and emotional integrity is not a society-wide priority. Respondents of color spoke of racialized safety hazards and often coordinated their activities to avoid spaces that they worried could put them in jeopardy. They orchestrated their lives to evade race-based harm, from taking precautions walking home at night to planning driving routes carefully. Respondents of color developed "racial 'intelligence.'"[54] Race scholars Michael Omi and Howard Winant describe racial "intelligence" as a skill crafted by people of color:

> At the "micro-level," each racial self engages in a certain amount of sociopolitical "navigation," so to speak. This activity takes place in everyday life . . . and requires what might be called racial "intelligence." When one acts self-reflectively in respect to race, she or he links the racial conditions of everyday life with those of the overall social structure. Often this racial intelligence is taken for granted, but it is also self-conscious much of the time, especially for people of color.[55]

By contrast, White privilege appears in a ubiquitous sense of safety: White respondents were confident that they could physically navigate space without consideration for how to circumvent possible harm. White privilege is apparent in the absence of fear.

Being a Racial Target and "Taxing Vigilance"

Since the safety of respondents of color is not secure, they undertake "taxing vigilance" to safeguard themselves from race-based harms. Taxing vigilance refers to the high-alert sensitivity of respondents of color to potential threats to their safety, a day-to-day phenomenon that incurs costs such as chronic stress.[56] "Taxing" refers to the health and well-being penalties that result from being chronically on guard and "vigilance" nods to the careful watching for possible dangers. Even as there are racial group-specific inflections to safety concerns, some of which are discussed below, this chapter focuses on the overarching theme of unguaranteed safety among respondents of color, a shared burden of belonging in a racially stratified society.

Worry about being a racial target (by government, institutions, or people) is a persistent reminder that one's group is marked as ill-fitting. Asian Americans sense a racial animus carryover from past military conflicts (see chapter 1), African Americans refer to slavery and the Confederate flag as a symbol of anti-Black hatred, Indigenous people continue to be victimized by colonization, Muslim interviewees report racial profiling and "citizen surveillance,"[57] and Latinos feel vilified by xenophobic and racist rhetoric around "the Wall" and a government that separates Latin American immigrant families at the US-Mexico border. These racial histories, symbols, narratives, and punishments not only cordon off American belonging as principally reserved for White people, as discussed in chapter 3, but also contribute to health and safety vulnerabilities.

Xavier discusses their alertness to safety, especially their worry that Blackness can have deadly consequences if police are involved:

> The hardest thing about being a problem for people is just—I just want to directly interact with you. I don't want to have this wall of a thousand layers . . . between us. . . . I just end up swallowing so much of this that I really don't . . . return fire. It's mostly just because I want to save myself the trouble. . . . What if they call the cops and the cops are gonna come and they're going to beat my ass, you know what I mean? Whereas they're going to leave alone the rest of the people in the situation. . . . I have to think about my own safety, you know? Even though in my mind part of me wants to be this revolutionary that doesn't care . . . most of the time I just don't try to respond that way because I have to be a little bit afraid for my safety.

Opting to "swallow" emotions and censor behavior, Xavier calculates that it would be worse to unleash unfiltered reaction and risk getting beaten. Reports show that Black people are subject to "overpolicing" and rarely seen as victims.[58] In prioritizing their own safety, Xavier implies that no one else will do so and that multiple systems collude to work against their health and safety. In a country where White people call the police on Black people for birdwatching or barbecuing in public parks,

Xavier has no confidence they can live their life without attending to the looming threat of White people weaponizing their Whiteness to punish Black people.

Showing a racial priority system that conceives of "public" as "White," the safety of respondents of color is curtailed on account of a concern for "public safety." Abdullah Jibran, a Muslim American with Middle Eastern heritage born in the United States, discussed post–9/11 suspicions that he may be a terrorist within ten minutes of the start of the interview. Suspicions activate during airline travel when he is "randomly" selected for searches on a regular basis. Post–9/11, Muslim Americans have been constructed as safety threats, and racialized-religious surveillance systems have been installed based on that premise.[59] Abdullah reports racial targeting by the Transportation Security Administration (TSA) during airline travel:

> It's disgusting. . . . They ask you questions and they put a sticker on the back of the passport. And depending on the sticker color they get to decide how to "randomly" choose you. It was very humiliating when I got "randomly chosen." . . . Every time it's "random check." And, I know it was not about randomness. I do engineering . . . I know statistics: It's impossible. It was about a sticker. It was about someone who perceived [that] I should be profiled.

In his everyday life as well, Abdullah has felt physically unsafe due to race-based threats of violence.

Bogga Deta has also experienced Islamophobia as a cultural trope that constructs her as a problem, treads on her safety, and compels her taxing vigilance. There is a "racial valence" to Islamophobia.[60] Muslim identity has become racialized, cultural trappings such as language, religion, and clothing becoming "racial clues" that are viewed as a threat to American values.[61] Reporting that people in the United States treat her with caution, Bogga's desire to cultivate community prompted her to take off her headcovering. The decision to disrobe herself of a culturally significant article of clothing can be interpreted as a combination of anticipatory racial stress and taxing vigilance because it was a reaction to Americans who may read her headcovering as a marker of foreign threat. Bogga says plainly, "I'm a Muslim and when I came to the US

I decided to take off my scarf because I was afraid to be identified . . . as a Muslim." She told her mother: "I'm making this decision . . . for my safety." Bogga also took safety precautions around language, such as not speaking or texting Arabic in public. She worried that a stranger might overhear her or see her phone screen and act violently toward her. Viewed as a "threat," she felt threatened. To quell xenophobic risks to her inclusion and physical safety, Bogga deployed taxing vigilance—she removed a culturally significant article of clothing and monitored her Arabic language use in public. Cultural stripping and vigilance around her presentation of self are taxes Bogga paid on her Muslim identity for an increased measure of safety.

Safety concerns illustrate how double consciousness is embodied. Double consciousness is born of, lives in, and acts on the body. Driving a car was a repeated theme: Many respondents of color only traveled main thoroughfares and did not deviate into unfamiliar, predominately White rural areas. Black respondents noted Confederate flags in small towns symbolizing their lack of welcome. John Blaze is typical of Black respondents' caution while traveling:

> I don't go very far off I-5 [highway]. I stay on the I-5 corridor. . . . You won't see me camping. [When we travel] we make sure we got enough gas so we don't have to stop. . . . We're very deliberate and intentional in our travel. . . . Going the back way to go to Bend [Oregon], there's a . . . big old Confederate Flag [off Highway 34]. . . . You not from the South, so.

On transporting the Confederate flag from the South to Oregon, John is incisive: "This is about White supremacy, [it] is not about Southern pride. . . . It's about White supremacy. It was about the institution of slavery." John engages double consciousness and taxing vigilance to protect himself from places that threaten his Black body. Another Black man respondent, an international student, quit driving altogether: "I haven't driven for almost two years now . . . just . . . to avoid cops."

As sociologist Elijah Anderson observed, "White people typically avoid Black space, but Black people are required to navigate the White space as a condition of their existence."[62] Not exclusive to Black people, fastidious preparation for travel and anxiety about traversing unfamiliar rural White spaces was a tendency shared by members of other racial groups. Anna Hernan, the US-born daughter of two Mexican immi-grants, was first taught about her non-Whiteness by a drive-by encoun-ter with White onlookers shouting "Go back to Mexico" to congregants parading in a church-sponsored event. In another incident, White driv-ers shouting racist epithets tried to run Anna's parents off the road when they were pedestrians. Raised in Oregon, by nine years old, Anna was taught that public space could be hostile to Mexican Americans. Now as a college student, Anna carries this racial anxiety and avoids small towns with predominately White populations out of concern they will endanger her:

> If . . . I'm [driving through] back roads . . . [that] go through really tiny, tiny little communities of mainly White people . . . I'm like, "Okay, so this is fine, we're in a car, we're moving." But . . . thinking about . . . [if] I would have to stop in one of those places [gives me a panic attack]. It really does . . . scare me.

Fear for her safety changes Anna's behavior, including where she travels and how she secures her home. Anna chides herself for being "irra-tional," but her instinct for self-preservation is rational and rooted in awareness of how her body is viewed by others:

> I know it's really irrational, but even sometimes walking home I [worry]. . . . Because recently . . . one of the students [enrolled at my university] was very . . . pro-White. So, if I'm walking home, is somebody going to see that I'm Mexican and see where I live? . . . It was really scary thinking . . . just because of who I am walking to my house . . . sometimes doesn't feel safe. . . . So when that [White supremacist incident] was hap-pening, I definitely kept [windows] closed.

Anger, grief, and fear are rational reactions to racial domination that are "not only sincerely felt but . . . are also appropriate emotions."[63] It is by "looking at [her]self through the eyes of others," as Du Bois wrote, that Anna was socialized into fearing for her safety.

The foregoing examples have centered physical safety, yet emotional safety (freedom from verbal and emotional abuse) is another frontier. Racial targeting can shatter a sense of emotional safety and negatively impact health. For example, Donald Trump vilified Mexican-origin people and employed "nativist racism," framing descendants from select nations (including Mexico) "enemies of America" and "as incapable of ever being American."[64] A climate of threat propelled by the Trump presidency, including his rhetoric and position on immigration, was an "anxiety trigger" for Latinos.[65] Trump's punishing rhetoric felt abusive to Mexican immigrant Roberto Torres, precipitating his depression. Roberto hopes to be "happy here without any fear," yet this condition is linked to race, legality, political rhetoric, and definition of American. Roberto connected the public demonization of Mexicans to his health burdens:

> When I hear the president [Trump] talk . . . or when I hear all his supporters . . . it makes me feel excluded for sure. . . . It makes me feel bad about myself. . . . I've had issues with mental health and anxiety and . . . it makes a negative impact on me personally. *And who wants to feel bad about themselves, you know?* . . . It makes me sad. I've dealt with depression as well and . . . those two things are connected for me. . . . Listening to all of his [Trump's] nasty words . . . reminds me of how I felt when I was going through depression. And that's . . . not good. It's something that I don't want. That's why I . . . shut everything out.

Finding himself a racial target, Roberto engages "taxing vigilance" by keeping antennae out for racialized political rhetoric that "makes him feel bad about himself." Sadness is not just a fleeting emotion but one that roots in the body as "feeling bad" physically. It is possible that "nasty words" condemning Mexicans do not just *remind* Roberto of depression but *triggered* it. Hence Roberto's regimen of taxing vigilance, or effort to protect himself: he "shut[s] everything out" and avoids listening to politics because it makes him "very, very angry and sad." More than sad, racialized political agendas have damaged his sense of self-worth, influencing, as Roberto said, "the way I see myself as not being worth as much as somebody else." Media and politics have been a drag on Roberto's health and yet he is civic-minded, volunteering to register people to vote in an effort to effect positive change for his Latino community.[66]

Safety concerns trouble mental and emotional equanimity and prompt taxing vigilance. As a cautionary effort, taxing vigilance is grounded in embodied fear—fear that stems from insecurity about how one's racialized body will be treated that lodges in the body as an extra burden. Respondents of color avoid racially coded places, abide by extra safety measures, and tune out grating political rhetoric. These safety precautions are a form of taxing vigilance undertaken in response to environments that center Whiteness and suspend the assumption of freedom from danger for people of color.

Whiteness as Safety

Safety is a benefit of Whiteness. Du Bois wrote of a "public and psychological wage" of Whiteness, where White people are given "public deference."[67] Conversely, Du Bois observed that Black people are subjected to "public insult."[68] This deference/insult dichotomy split along the White/Black color line correlates to safety as secured versus safety in jeopardy. Nearly one hundred years after Du Bois's analysis of public deference and public insult, White respondents reported to me that their personal safety was secure without much effort on their part, whereas many respondents of color attested that their personal safety was daily imperiled by racialized treatment.

White respondents spoke of safety, lack of racial stress, and therefore health benefits. In contrast to the safety precautions respondents of color routinely take as they navigate their surroundings, Elizabeth Cooper (White) calls out her unearned privilege: "I absolutely just had an experience of . . . 'driving while White.' . . . People assume I'm well-intended and I can get out of it. I've gotten out of like four speeding tickets in my life and . . . that's driving while White [chuckle]." Elizabeth has confidence that (unfair as it is) her White privilege will behoove her. She flips the phrase "driving while Black" that refers to the disadvantage of frequent, unprovoked traffic stops for Black drivers to "driving while White," to mark that White people are advantaged in this facet of travel. While Elizabeth uses the example of escaping traffic tickets when pulled over by law enforcement officers due to her Whiteness, her racial status also protects her from physical assault and even death at the hands of police. The overpolicing of people of color has severe consequences, one statistic noting that Black men are twenty-one times more likely to be killed by a police officer than White men.[69] In terms of gender and sexuality, Elizabeth identifies as a queer pansexual, to which she attributes only "moments of discomfort." Whiteness is a zone of safety for Elizabeth: "On some level I can control my gender presentation and . . . I can control how I engage in PDA [public displays of affection] or not. For folks of color, you can't take off your skin." Unlike non-Whiteness as a liability that leaves people of color at risk of harm, Whiteness as a protectant insulates White people from injury.

Consider also Nellie Locke, with Rapunzel-like long, blonde hair, who remarked: "[To] touch on well-being, I don't experience . . . discomfort a lot. . . . There's an absence of stress. Typically, I'm not stressed. . . . I think it would be more difficult for people that aren't White. . . . They probably have to think about [stress] more than I do." Nellie's Whiteness acts as a shield against racial stress. In a culture where Whiteness is privileged, one embodied feature of that unearned privilege is protection from racial stress. White respondents' privilege shows in their lack of premeditated thought and action to assure their safety. Making the comparison with people of color stark, some White respondents compared their sense of safety to their non-White friends' jeopardy. When I asked Jubilee Thompson if she had a "magnified moment" that highlighted her inclusion in the nation, she juxtaposed her experience as a White college-age woman with that of her Black roommate when on a "mission year" in Houston with her Christian church:

> I was walking . . . with my Black roommate . . . and I just remember this huge paradigm shift that I had: I'm safer than she is. And it was just that radical moment of [awareness]. . . . I was one of . . . three or four White people who lived in this neighborhood . . . [in a] five mile radius. . . . I stuck out like a sore thumb for that entire year. But even . . . though I had that really oppressive feeling of "all eyes on me"—like "Why are you here?"— . . . even so I was still favored. And that was this paradigm shift . . . like, wow, wow, this goes really deep. . . . Even being the outlier, I still carry this power just by the color of my skin. . . . It was just a really powerful thing to realize.

Critical Whiteness studies literature finds that White people see themselves as an "invisible, raceless norm," yet when they are spatially situated as a numerical minority they notice the salience of their race.[70] Jubilee's "paradigm shift" punctured colorblind ideology that says that race does not matter. Jubilee's college-age recognition comes late in comparison to the racial awakenings of people of color who all reported their first insight into the power of race in early childhood. Du Boisian scholars José Itzigsohn and Karida Brown suggest that White subjectivity is "based on willful ignorance toward life behind the veil," rendering colonial and racialized subjects invisible.[71] Willful ignorance that supports the racial status quo will persist unless White people are willing to become uncomfortable for the sake of racial justice.

Some White respondents were comfortably ensconced in the safety that Whiteness confers them. Doug Miller prefers the company of White people for himself and his children because Whiteness equates to safety. He holds such a strong preference for associating with White people that he moved from diverse places to a mostly White environment. Prior to moving to college-town Oregon, Doug lived in Chicago and San Antonio, calling those cities "international," "really diverse," and complaining of people with "thick accents." Doug's preference for Whiteness, racial homogeneity, and non-accented English drove his decision to move to a White space where he feels safe:

> I moved to Oregon, right? So I moved here consciously. So why did I move *here* of all places? Why didn't I move to . . . Manhattan or New York or to . . . Southern California or Arizona . . . ? Well . . . maybe I feel more comfortable . . . because that's where I feel like my community is. And certainly I think we can draw a direct line back to my youth and where I grew up [Wisconsin] and my family. . . . That's why it's more comfortable for me—and this is not easy to talk about or consider. . . . I think there's a reason that I chose to move here. . . . Frankly . . . when there's a more homogeneous society it tends to be more peaceful. And that's attractive to me.

Even as it is "not easy to talk about or consider," Doug equates racial homogeneity with White comfort and his access to "peace." White people seek comfort in racial segregation, White enclaves prioritizing White contentment.[72] Even as Doug insulates himself with other White people, he "tap[s] into that culture, that diversity" of the university town in which he resides, interfacing with "diversity" in opportunistic fashion. Living behind a bulwark of Whiteness and foraying out at will, Doug commodifies people of color and their cultures and "consumes" them by "tapping into" them without reciprocity or relationship.[73]

There are health benefits to White safety. Tess Smith, who worked as a midwife in reproductive health centers on the US-Mexico border, pontificated on how life expectancy is conditioned by race. Tess teases out how her health is shaped by her Whiteness, her body protected from certain harms more likely to afflict bodies of color:

> If we imagine manifestations of oppression for what they are . . . it's like Ruth Wilson Gilmore[74] wrote: that racism is group-differentiated vulnerability to premature death. I think about that a lot. . . . Part of the way that [racism] functions is to reduce life expectancy, literally. And there are different ways that people are killed. . . . If we imagine oppression as creating sets of material realities that rob people of bodily safety, spiritual safety, family safety, those work in different ways by groups.

Alluding to incarceration and deportation rates that disproportionately affect people of color, Tess sees that her Whiteness shields her from group-based "manifestations of oppression" that result in "premature death."

Most White respondents did not remark at length about health and safety concerns. This relative silence of White respondents stands out in stark relief against respondents of color who had much to say on the topic as well as strategies to deal with the racial stress that imperils their well-being. Lizzie Rhodes, a White woman who works with a social services organization interfacing with Latino immigrants, offers an interesting perspective. She sees it as her duty to "[try] to eliminate any potential for fear" her White presence may stir for people of color. Lizzie remarks: "I see it as they [people of color] have every reason to be afraid that I'm going to be racist or come on with . . . entitlement. . . . I want them to know that I'm a safe space." The safety Lizzie addresses here is not *her own*, as a White person, but that of people of color. Using her body as a vehicle to communicate an "identity safety cue" that the other person is welcomed and the threat of discrimination is limited,[75] Lizzie attempts to convey that she is a "safe space," approachable, and anti-racist. In so doing, she flips the script that calls on people of color to make themselves appear non-threatening [to White people] in order to secure their own safety. Lizzie prioritizes the safety of people of color with whom she interacts: "I try to just be as welcoming as I can in my ambiance and I always try to approach people and just smile as much as I can. . . . If you smile at someone, it's indicating that you're a positive energy and that you're trying to connect." In the spirit of symbolic interaction,[76] people are constantly interpreting messages they receive from others that then organizes their own actions and feelings. As part of her anti-racist agenda, as a White woman, Lizzie converts the surety of *her own safety* into a vow to interact with people of color in a fashion that values *their safety*.

White privilege is not conferred on all White people equally. Annie Herman is a Jew whose White privilege has limits in the United States, a Christian nation. She has benefited from White privilege, confirming, "Nobody's questioning whether I'm American . . . nobody's giving me flack." But, she feels the historical persecution of Jews and the contemporary uptick of anti-Semitism. Our interview occurred within two weeks of the attack on a Jewish synagogue during morning Shabbat services in Pittsburg, Pennsylvania, that killed eleven Jews and wounded six more (October 27, 2018). In terms of "real danger," she "got it like a load of bricks to the head" when the Pittsburg synagogue was attacked by a shooter who was later charged with federal hate crimes. Because of her Jewish heritage, Annie does not feel the safety of which other White respondents spoke. Saying plainly, "I'm scared of anti-Semitism," Annie's White privilege is circumscribed by her religious heritage and her perceived safety is downgraded as a result.

Access to safety is not universal. From physical to emotional security, respondents of color expressed vulnerability and racial targeting. By contrast, White respondents felt assured of their safety on account of race, even as other social identities may make them susceptible to injury. Respondents of color deployed taxing vigilance tactics ranging from customizing travel routes to stripping off cultural signifiers to filtering out abusive media coverage. While these efforts may act as a shield against racism, preventative measures cannot protect against all possible racist incursions, and to try to foresee them all only perpetuates a cycle of anticipatory racial stress.

Conclusion

Colonial and racial trauma and lack of safety accumulate into racial stress and damaging health outcomes for respondents of color. Settler colonialism and systemic racism work on bodies to ill effect. Respondents of color feel (in their minds, emotions, and bodies) their vulnerability to racialized harm that presents in the forms of intergenerational trauma, racial stress, anticipatory racial stress, and lack of personal safety. Respondents who identify as Black, Latino, Asian American, Muslim,[77] and Native American wrestled with being racial targets. Racism places racial baggage on the proverbial backs of respondents of color, stressing and depressing minds and bodies. Left to swallow emotions or engage in taxing vigilance to protect one's self, respondents of color are *viscerally aware* of the embodied trauma, health, and safety burdens of their belonging. In response to racism, respondents of color are pushed into developing "racial 'intelligence'" as they navigate their lives.[78] In contrast, trauma, health, and safety burdens of belonging do not encumber White respondents who sit at the zenith of a racial hierarchy.

Racism is embodied. It is lived, felt, and manifested in the body. Trauma, health, and safety are experienced by respondents *due to* their racialized body and also *through* (or *in*) the body. Intergenerational trauma, racial and colonial memory, and racial targeting shape life experience and dwell in bodies, minds, and spirits. White privilege includes safety; it is an escape from negative racial meanings that direct how a body is perceived and treated. While other oppressions may exist—race is not the singular story—White respondents walked through life with racial confidence, skirting worry over harm and obviating (anticipatory) racial stress and taxing vigilance.

Colonial trauma and racial stressors precipitate anxiety, depression, frustration, and anger. These racialized emotions then lodge in the body as mental health imbalances and physical maladies. While the specifics of racial targeting vary by group, the consequences of vilifying non-White people unify the experiences of respondents of color. The burden of navigating racially stressful situations, carrying anticipatory racial stress, and engaging in taxing vigilance was a common experience among respondents of color.

Negative health markers, intergenerational trauma, and safety concerns all function as *symptoms* and *reminders* of the subordinated status of people of color in the United States' colonial and racial systems. This stratification system metes out protection from and subjection to racial stress unequally, thereby creating "racial fault lines"[79] that put communities of color "at risk of risks."[80] Indices of colonial and racial status in hierarchal systems, oppression and victimization surface as racial stress, intergenerational trauma, and health and safety concerns, all of which blockade health and well-being. These socially produced, racialized vulnerabilities accumulate to burdens of belonging and bog down the physical, mental, and emotional health of marginalized populations. Indicative of belonging that is imperiled by costs, intergenerational trauma and lack of health and safety are painful symptoms and reminders of non-White status in a society that prizes and prioritizes Whiteness.

6

Racial Biography and Goal Formation

"Organic Goals" and "Acquired Goals"

Anna Hernan is the US-born daughter of two Mexican immigrants whose "organic goals" sprout from her experience with educational tracking based on race. Anna's goal of providing educational mentoring to Mexican-origin people directly derives from lack of institutional supports for her success. Up through high school, Anna was placed in special education and English as a second language classes despite her fluency in English and her complaint that those classes were beneath her academic level. A teacher eventually noticed her incorrect low placement and transitioned her into the regular academic track. A consequence of years-long racialized tracking, however, meant that Anna missed out on fundamental instruction, which caused her to slip behind her peers.

Anna was one of few Latinas studying science at her university. She faced stereotypes that she aims to overturn: "It was harder to find a stereotypically nerdy Hispanic or Latino. [laughter] So, [now I am] able to be like, 'Hey, look, I'm really nerdy too . . . and then also Hispanic!" Fighting a tide of low expectations, Anna wants to role model being an educated, professional Latina who inspires children of color. Already mentoring through a science club that hosted an event at a science fair for Latino families with young children, she enthused, "Just being able to interact with these kids and be like, 'Look, I'm a Hispanic too. I'm a first generation. I was able to do it. You're going to be able to do it.' . . . That was one of the best moments of my life." Her goals hitched to her experience, Anna focuses her mentorship efforts on Latino youth who have busy, working-class parents precisely because that had been her reality. Anna's satisfaction in coming full circle by being part of a support system for Latino youth was palpable:

It's *really* emotional to me. It's like, "Yes! I did it! I did it!" . . . I'm just overwhelmed by that feeling sometimes. I'm like, (whispering) "I can't believe I'm here and I can't believe I'm talking in front of all these kids and trying to tell them, 'You can do this too.'" . . . If they ever do feel a doubt about it, I'm like, "Dude, I was in special ed . . . all this time. If I can do it, you can definitely do it." . . . [I feel] a sense of accomplishment, a lot of pride, and . . . a lot of happiness and hope that they can also do something really amazing with their lives to show the world Hispanics can do amazing things.

Anna's racial biography that encapsulates her own and her parents' lived experience with racism and anti-immigrant harassment is the foundation for her organic goal of being a role model and mentor: "For most of my life, I didn't see high-class professional Latinos and so it's hard to really envision myself as being that. And so I feel if I can provide that visual for [Latino youth] and . . . show them . . . this is what I'm doing . . . [it will send the message] 'you can do it too.' . . . I didn't really [have] that support system and . . . I really want to focus on giving that to those kids."

This chapter argues that goals for respondents of color are shaped by their racial biographies, or the sum total of lived experience of race and racism. The same is not true for White respondents whose goals are unhitched from race or involve race only through observation. Certainly, White people also have a racial identity and are deeply affected by it, albeit in ways often invisible to them, yet the structural advantage of Whiteness disrupts the direct linkage between racial experience and goal formation so clear among respondents of color. Because Whiteness is a privileged status it does not drive goal formation, whereas experiences with racial oppression saturate the goals of people of color who are motivated to address racial inequality.

This chapter begins with the premise that a person's "racial biography" stimulates goal formation in patterned ways, reflecting racial advantage and disadvantage. "Biography" is defined as "a human life in its course" or "an account of the life of something." My term "racial biography" centers the racial character of lived experience in the "accounting" of a life trajectory. Interviews with people across racial categories reveal that racial biographies produce two distinct types of goals that are conditioned on racial status: "organic goals" and "acquired goals." As this chapter will demonstrate, respondents of color developed organic goals that grow from the soil of race-based lack of institutional supports for success and wellness, whereas White respondents held goals removed from race or expressed acquired goals concerning race that are *detached* from personal racialized experience. The process of goal formation is characterized by a racial division: Respondents of color transfigure their racial biographies into organic goals that reflect and address their racialized experience, whereas White respondents, in a location of racial advantage, develop goals untethered to their racial biographies.

Definitions of "organic" include "relating to or derived from living matter" and "characterized by continuous or natural development." Considering the influence of race and racialized experience ("racial biography") on a person's aspirations sharpens the focus on organic goals as a product of "continuous or natural development." I define "organic goals" as goals developed out of prior racial experiences over the life course (one's racial biography) that express real-life racial knowledge, often with the aim of remedying a harm or shortage of support. The concept of organic goals takes inspiration from Antonio Gramsci, who used the term "organic" intellectuals to refer to homegrown knowledge-holders who articulate the feelings and experiences of their ranks of common people (as opposed to the intelligentsia).[1] According to Gramsci, organic intellectuals come from excluded social groups (the "subaltern") and voice the common knowledge of their overlooked groups. Organic goals spring from wisdom gained from real situations, with first-hand, lived experience the "only sort of knowledge which really 'sticks.'"[2] Respondents of color overwhelmingly expressed organic goals.

"Acquired goals," by contrast, are gained through observations. When related to race, acquired goals rely on an outsider-looking-in viewpoint on oppression. White respondents were more likely to express acquired goals relating to race if they traveled domestically or internationally. Travel disrupts White respondents' "White habitus"[3] by making them a numerical minority in a new space and opening the possibility of witnessing racial inequality in a new context. Insights derive more from *observation* than lived experience here. White respondents' racial privilege insulated them from struggling against racial inequality directly, so to the extent that they held goals related to race, they were acquired from witnessing—but not living at the butt end of—racial inequality.

I contend that race-related goals are action-oriented responses to emotions. Goal-setting literature emphasizes that motivation is key to high performance and goal attainment.[4] The insight that "a specific . . . goal activates the knowledge and skills a person possesses that are necessary to attain the goal" opens the door for my argument that a person's racial biography is relevant to their goal formation.[5] Emotions are credited with having "motivational properties" and yet researchers still need to parse out how emotions integrate into motivation.[6] A step in this direction is the concept of "racial emotions" or "racialized emotions," referring to how race "comes to life" through an injection of emotions.[7] As "fundamental social forces," racialized emotions are rooted in and reflect location in a racialized social system.[8]

Conceptualizing racialized emotions as "group-based and relational"[9] and "embodied expressions of knowledge and social power" that can be leveraged to "inscribe or resist" power relations,[10] this chapter takes seriously the interplay between emotions and action. As Bonilla-Silva writes, "race cannot come to life without being infused with emotions, thus, racialized actors feel the emotional weight of their categorical location."[11] This chapter illustrates that not only do emotions reflect structural location, but they can motivate action. Using racialized emotions as a launching pad, this chapter traces how racial oppression can produce feelings about race and racial inequality that respondents of color use to build, express, and actualize organic goals.

A through line connects the racial biography of respondents of color with how they aim to spend their career, volunteer activities, or family life. This link of past racial experience to present goals is fundamental to what W.E.B. Du Bois called a "sincerity of purpose."[12] Again to quote Du Bois, disadvantage steers conceptions of an "honest endeavor," that is, "doing something worth the doing."[13] In contrast, the unifying theme among White respondents is that Whiteness does not direct goals. White privilege buffers White respondents from the racial disadvantage necessary to grow organic goals. Without deep personal acquaintance with racial subordination, White respondents skirted the first-hand experience and racialized emotions that stimulate and steer goal-setting. A racial biography characterized by suffering racial discrimination incites organic goals related to race among respondents of color, whereas White respondents' racial biography, marked by racial privilege, results in either goals unrelated to race or acquired goals that concern race due to witnessing racial inequality.

Racial biography and accompanying racialized emotions are directive for people of color. Life history and emotions inflected by race do not sit idle but, instead, undergird goal formation. Racialized emotions and ensuing action are part of the "process of racial contestation" that energizes the direction and flow of racial progress and power relations.[14] Goals—from job selection to mentorship efforts—are not random but are guided by racial biography and racialized emotions. Leveraging the concepts of organic goals and acquired goals, this chapter asserts that goal formation is structured by race, with the racial biographies of people of color leading to organic goals that center race and the racial biographies of White people allowing for wide variability in goal formation. Racial biographies structure goal formation, with racialized emotions yoking the two.

"Organic Goals": Goal Formation among People of Color

People of color use their racialized life experience and emotions as groundwork and inspiration to craft their goals. Often, aspirations grown from the soil of life experience are intended to work against systemic racist oppression and toward racial group uplift. Cognizant of their own struggles against racial blockades, stigmatization, and legal issues, respondents of color wanted to assist others in surmounting those same issues. We know that when people of color perceive their disadvantage they can be compelled to disprove low expectations, putting pressure on themselves to gain recognition.[15] We know less, however, about goals beyond exceeding expectations or navigating racism such as pursuits that catapult from racialized personal history to support others or help build more welcoming institutions.

Organic goals evolve from trauma and withheld resources. I use the phrase "withheld resources" as opposed to a deficit model that attributes failures to lack of effort or individual-level deficiency. "Withheld resources" suggests that settler colonialism and systemic racism are the culprits that withhold precious resources from people of color, thus contributing to hardships, rather than blame a person's behavior, family, culture, or community by default. Organic goals expressed by respondents of color include efforts to aid in intergenerational trauma recovery, decolonize US culture and spaces, overhaul the immigration system, institute educational and career mentoring and health-care outreach, and collective action to advocate for one's community. We turn to those efforts next.

Surviving Trauma and Aiding Trauma Recovery

As discussed in chapter 1 on settler colonialism, Native American respondents were blunt about suffering intergenerational trauma. Experiences with intergenerational trauma pivot Native American respondents first to their own self-care practices and then toward assisting their community in recovery.

Evelyn Xus's family history motivates her concerns around healing and femicide whereas Beau Landon's addiction and recovery leads him to nurture Native youth who encounter similar struggles. Intergenerational trauma feeds into these Native American respondents' goals of using their experience to benefit other Natives in their paths of recovery. Evelyn links her life to the survivorship of her ancestors: "[Intergenerational trauma] definitely is present. . . . How can you not feel upset or hurt . . . knowing this history? . . . And knowing that somebody survived it for you to be here." Evelyn refers to "alarming statistics that come along with being Native," such as mortality rates from suicide, health problems, assault, and accidents. She remarked that "death and grieving . . . has been very present for a lot of Native folk throughout history . . . since contact [with White settlers]." Evelyn tries to keep despair at bay by maintaining "critical connections" with other Natives, ceremony, and engaging land-based practices like "hanging out by the river or . . . sitting under a tree." Evelyn's reclamation of land and nature-based practices that renew her soul are poignant in light of the settler-colonial priority of usurping Native lands for White settlement.

Surviving intergenerational trauma is an immediate goal, followed by the aim of using personal experience to aid the recovery of others. Native Studies classes that taught *her* history as *"real* history" and Native American mentors aided Evelyn's college success. Wanting to do the same for other Native students, Evelyn has held various positions with local tribes and at a university in order to work with hundreds of tribal members attending college. In shepherding Native youth through university, Evelyn is serving as an "agent of ethnic mobility"—she is a highly educated minority professional who guides minorities through bureaucratic institutions.[16]

Promoting protections for women and caring about murdered and missing Indigenous women is part of Evelyn's racial biography inheritance. Her ancestors' and friends' autobiographical sharing shapes Evelyn's desire to fight violence against Indigenous women:

> It's hearing my mom's stories. It's hearing stories about my grandmothers. It's hearing the stories of my friends and family. . . . Hearing their . . . stories of survival and just seeing the beautiful people that they are now too. There's just a lot of healing we need to do. . . . How do we get to a place where we're not just looking to what *was*, but what *can be* too?

As my prior work on multi-generation families shows, sharing tales of lived experience across family generations is an engine for cultural shifts.[17] Evelyn's goals are bound to her individual and group history as Native American. She summarizes with laughter, "That's a long way of saying, 'Yeah, my identity has shaped everything.'"

Racial biography gives rise to emotions and directs goals for respondents of color. Beau Landon had succumbed to substance abuse, an outgrowth of colonialism. Consequently, Beau's form of giving back to his Native community uses his addiction as a resource to help others who face the same struggle. Beau recognizes his excessive drinking as related to intergenerational trauma, calling it a "coping mechanism." Beau relates, "My dad did better than his dad did. And then I'm just going to try and do better than my dad did to stop that cycle of generational trauma." Beau's personal goal of "doing better" is a blueprint for helping other tribal members.

Beau lost his father when he was seventeen and lapsed into a downward spiral of drinking heavily during his first year of college. He dropped out of college, sold marijuana, and "eventually got arrested, all blacked-out drunk with felony charges for marijuana possession" when he was nineteen. In rehabilitation and on probation two years later, he was "in chaos": "I [was] drinking *every day* and I'd go to jail once every couple of months for just a probation violation—my P.O. [probation officer] would catch me drinking or smoking pot." Beau beseeched his probation officer to get him into treatment. The probation officer, who treated Beau as "at promise" rather than "at risk,"[18] sent him to treatment after eighteen days in jail. Eight years later he had not taken a drink since. With a second chance, Beau rebounded and graduated with a bachelor's degree. Beau wants to use his struggle with addiction for the benefit of other Native youth. Beau says that he aspires to:

> come back to the tribe and start a STEM [Science, Technology, Education, Math] program . . . with the high school. I feel like—and I've been told this—that my story would be very impactful to tribal members and kids who grow up seeing those issues, you know? I've been to jail and been on probation and smoked pills and drank belligerently. And I made it through. I was able to get past all that and still do something productive. . . . [I want to] give to the tribe because I feel like I have something that the people could benefit from.

Beau's goals are bound to hardships that are aftereffects of colonialism. Substance abuse is linked to the oppression of sovereign nations and may have contributed to his father's early death, the traumatic event that precipitated Beau's addiction. Beau reasons that he can be a model of someone who hit bottom and recovered, a life story that would resound with Native youth. From this perspective, Beau is emblematic of group-level phenomena. He is part of a larger pattern of being beset by the intergenerational trauma of colonization and wrestling to overcome that settler-colonial burden.

Decolonization Efforts

The thrust of decolonization is to reimagine and reconstruct society free of imperial influence. Using a postcolonial sociology of race perspective, this section showcases goals of Pacific Islander and Native American respondents to reclaim culture and knowledge. As Julian Go writes, a postcolonial sociology of race would "analytically recover empire and colonialism and their legacies," "excavate colonial racialization (including racialized systems of knowledge and power) and trace its continuities into the present," and "critique the imperial standpoint and seek out the subjugated epistemologies of racialized subjects."[19] Colonized peoples' lives are rife with "subjugated epistemologies" that inform their decolonial goals.

Pacific Islander Mariana Palacios shows how colonization is not only historical but a present-tense action verb. On the day I met her, Mariana's black hair was up in a large bun and she wore a grey t-shirt that read (one word atop the next): "strong resilient indigenous" in white block print. She wore tropical flower jewelry as expressions of her island background. A central theme in Mariana's interview was her effort to "decolonize" herself, to evict colonialism from her thoughts, diet, and attire. Mariana tells me:

> I'm trying to decolonize my diet. I'm trying to eat healthy, but in a decolonized way. Have you heard of how "healthy eating" is very White? Yeah. So, I'm learning how to do that. . . . I *love* pasta, and I love salads, but . . . I need to have some tortillas . . . and rice and some soup.

As a goal for daily life, Mariana is trying to undo the White supremacy that has infiltrated her diet that would otherwise be more Indigenous.

In addition to decolonizing her own thoughts and habits, Mariana pushes back against Whiteness that is embedded in education. As a child, her parents did not expressly teach her about her Indigenous ethnic group (Chamorro) because on the island, as she says, "it was all around me." Mariana was pained to see that her "culture was being depleted in the curriculum." Already carrying that critique, Mariana moved to Oregon for college and accepted employment as a summer program coordinator at an elite university. Mariana was drawn to the summer employment, which received federal funding to enroll students from the territories (such as Micronesia, the US Virgin Islands, and the Mariana Islands), because she could provide "culturally competent guidance." She strove for Pacific Islander visibility, choosing a Pacific Islander as a keynote speaker on climate change, intentionally positioning this Indigenous scholar as a knowledge-holder. A White male coworker complained that the invited speaker spoke about "island issues." The White staff member fretted that he could not relate to "island issues"— forget the dozens of student participants whose experience was moved "from margin to center."[20] Mariana shot back, "Don't you realize it's all about *you* [all of the time]?! . . . Do you realize what you're saying?!" When Mariana disrupted White-centric curriculum, it is telling that a White peer protested over his exclusion, exposing his assumption that his standpoint should be reflected in the academy. It is the "*omission of race in the color-blind classroom* [that is a] strategy that preserves whiteness's position of unspoken privilege."[21] To include non-White perspectives in education is to call out and puncture White privilege and decolonize teaching and learning. Presenting a Pacific Islander as a knowledge-holder who takes center stage showcases a non-White role model and makes curricula more multivocal and inclusive.

Postcolonialism contends that colonialism "persist[s] in various guises today."[22] Colonial dynamics and ramifications are never finished but require ongoing reckoning. It is in this vein that Kaulana Tamata, born in American Samoa and raised in Hawai'i, sees postcolonialism fueling her present-day goals. She communicates her emotional drive and decolonial goals: "They came to our islands to basically teach us religion . . . put us in clothes. . . . Why would they do that unless they thought we were the problem or that we weren't civilized?" Discontented with colonial occupation and forced assimilation, Kaulana wants expanded opportunities outside of well-worn pathways of military or football:

> Overall my goal is to become . . . a successful business owner and take [that success] home to Samoa and help the community back home see more opportunities. . . . [I want to] take away that idea that you need to leave [and] the way to leave the island is through . . . football and the military. Giving more options. . . . Because [with] education you can use your head without damaging it and damaging your life; [you can] use your head and keep your culture, keep your identity.

Her exhortation that "you can use your head without damaging it" is a double entendre referring to high rates of concussions for men of color football players and post-traumatic stress disorder that numerous military veterans suffer. Kaulana pushes against the postcolonial structure of opportunity that limits Pacific Islander futures largely to the military or football, both of which treat her people as expendable and useful principally for their bodily might.

The goal of offering expanded opportunities stems from colonial exploitation that shrank opportunities and homogenized Pacific Islanders to "just big people that like to eat, play football, and can sing and play instruments and dance," as Kaulana quips. Kaulana desires to explode that circumscribed vision:

> My goal for . . . my community is basically create a different perspective of us. . . . We're educated, we're intelligent, we hold high positions. . . . I've been reaching out to . . . professors and staff who are P.I. [Pacific Islander] and . . . giving them acknowledgment and showing them to other P.I.s and saying, ". . . There is a professor. She did it! Or, he did it! You can do it too." . . . Starting with little steps to just show that we can do it.

Kaulana calls attention to Pacific Islander futures unrestricted by postcolonial stereotypes.

Native American and Pacific Islander respondents formed organic goals grounded in their colonization. With the objective of decolonizing everything from the self to society, Indigenous respondents looked to their colonized life experience to generate specific goals. Decolonization efforts are an organic goal for Indigenous respondents who want to break out of settler-colonial subjugation and craft more liberated futures.

Help Migrants Navigate the Legal System . . . and Change the Legal System

Another goal stemming from trauma and withheld resources—or, more accurately, trauma *because of* withheld resources—is to assist migrants navigating the US immigration legal system. Roberto Torres and Candi Perez arrived in the United States as young children, known as the "1.5 generation" who are foreign-born but arrive to a host country pre-adolescence. Both of Mexican origin, they were undocumented for years and identify as DREAMers. Roberto's and Candi's experiences with immigration and illegality fuel their goal to mentor others in hopes of using their knowledge born of struggle to benefit people in similar situations.

Roberto Torres is a Mexican American DACA (Deferred Action for Childhood Arrivals) recipient. He works for a Latino-serving organization that provides legal aid, translation services, cultural celebrations, and immigrant outreach and volunteers during elections to educate voters about ballot initiatives, despite his ineligibility to vote. Being undocumented has been described as "living in the shadows," with youth learning about their unauthorized status akin to "waking up to a nightmare" where they must "learn to be illegal" and come to terms with their limited options.[23] A legal system that enacts structural and symbolic violence on undocumented migrants is naturalized when these harms are encoded in laws, manufacturing "legal violence."[24] As touched on in chapter 5, Roberto describes the immense stress of legal violence that worsened into depression:

> I would hold everything in until I would just break down. And that eventually led me to my depression, to my anxiety. . . . Talking things out was something that helped me overcome all of those issues. . . . I feel like if it helped me, I can help other people with that.
>
> JVT: And that's what is driving you to psychology?
>
> ROBERTO: Mm-hmm.

Because of his racial biography, Roberto is inspired to assist others in coping with issues involving immigration and legal status. Roberto's racial biography (which is enmeshed with immigration and legal status), burdened him with anguish and then evolved into the organic goals of Latino migrant advocacy and counseling.

Roberto's racial biography blooms into the organic goal of helping undocumented immigrants. With race-based hardships acting as a rudder, Roberto's racialized emotions transmute into organic goals. He refers to the time prior to receiving DACA (temporary legal status): "I didn't know if I wanted to go to college. I wasn't sure if I was going to graduate high school . . . I went through all of that [turmoil], so . . . I want to help others *avoid* that hardship, so that . . . they can work on bettering themselves." The people Roberto assists are reminiscent of his migrant family's journey: "We mostly get . . . undocumented people—immigrants. . . . Mexicans . . . people from Guatemala. . . . [and] refugees. . . . [I work on issues like] fighting an eviction from a home." Now holding an associate degree with plans to transfer to a four-year university to earn a bachelor's degree, Roberto's experiences around legal liminality impel him to mentor newcomer Latinos.

Roberto's career objective of becoming a school guidance counselor is linked to perceiving, during registration for kindergarten at five years old, that even very young Mexican immigrants were frowned upon. Roberto answers my question about his "first memory of race" by telling me about his pre-kindergarten self being discriminated against by a school official: "I distinctly remember [the school administrator] saying, 'Oh, so you're Mexican.' . . . But it was in that tone of voice where you *know* they . . . had an issue with it. . . . It's burned into my mind." This searing memory "burned into" his mind is a motivating force behind supporting Latino immigrants in the realm of educational access. As an adult, Roberto's organic goals that arise from his racial biography are intended to ameliorate (for himself and others) the harm that can be incurred by uncaring, racist gatekeepers and racialized institutions.

In addition to current employment and career goals, Roberto's volunteer work is rooted in the emotions and practicalities of having been undocumented. Immigrants develop a sense of "legal-spatial consciousness," meaning "individuals' sense of how space and law are interconnected and experienced at the personal level."[25] Roberto's angst over not being able to legally drive before he received DACA inspired his civic participation around voter education and voter registration when a driver's license measure was on the state ballot. For both Black people and Latinos, political participation has been linked to representing the interests of their racial/ethnic group ("linked fate") as well as those of immigrants more broadly.[26] Revealing his legal-spatial consciousness, Roberto connects his prior blocked access to driving with his civic engagement around voting:

[Something] that had a big impact on me back when I was younger . . . before DACA . . . [was] not being able to drive. Yeah. That was huge. . . . [Now] I love to [drive] honestly. . . . When I got my license . . . I was just ecstatic. . . . I was so excited to make simple runs to the grocery store, because I couldn't do that before, you know? . . . It enabled me to help my parents with things that they couldn't do . . . like just simple trips driving. . . . It was amazing for me.

In the context of illegality as a "'moving' target across space that individuals navigate,"[27] possessing a driver's license removes barriers to traveling locally and decreases fears.[28]

Roberto's life course moving from searching out bus lines and "safe walking routes" to fervor for driving as a legal privilege motivates his organic goal of voter education volunteer work. Voting can alter the legal system. Roberto campaigned when Measure 88 (Oregon Alternative Driver Licenses Referendum in 2014 that would have made four-year driver licenses available to those who cannot prove legal presence in the United States) was on the ballot (the measure was defeated). Through voter education, Roberto advocated for undocumented immigrants and hoped to affect voters and vote outcomes: "Even though I can't [vote], I can always go out there and . . . educate [voters] to make a difference. . . . If people don't vote, that . . . gives a clear pathway . . . for those laws that have a negative impact on our community to be able to be passed." The link between racial biography, racialized emotion, and organic goals is a straight line.

Candi Perez, a young woman who wore her jet-black hair in a single braid that hung to the side in front of her shoulder, was born in Michoacán, Mexico, and is part of a mixed-status family. After nine years of processing, she was granted documentation status as a permanent resident with a "Visa U" (or U Visa) that protects victims of domestic violence and trafficking. Living in the United States since before age two, the fear of deportation she endured before permanent residency is the foundation for her organic goal of assisting immigrant youth. Candi wants to be for others the mentor she wished she had.

Candi harbors complicated feelings around the long, bureaucratic march through immigration processes through which she eventually attained her permanent residency. Attesting that the process could have been easier, Candi laments:

> It's just really frustrating. . . . A lot of people are like, "Oh, it's so easy, I don't know why people cross the border and blah blah blah when they can just . . . go through the process." But they don't know that it takes years and thousands of dollars and it's not as easy as it seems. For me it was a really long process.

Until Candi obtained legal status, she feared deportation raids:

"Oh my gosh, Immigration [and Customs Enforcement] is gonna come get me in class, and they're gonna take me!" . . . When it hit me that I was safe was when I got the Visa U, that's when I cried. That's when I was like [breathes a sigh of relief], "I'm safe, I can go to school now and I can get a job and everything." I cried a lot that day. Just thinking about it makes me wanna cry.

Candi spent nine years in legal limbo as her case was processed. Even now possessing legal status, her "liminal legality"[29] is so deeply felt that she "forgets." Fear is so firmly embedded in her psyche around her (former) undocumented status that it crops up periodically: "Sometimes I'll be watching the news like, 'Oh my gosh, what am I gonna do?' I forget just because I've always had that fear. I guess it's just still in me. It's scary." As sociologist Laura Enriquez who studies undocumented youth shows, after legalization some people "felt their fears of deportation melt away, while others suffered 'posttraumatic stress' from a lifetime of surveillance."[30] Our tearful conversation reveals the first-hand experience and raw-emotion motivation that propels Candi's aspiration to mentor migrants navigating the immigration system.

Candi's organic goals are directly related to her racial biography, which is wrapped up with an immigration and legal journey. I inquired about a connection between her experience and goals. She was definitive:

Definitely. . . . I want to become somebody who is able to help. I think about it this way: *when I was little, I wish I would have had somebody like me now to help me. And I want to be that person for somebody.* . . . One time, a *padre* . . . a pastor . . . told me "you're a warrior." . . . That's stuck with me. I definitely feel that way. I've . . . been through so much [and] I want to be able to share my story, inspire others, like, "You're not alone. I was able to get through it, you can do it." (emphasis added)

Candi's racial biography, laced with migration and legal status complications, impels her to "inspire others" and "help." She aims to pass forward the tactical knowledge she gained through her trying experience. Practically speaking, legal status facilitates Candi's achievement of her goals. Legal status and lack of legal status offers or forecloses opportunities, respectively.[31] Candi's educational goals are more attainable with legal status: "In order to receive financial aid [to attend college], [you] have to be a permanent resident or a citizen. Now that I am a permanent resident and can receive financial aid, I'm going back to school. I'm jumping right in."

Build Support Programs for People of Color: Compensatory Mentoring and Health-Care Access

Success is not due to "pluck and perseverance" alone but is a credit to "individual agency, family agency, and institutional supports *combined*."[32] Respondents of color who feel they would have benefited from mentoring programs they never had tend to participate in compensatory mentoring: They want to provide to others the mentorship, training, relationship- and skill-building opportunities that they wished they had. This mentoring is compensatory because it is driven by respondents' prior subjection to group-based institutional lack of support. Similarly, respondents working in health care suffered inadequate health services in earlier years.

Two Asian American respondents exemplify the conversion of deficiency of support for (and in) college into mentoring college students of color. While Asian Americans are a broad category, many of whom are buoyed by a "stereotype promise" in school,[33] this positive labeling conceals resource disadvantage and can exacerbate challenges. That is the case for Paul Lee, Vietnamese American, who was expected to attend college but lacked the knowledge to navigate that pathway well. Paul lays out the conundrum: "I think there's a lot of opportunities in the US. Whether it's *accessible* . . . depends. I think for Asian Americans . . . mostly because of the model minority myth, I think we have it easier than other folks. But it's just a broad myth that impacts us in a very negative way, too." Vietnamese refugees are upheld as a success story but this casting glosses over their economic insecurity, including a poverty rate higher than the national average.[34] The overly general model minority myth backfired for Paul. He attended an upper-middle class "only-White" high school and administrators assumed he had the skills to pursue college with little guidance. Positive assumptions about Paul based on Asian heritage undermined him: "No one talked to me about going to college. They wanted to assume that I knew what I was doing—that I'm Asian American [so] I'll just get into any school that I want. And being a first-generation college student, I had no idea what I was doing." High school administrators "want[ing] to assume" that Paul had knowledge about the college admissions process let them off the hook for supporting him. Paul's first-generation Asian American aspiring college student status was read as an oxymoron.

Because Paul did not receive guidance counseling, he mimicked his wealthy White peers and applied to expensive, prestigious universities his family could not afford. Because administrators stamped Paul with the model minority myth ("They just assumed I always do well academically, I was Asian . . . you're good."), he almost fell through the crack between high school and college. His family could not afford an out-of-state private college so Paul applied late to an in-state university and attended it. Paul experiencing the underbelly of the model minority stereotype—rather than its potentially protective halo—nearly derailed his education. Once in college, an organic goal relative to education burgeoned. He reflects: "[I did] high school outreach because I remember my experience: . . . I had no idea what I was doing. . . . [In the] outreach program [we went] out to different high schools and talk[ed] to students about college. . . . A current goal [is] to create meaning and impact." Due to his racial biography of being overlooked when accessing college, Paul now holds a career in higher education devoted to building community for students of color that supports their racial/ethnic heritages and educational success.

Like Paul, James Tran's organic goal of a career in higher education took shape because he wanted to be the kind of mentor he wished he had. Also like Paul, James is the US-born son of two Vietnamese refugees. The model minority stereotype posits that Asian Americans overperform relative to other groups. This postulation overshadows the hardships of subgroups. Contrary to the provision of resources that some Asian Americans may be awarded because of a halo effect (such as teachers' belief in certain students' smarts that triggers extra, positive attention), James faltered when school officials left him on autopilot. The absence of mentors sparked his career goals: "[I did] not really [get] to connect with someone who has gone in the trenches and has fought the battles. . . . I felt like I could offer something to . . . minority groups who [will see] that I've gone through it and that they can do it as well." James's compensatory mentoring is an organic goal driven by his yearning for mentorship earlier in his life. He says, "I've always wanted mentors. . . . I haven't had one." James's goals are wish-fulfillment that compensate for the void of support he faced. His prior experience converts into a professional responsibility: "Working with students . . . is what I can offer and this is what I'm doing to represent my group."

A multiracial Asian-Latinx woman, Luna Espinosa's career of supporting students of color in higher education blooms from her struggles around race. In college, as a multiracial person, she faced ultimatums from student race–based organizations which led her to isolation. Confronted with "lots of in-group, out-group" tensions, Luna was disappointed by the racial conflicts because she had anticipated college as a time and place for racial exploration.[35] Luna ponders the link between the dearth of multiracial spaces in college and her career in higher education:

> All these [work] projects [were] really initially about me: about how I didn't belong and I was curious whether other people felt like they did or did not belong. . . . The goal for me was always to create more inclusive spaces in those monoracial spaces. . . . I think that the right thing to do is dismantle racism and offer an opportunity for us to be really critical in all spaces, whether it be really talking about where anti-Blackness shows up or where we're not doing coalitional or solidarity-based work.

Luna's college student pain became a springboard into her profession which aims to facilitate awareness around race, racism, multiraciality, and coalition-building.

In addition to education, respondents of color identified health care as a source of inequality, their families and communities bereft of access. Latinx Melanie Rodriguez, who is pursuing an advanced degree in health, refers to her racial biography and ensuing organic goals as related to her family's health barriers:

> In high school I was very aware that Latin people face greater health disparities than White people do. I didn't have the language for it back then

like I do now. . . . My own family . . . had so many more health problems that nobody else I . . . knew had. So, that . . . piqued my interest in this field. . . . So, I think that mostly shaped my goals.

Knowledge of her Latinx family's health problems spurred Melanie's desire to ameliorate health inequities through a career in health.

Jasmine Salazar, the twenty-six-year-old daughter of two Mexican immigrants, offers an account of how her empathy for immigrants and poor families in need of health care is rooted in her racial biography plus newcomer status in the United States. In leveraging her own life experience as a basis for connection to communities in need of health care, she is enacting a recommendation by health researchers who favor "diversifying the healthcare work force to more closely reflect the demographic composition of the patient population."[36] Wanting to be "that voice and advocate for my community," Jasmine was beginning a new job in public health as an outreach coordinator who conducts home visits. Jasmine's racial biography and immigrant background inform her career choice of health services access for underprivileged communities. As an immigrant from a working-class background, Jasmine says she "gets it":

I think [social justice has] always been . . . my driving force behind public health. . . . I always aimed to work with minorities—specifically Hispanics and African Americans—because that is what I'm familiar with and I see firsthand . . . the need. . . . The health disparities are more present in those communities.

Public health literature supports Jasmine's first-hand observations of need in communities of color. She links her life experience to her empathy and ability to build rapport with those in need of health-care assistance. Her racial biography positions her as an "insider" with the clientele she serves: "More than anything, it's like, 'I'm one of your kind. . . . You can trust me' . . . because when I say, 'I get it' . . . I actually get it . . . because . . . I've been there.'" Jasmine's goal "to have an impact" is driven by her position as the daughter of Mexican immigrants who survived tough times. Jasmine's background boosts her ability to connect with those in need:

I was drawn to . . . community health [and] health promotion. . . . I worked with . . . marginalized families . . . [that were] lower class. . . . I really liked that. . . . For me, that speaks close to home . . . because . . . *those are more of my people.* . . . I was one of those [people] when my parents first came. . . . We literally had nothing. . . . We had to make a lot of sacrifices. . . . Now [my parents] have a nice home and . . . we're all doing pretty well. So . . . I feel like if there's anything I can do to . . . open up that path of hope for other families [I want to]. In my case . . . that's health-care access, which is very important and helps . . . provide stability. . . . Being able to go to work every day and know that I'm going to be in contact with people that I want to help and that I can especially connect to closely and . . . easily . . . is a huge blessing.

Jasmine's organic career goals are directly tied to her experience of race, class, and immigration. Not only do racialized emotions "draw" a person of color to a career, but there is an emotional payoff ("huge blessing") to effectively conjoin one's racial biography to desired equity-oriented outcomes by way of organic goals.

As an "insider" to the community she helps, Jasmine lives out the trend of socially mobile Mexican Americans who grew up poor or working class and upon entering the middle class are "giving back" to their racial/ethnic communities.[37] Jasmine may be adopting the role of a "cultural guardian"—a term originally coined to refer to working-class origin Latina teachers whose own "marginalization over the life course" helps them "realize how valuable they can be" to students who share their cultural roots and whom they consciously try to help.[38] Additionally, as a Latina professional, she is poised to resist institutional discrimination through executing anti-racist projects from within her profession.[39]

Jasmine's second intention is to empower youth from similar backgrounds. As seen, serving as a role model is an organic goal for many respondents of color because they seek to fill a void that they faced. Jasmine comments:

[I want to help] empower . . . the little ones. Just empowering them: "Yes, you can do it. Pursue your dreams and goals . . . whatever you want to be. . . . You have the right to do that and don't feel limited or constrained because maybe you don't have health-care access or your parents are immigrants. . . ." [I want to] remind that they have a community and support system.

Her lived experience positioning her to be a culturally competent, bilingual heath-care service provider, Jasmine aims to affect change in health care and life trajectories.

Collective Action

The question I asked ("When you think of your 'life goals' or aspirations (career, family, or otherwise), are they related to race, in your view?") solicited individual-level responses about ambitions, past accomplishments, and future plans. Despite the focus on the individual, some answers linked up to collective action efforts. Some respondents were involved in organized efforts (e.g., voter registration, tribal restoration, immigration reform) or affiliative groups cohering around race/ethnicity. Community involvement fueled community-oriented goals. Thus, even as my interview question targeted the individual, some respondents' endeavors are linked to collective action efforts.

Engaging in collective action serves the dual purpose of striving to ameliorate social problems that are deeply felt and to promote affective inclusion in a community, be it racial/ethnic, a tribal nation, or the US nation. Grassroots collective efforts are also vehicles to "continue to be a problem," discussed in chapter 2, a way to agitate for group-level respect and needs. For Candi Perez (Mexican American), discussed above, collective action makes her feel included in a caring community as she vies for immigration reform. She engages in claims-making for a collective. Referring to protests against family separation at the border and collective action in favor of immigration reform, Candi remarks:

Everything that's going on is bringing so many people together and it feels like I'm a part of that history. Bringing the families together . . . and immigration . . . it's bringing so many people together. I feel like a lot of people are losing fear just because they know they're not alone. They know they have that support system. So, I don't really feel excluded anymore.

As a former undocumented immigrant engaged in a social movement that has gained a groundswell of support, Candi's individual-level goal of helping others navigate the immigration system intersects with a collective effort calling for immigration reform, including pathways to citizenship and family reunification. Engaging in collective action that parallels her own individual goals provides a sense of inclusion for Candi, who feels she is "part of that history," "not alone," and has a "support system."

Similarly engaged in collective action as a conduit for group-level goals, Leles Talbot (Native American) worked for federal recognition (restoration) of her tribe (Miluk Coos). The collective—her tribe—orients both her organic goal formation and her cooperative approach to pooling efforts for tribal restoration. Leles worked with tribal members as she kept her eye on benefiting her tribe ("it's so good for my tribe"). She lists the tribes involved in collective action:

> Several of the tribes here in Western Oregon got very active in restoration. And we got involved with some very competent lawyers and . . . ethnohistorians. . . . Siletz went [for restoration] first [1977], then everybody queued up: Grand Ronde, Cow Creek, us [Miluk Coos]. We . . . went bing-bing-bing [in '82, '83, '84]. . . . We kind of *built on each other's success*. And then it took a few years . . . for Klamath and Coquille to get restored. . . . For a while there we only [had] three federally recognized tribes and now we have nine. . . . Chinook and the Confederated Tribes of the Lower Rogue are also now pushing for restoration. . . . That circle's come around again—it's time for us to all push . . . to help them.

Leles' collective action organic goals are inextricably linked to her tribe. Yet, her collectivist mindset broadens what she views as "the collective" to encompass additional tribal nations and their legal objectives ("it's time for us to all push . . . to help them"). Leles took her first-ever airplane trip to go to Washington, DC, with four tribal elders to testify in favor of tribal restoration. Upon achieving federal recognition for her tribe, Leles said she "completed [her] life goal" and now, decades later, she keeps "going forward for Natives."

Deriving from racial biography, organic goals are wedded to bettering the fortunes of one's group. Many organic goals are sized as individual-level aspirations aimed toward one's community while others, like those in this section, are contributions to collective action. The overlap of self and group is seen here, demonstrating how individual and group experiences are braided together. Racial biographies stimulate organic goals that surface as both personal and collective ambitions that keep the welfare of group members as the lead concern.

Role of Family in Racial Biographies and Organic Goals

While racialized life experience, including withheld resources, is the basis for organic goals, the role a family plays in socializing children into awareness of race and racism is like adding fertilizer to the soil that grows organic goals. The open discussion of racial inequality that respondents of color had with parents developed their racial consciousness and, in turn, goal formation. The fact that race and racial justice efforts are common topics of conversation in families primes people of color to detect and combat racism.

Maggie Rose (Chicana) grew up working class in a diverse area in California to Mexican immigrant parents who spoke frankly about race and racism. This open dialog within the family means that Maggie's racial biography *includes* bits of her parents' racial biographies that they relayed to her. The overriding message her parents jointly conveyed was: "Racism is real. People [are] trying to treat Mexicans like shit. So be aware of it and speak up." Maggie hypothesizes that her parents' "lived experience" caused them to be forthcoming about anti-Mexican racism. Maggie's parents' "fear that it would happen again if they didn't intervene" prompted kitchen-table race-conscious conversations. Maggie offers an example of these everyday conversations about race:

> If we said like, "How was your day?" . . . [My dad] would actively talk about, "Oh, a customer came in today and asked to talk to a manager, but I knew more. . . . Or they asked to talk to so-and-so because he's White and wearing a suit and I'm Brown and not wearing a suit." . . . [My parents] just made . . . conversation *include* race all the time.

Maggie credits these discussions with her preparedness: "I was able to then navigate [racism] differently because it didn't catch me off guard as much." She analogizes the need for race-consciousness to looking both ways before you cross the street:

> [Race and racism] was always in my understanding of the world. . . . You know that you're supposed to . . . look both ways before crossing the street. . . . It's going to keep you safe and it's going to keep you protected. But if nobody teaches you that you're supposed to look both ways before crossing the street, you're going to put yourself in a lot of harm's way, right?

Grateful for the racial socialization her parents provided her, Maggie funnels her energy: "Anger . . . fuels my work." Because of her parents' persistent talk of racial injustice, Maggie was taught to identify and condemn inequality. Working toward a graduate degree and teaching college classes, Maggie connects the dots between her parents' racial biographies, their race-conscious teachings, and the organic goals she is pursuing in higher education:

> Luckily, I had parents who talked a lot about racial injustice. . . . I never had a moment where it really *hit me* that America hated Mexicans [chuckles]; it was more like always a part of my truth because of the way that my parents spoke about things. . . . I know America hates Mexican people. [It does not] find much value in them—in me—until I can produce something for them. And that's just the anger that supports my work every day. Why I want . . . to engage in telling stories and social justice work.

With a swift critique of racial capitalism, Maggie connects her parents' racial truth-telling, contoured by their lived experiences, to her emotions and organic goal of racial justice.

Family socialization into race-consciousness is an important but not singular influence on organic goals. Like other respondents of color, Maggie faced a dearth of Mexican-origin mentors and role models: "It was really hard to feel like I knew what it looked like to be a Mexican student doing work because I didn't see other Mexican students doing the work. . . . There was no example . . . to lead me, to show me." A first-generation college student, Maggie enrolled at a university campus as a math major and recalls, "I had never seen that many White people in my entire life. . . . It was like extra White and extra men." She felt "extremely overwhelmed" and out of place: "I didn't even know that many White people could be in one place. . . . I was like, 'Oh my God, I can't go to college.'" As discussed in chapter 4, the racial demographics, power skew, and culture of an institution either roll out or withhold the welcome mat. Maggie's epiphany during summer orientation was the lightbulb moment of an organic goal: "It just clicked. Because I didn't see any summer orientation leaders that looked like me or sounded like me, I wanted to be one."

The lessons of her parents' racial biographical self-telling, combined with her first-hand experience with underrepresentation on campus, culminated into Maggie's organic goal. Moving from dissatisfaction and overwhelm, Maggie converts her bundle of knowledge into a career path: "I could complain and be miserable the whole time and finish with a math degree and be really sad and isolated. Or I could turn what I do in the classroom and out of the classroom into creating a better context for me and for others like me." Maggie's career aspiration of race-conscious higher education work is linked to her racial biography in two manners: first, her family racial socialization gave her a critical eye with which to see racial problems and a racial vocabulary to articulate them, and second, her first-hand experiences with underrepresentation and disadvantage in education boosted her desire to smooth the pathway for students of color.

Respondents of color overwhelmingly articulate organic goals in that their career, avocational, or personal aspirations were fashioned out of the raw material of their racial lives. The particularities ranged from surviving trauma and aiding others' recovery, decolonization efforts, helping migrants navigate the legal system, supporting education and health-care access for people of color, and engaging in collective action to pursue community-oriented objectives. The goals and convictions of these respondents sprout organically from the fertile soil of lived experience around race—their racial biography.

"Acquired Goals": Goal Formation among White People

In contrast to respondents of color, White respondents possessed goals that were disconnected from racialized experience. White respondents articulated non–race specific goals as well as (less often) race-specific "acquired goals" that stood apart from their racial biography. The goals of White respondents that concern race spring from an origin that is not from first-hand experience with racial oppression. The inspiration for racial justice work among White respondents arises not from racial subjugation but the second-hand witnessing of it.

Race and racial biography do not direct goal formation for White respondents. Two White men interviewees offer incisive comments about how race does not shape their objectives. To my question, "Have you been steered toward . . . life goals . . . that you feel have to do with your racial background?" Dylan Johnson replies, "Mmm, no. Off the top of my head, no." Doug Miller, who works in retail, explains how White privilege allowed him to fritter away opportunities rather than work hard: "I was privileged enough to be able to just say . . . 'Whatever. I can blow this off now. There will be other opportunities in the future.'" Whiteness is a force of domination with material consequences.[40] Doug's access to achievement and lackadaisical attitude is colored by White privilege. Doug was confident that, with White privilege as a backup plan, doors would remain open for him: A detour would not mean derailment, only a willful delay. With racial status conferring advantage, Doug was cushioned by White privilege, a position of complacency that left racial matters by the wayside.

In contrast to respondents of color, White respondents needed to look outside of their own lived experience to observe race and racial inequality. Occupying a privileged racial category that is viewed as "default" means that White people do not necessarily see how race operates because their race shields them from the blunt end of racial inequality. In a position of privilege, White people may not comprehend race without a precipitating consciousness-raising moment. For White respondents, this racial epiphany usually occurred when they were traveling and became a numerical minority in a largely non-White context. Because Whiteness is a privileged racial status, White respondents' goals were not saturated with racial inequality concerns born of lived experience. Some White respondents came to see and care about racial inequality but, lacking experiential knowledge, their goal generation is qualitatively different from respondents of color whose goals are directly shaped by racialized life experience.

In addition to some White respondents who were unmoved by racial concerns, others developed acquired goals that touch on race.

This notable variation avoids essentializing the experiences of White people. White respondents do not experience racial disadvantage, but they can observe it. Kathleen Post's international travel led her to observe racial, class, and health inequities that stimulated her interest in a health-related career trajectory. Living in predominately White locales throughout her childhood, it was not until after college graduation, when Kathleen traveled in Guatemala, Bolivia, Chile, and Ecuador, that she "learned about race." She observed gross disparities, which made her angry and catapulted her career path into global public health. In Bolivia she went on walking tours where she learned of the appropriationist role of the United States extracting resources, all while seeing "Indigenous people on the street." Living in predominately White environments, it was not until Kathleen traveled abroad that she looked outward to comprehend race and colonialism. Travel disrupted her "White habitus."[41] In a foreign country where she was a numerical minority visitor, Kathleen was removed enough from her comfortable White milieux to observe and digest racial disparities and colonial legacies. Kathleen remarks that her travels in Central and South America were pivotal to her acquired goal of work in global health:

> I learned so much about race and ethnicity just by being there and talking to people. . . . That was a huge motivator because I learned so much about race and ethnicity down there in South America. . . . Just . . . the disparities between different groups and how grossly unfair it is and terrible. [It] just made me *mad* and so I came back and it was like: "Okay I think this is what I want to do."

She saw the Indigenous populations as "really, really, marginalized." She says, "It was just crazy to see the colonialism just still *so apparent* down there." Kathleen ties her international travel observations to her career aim: "Discrimination . . . colonialism, neo-colonialism . . . affects people's health and . . . I think my travel definitely is . . . the reason that I'm doing global health." Kathleen assimilated newfound information on race and colonialism through travel, which became the foundation for her acquired goals around racial equity in health.

Elizabeth Cooper's story of acquiring goals around race starts with being called out for having a racial identity, piercing the colorblindness that keeps White privilege intact. Elizabeth stepped out of her largely White social environment for a humanitarian project, which is where her race was first publicly identified:

> My first memory of someone pointing out to me that I was White—because I think largely I didn't even think about being White—[was when] I was about sixteen years old. . . . We were doing a Habitat for Humanity project in . . . very low-income projects. . . . We were doing a house build. . . . My dad had picked me up . . . and I remember just gazing out the window. . . . I was pretty aloof and I remember this [Black] teenager . . . speaking with a level of assertiveness: ". . . What are you looking at, White girl?"
>
> . . . It is a moment that I have reflected on and have come back to so many times in my life. . . . That's the first time ever anyone ever mentioned that I was White. And that felt offensive to me [laughter] almost. I was like, "What—why are you calling out my race?" That was like a form of border crossing . . . [into] a . . . community made up largely of . . . working poor and almost exclusively Black. . . . I was a do-gooder, like a White knight. . . . My work now is about preparing students to not do [that] [chuckles]. [I emphasize] understanding your identity and understanding the communities that you're working with rather than assuming you know what they need.

In this vignette, Elizabeth moves from racial colorblindness to a racial awakening. In that moment of being called out as a "White girl," Elizabeth's White invisibility was upset. As sociologist Monica McDermott instructs, "The invisibility of whiteness is such that the privilege it involves is often hidden from view—it seems like the natural order of things."[42] In the situation Elizabeth recounts, her race was no longer unspoken because it no longer aligned with the local environment. Elizabeth links the epiphany around her Whiteness and the lack of critical reflexivity she had when doing volunteer work in a low-income Black community to her career where she facilitates service learning experiences for students, but with a critical lens. That moment with the Black teenager at the Habitat for Humanity site sparked Elizabeth's reflexivity and grew into the acquired goal of coordinating university service learning programming with a critical approach.

In addition to local volunteer work, domestic travel for disaster relief interrupted Elizabeth's insulation in a White environment and exposed her to racial and class inequalities and inspired her acquired goals. Elizabeth explains:

> Hurricane Katrina hit my senior year of college and my school organized . . . fundraising campaigns and then a few trips to . . . help with some of the immediate cleanup efforts in the Gulf coast. I went to New Orleans January of 2006 . . . five months after [the August storm]. . . . [I was] seeing who got support from FEMA [Federal Emergency Management Agency] . . . learning about who was living in the 9th Ward, why they were living in the 9th Ward. [I walked] through parts of New Orleans where it looked like an atomic bomb had gone off. It was unbelievably shocking and horrific and unsettling [to witness] what races and what class statuses were completely devastated and unable to return and . . . having such a hard time getting FEMA support. . . . Being down there and talking in person to people whose lives were just destroyed and hearing . . . "Oh yeah, our family was forced out of the French Quarter because they were trying to increase tourism and don't want Brown people there" and [I am] just like, "Holy shit."

"Borrowed" experiences (such as racial biography tales told from one person to another) can lead to a recipient "acquiring" knowledge second-hand.[43] This newly acquired, non-biographical knowledge is meaningful and can contour goals: Acquired goals are gained from a journey of observations. While not a guaranteed outcome, instances of observing racial inequality can prompt White people, who are structurally buffered from racial disadvantage, to integrate an acquired concern for racial justice efforts into their goals. Mirroring her own eye-opening immersive experience with humanitarian projects, Elizabeth now oversees "educational experiences where people are out in communities and learning about what's really going on."

Racial privilege shields White respondents from first-hand experience with racial harms that fueled the organic goals of people of color. Most White respondents were not committed to racial equity aims like respondents of color. The few White respondents whose goals were race-oriented had traveled to racially heterogeneous landscapes. During these explorations, often as numerical minorities (White people in predominantly non-White spaces), White respondents observed racial inequality. Observations when traveling led White respondents to pick up second-hand knowledge and acquire goals that fold in racial concerns. Yet, even if moved to action, White respondents' lives were not significantly negatively impacted by the observation of racial inequality, unlike respondents of color whose lives and emotions were often deeply and continuously shaped by disadvantage. This power of selectivity is a privilege because White respondents have great latitude in choosing their goals rather than being directed toward goals by virtue of racialized life experience.

"White-Passing" People of Color: Racism against Family and Community Fosters Organic Goals

The dichotomous framework non-White/White belies messiness such as racial admixture, people who identify as White yet have ancestors of color, and people of color who believe they "pass" as White. Eight respondents of color (including three multiracial respondents[44]) identified their "street race" (the race they believe someone observing them on the street would classify them)[45] as White. Believing they are viewed as White, these respondents of color find a disjuncture between how they self-identify and their perception of other people's assessment of them. All these respondents of color who are White-passing feel allied with people of color. The route into organic goals traveled by these White-passing respondents of color is via stories of discrimination told to them by their darker-skinned parents and grandparents or their witnessing of family members' subjection to racial inequality. These White-passing respondents told me many stories of their ancestors' racial hardships and times they watched family members bear the brunt of discriminatory treatment. These passed-down accounts and first-hand testimonials bolster these White-passing respondents' self-descriptor as a person of color as well as fuel their organic goals.

Respondents of color who listed their "street race" as White exhibited awareness of racism and organic goals akin to their non–White-passing counterparts. Based on inherited stories of injustice experienced by ancestors or eyewitness accounts of differential treatment, this subgroup expressed empathy for racial group members subjected to discrimination. Some also perceived discrimination directed toward them personally, showing inconsistencies around passing as White. Among White-passing respondents of color, emotional ties stemming from family connections to a racialized group can be sufficient to inspire organic goal formation.

Family-based emotional connection to ancestral heritage can direct attitudes and actions. Sentimental ancestral connection can counteract the "disappearance" (or disaffiliation) of people from racial groups, such as Mexican Americans, as the result of racial intermarriage.[46] Rachel Jones, whose parentage is a Mexican American mother and a White (Irish) father, identifies herself as mixed race (White/Hispanic) and her "street race" as White. She explains, "I pass as White—I'm mostly White—it's not fair to say I'm Mexican." Fair-skinned, she surmises her "day to day" is that of a White person. Yet, her ancestral connection (a Mexican great-grandmother) motivates her to "humanize" Mexican Americans for people who lack a link to the group and may rely on damaging political spin to fill their information base. Interviewed during the Trump presidency when anti-Mexican sentiment was flagrant, Rachel was catalyzed to grow more familiar with her Mexican-born great-grandmother to humanize Mexican-origin people and Mexican migration for herself and others. She contemplates her racial identity journey:

> [I am] making something that isn't familiar, *familiar*. . . . Bringing it closer to me. Because it feels so distant . . . "My great grandmother is Mexican-born." . . . I wanna bring that closer and make that familiar and be able to know and talk about who those people were. . . . My focus is so much on this because of the . . . outside influences that are going on.

Rachel expresses a family-grounded sentimental concern for Mexican-origin people, despite her light skin tone and Anglophone first and last name. Rachel is willfully opting-in to this anti-racist "racial project,"[47] aided perhaps by her color privilege, which allows her to select what she cares about and when. By contrast, people who directly experience racism do not have the *option* to opt-in—racism ropes them in to awareness of racial injustice.

Family-grounded sentimental concern about racism based on ancestral ties can cause a ripple effect. Rachel has conversations with her in-laws, who hold anti-immigration stances: "I can personalize it for them. Like say, 'Well, guess what? I'm part of your family and this is part of my family and there's a tie here. How does that make you feel now you have a direct association with . . . this race that you feel this way about?'" While the jury is out on the impact of these conversations, the point is that mixed-race, White-passing respondents tend to reach to higher branches in a family tree to fasten their sentimental attachment and learn more about their family history. This family tie to a subordinated racial group, emotion, and expanded knowledge base activates organic goals for White-passing people of color.

Family exposure to racial injustice erodes some skin tone privilege of White-passing respondents of color; instead of being insulated from racial concerns or reliant on travel like White respondents, the goal formation of White-passing respondents of color is racially motivated. Beyond the individual, family-level racial oppression contributes meaningfully to organic goals. Divina Garcia, who identifies as Hispanic and notes her "street race" as White due to her light skin and red hair, is an example. With the career goal of being a pediatrician or epidemiologist, Divina wants to "give back" and "make good" on her family's sacrifice by helping people. Her family's racial and class disadvantage explains why fair skin does not temper the instinct to "give back" to racial and class brethren, a hallmark of organic goals. Divina explains:

> Both sets of my grandparents worked . . . construction jobs or picking jobs . . . really hard manual labor jobs. . . . My dad was raised picking and in canneries. . . . People don't think I've struggled as much as other people . . . that I don't share . . . in that struggle. . . . Our stories aren't very different just because I look a little different.

Divina's family is situated in a low-income, predominately Black and Latino neighborhood marked by "drugs and crime." Her neighborhood environment is marred by withheld resources: Education is poorly funded, jobs with living wages are scarce, a black-market economy fills gaps, and violence expresses frustration and lack of opportunity. In her words, "You feel like nothing's going your way because you don't have the same access to education, you're not given the same opportunities, you don't get to . . . do after-school activities and sports . . . that are going to help you, get you out." Calling herself a "cactus" who is used to deprivation, this background sets the stage for Divina's organic goals which she already lives out through periodic volunteer work geared toward Latino youth. Envisioning a career in health where she helps people in her community, Divina's organic goals make use of her history as a "cactus," as she hopes to provide nutrients to other cacti.

Due to a family history of racial subordination, White-passing people of color develop organic goals like their peers who are not perceived as White. White-passing is a tricky concept because people do not have full information about how others perceive them, and this perception can vary by observer, time, place, and context.[48] My data suggest that belief that one is treated as White does not translate to an unwavering or holistic experience of Whiteness, such as that which orients White respondents toward acquired goals. Instead, a family history that includes racial disadvantage constitutes a warehouse of knowledge for White-passing people of color and contributes to organic goals. Some light-skinned respondents upheld an ancestor as paradigmatic of racial suffering in a family line and clutched to this family forerunner as a source of sentimental attachment which then extends to a larger community of color. For respondents of color whom others may perceive as White, their family's experience of racial domination suffices to stimulate organic goals.

Conclusion

Racial biography and racialized emotions have the potential to be directive. For people of color especially, racialized life experiences and emotions do not merely sit idle but are a launching pad for future direction. There is a racial cleavage in the goals of respondents: Respondents of color expressed organic goals grounded in their lived experience of race, whereas White respondents' goals were unrelated to race or, if they concern race, were acquired after witnessing—but not living at the butt end of—racial inequality.

Revealing a burden of racial inequality, organic goals reflect intimacy with the underbelly of oppression that becomes fodder for goal formation. Respondents of color want to improve the experiences and life chances of people of color who face similar circumstances as they did. Racialized emotions, fomented by racism, connect past experience with goals. White privilege is discernable in that White respondents' goals were not tethered to race. To the extent White respondents expressed race-related goals, it was because they traveled outside of predominately White spaces and observed racial inequality. To witness race-based harm is not the same as to live it. As observers, these White respondents "acquire" goals that may be race-related, but they are vastly different from the companion concept of "organic goals" developed by respondents of color. First-hand experience of race and racism (organic goals) is distinct from second-hand observation of such phenomena (acquired goals), this difference that flags profundity of impact hinging on racial status. The organic, lived experience of people of color equips them with knowledge that can expertly support and mentor people of color living within systems of oppression. On the other hand, second-hand observations lead to insights and inspirations that can lead to goals but are limited by an outsider position and rely to some extent on altruism and prosocial emotions.[49]

Racial biographies and accompanying racialized emotions are *directive* for respondents of color. Racial disadvantage steers life goals. Respondents of color developed goals that stem from their lives under a regime of White supremacy: trauma, withheld resources, and racism. Goals are sown from the racial biographies of respondents of color and the related desire to uplift their racial communities. Reflecting on their real-life experience, respondents of color endeavor toward an improved society by remedying gaps in knowledge, mentorship, and training, aspiring to decolonization, and participating in collective action to advance community goals. Exposure to racial disadvantage (personal or familial), rather than skin tone, mediates organic goal formation. Respondents of color who believe they "pass" as White due to their light skin are not exempt from this pattern—their portal into organic goals is hearing about ancestors' racial oppression or being party to their natal family's racial subordination. Family history shaped by racism anchors attachment to a community of color and promotes organic goals. There is variation in the intensity or frequency with which race-infused organic goals are engaged (periodic conversations around race as compared to a career serving historically underserved racial populations), yet the through line remains that racial biography influences goal formation among respondents of color. These efforts by people of color to improve society is simultaneously a form of advocacy for the oppressed and resistance against unjust social structures.

To state the obvious, race functions differently for White respondents. For White respondents, goals were absent race or, less often, acquired through travel that revealed inequality they could observe once there was distance from the White context to which they were accustomed. Rather than living in a body or space of racial disadvantage like respondents of color, White respondents have the option to travel to more racially heterogeneous or majority-minority spaces and better perceive racial disadvantage. While White respondents do not *live with* racial disadvantage, they can *observe* it. Yet learning about racial inequality does not guarantee deviation from colorblindness or changes in attitudes, behavior, or goals.[50] A direct link does not exist between racial background and goal formation for White respondents as it does for respondents of color. Yet, White people can work in anti-racist ways by disavowing White privilege and working alongside communities of color as allies. Even so, the discretionary element here shines a light on racial inequality. White people are privileged in their ability to opt in or out of racial struggles, whereas respondents of color sharpen their organic goals with a mix of desire and obligation to aid others facing racial struggles and even alter institutions from within. A significant distinction between respondents of color developing organic goals and White respondents holding acquired goals is that people of color *live with* the brunt of racial inequality, whereas White people *witness* it from a place of privilege.

Conclusion

Learning from Burdens to Remedy Inequality

W.E.B. Du Bois's inquiry in 1903, "How does it feel to be a problem?," was the inspiration for *Burdens of Belonging*. Most news headlines are replete with stories that scream out answers to this question: Society views and treats people from various communities of color differentially from White people who sit at the apex of the racial hierarchy and are considered the national culture core. Much is at stake in inequality of belonging: self-concept, emotional life, an affirming education, safety and well-being, and sense of community in local space and the national imaginary. This book is based on seventy interviews, with ten to fifteen respondents in each of the following categories: Latino, White, Black, Indigenous (Native American and Pacific Islander), Asian American, and mixed race and Middle Eastern (combined). More than a hundred years later, Du Bois's contemplations about being cast as a problem resonate for respondents of color. The respondents of color interviewed for this book testify to the veracity of legal and ethnic studies scholar john powell's observation that "what is being sorted in the making of a nation-state is not just the question of who is in a *physical space*, but who is in the *psychic space*, in the *imagined community of that space*."[1] Spaces (national, regional, local, and psychic/imagined) are racialized, layers of history setting the stage for the privilege or precarity of belonging in the present.

Belonging in the United States is conditioned on racial and colonial status. White people occupying the zenith of the US racial order, typifying an "ideal" American, calls into question the belonging of people of color. Burdened belonging describes the situation of members of the nation who experience marginality, exclusions, or penalties as a condition of their belonging. While similar burdens were shared across non-White racial groups, distinctions also contour experience in the nation and local space. Black respondents face persistent anti-Black racism and institutional barriers and interactional assumptions that frustrate their experience and counteract signals of belonging. Yet, some US-born Black respondents claim belonging due to long-running presence in—and ancestors' forced building of—the nation. Latinos expressed dissatisfaction and vexation with being socially unwelcome and legally suspect. They too offered narratives justifying their belonging, even as they critiqued its exclusivity. Despite some change over time, Asian Americans expressed disgruntlement at being frozen in the image of a military-racial opponent, a representation that legitimizes subjugation and infamy in the context of global imperialism. Contending with the continuing trauma and disruption of colonization, Indigenous respondents (Native Americans and Pacific Islanders) felt a range of ways about being American. Yet one unifying element is that Native American and Pacific Islander respondents cultivated critical colonial consciousness, viewpoints arising out of lives framed by settler colonialism. Muslim respondents (Middle Eastern and Black) felt castigated by Islamophobia enforced by both agents of the nation and community members. Mixed-race respondents often felt allied with the communities of color from which they hailed (more so than Whiteness, if they had White heritage) due to familial connections. Uniformly, White respondents felt a seamless racial fit in the nation, effortlessly advantaged by satisfying the ideal-type American image. With intersectionality always at play, people with disadvantaged identities with respect to gender, sexuality, and class received compounded messages of ill-fit in spaces that reify and reflect a narrow White, middle-class, cisgender, heteronormative image. This research was based in predominately White Oregon, where the context of largely White space reinforced and naturalized the notion of Whiteness as a predicate to belonging, a spatial influence that emboldened gatekeepers to interactionally police boundaries of belonging through words and actions.

Conditional or tenuous belonging, peripheral status, and even non-belonging due to damning racial and colonial realities involves a cascade of burdens for people of color. With imperialism, settler colonialism, and racial domination organizing life, a basic lesson from this book is how race saturates social life, seeping into far corners of bodies, minds, and lived experience. Resisting marginalization, devising counternarratives or coping strategies, and crafting a sense of community are incumbent on people of color. By comparison, the belonging of White people is a central premise of the "inherently racial" nation[2] and freely granted. Variation in belonging indexes inequality.

Historic and contemporary maneuvers of the nation, spurred on by racist beliefs in biological essentialism and cultural inferiority, *constructed* (and continue to construct) groups of color as problems. Racial ideology, policy, and practices drew and hold artificial lines between problem/non-problem, non-White/White, and subjugated/dominant. Institutions and interactions invested in White racial dominance do the dirty work of systemic racism and settler colonialism, propping up racial inequality vis-à-vis foisting "problem" status on communities of color. *Burdens of Belonging* probes the continued relevance of "being a problem" and elaborates on what this means, how it manifests, what it feels like, and how people respond. Double consciousness is an intersectional phenomenon, the experience of race affected by additional systems of power and "second sight" folding in awareness of these added dimensions. With varying group histories and multiple systems of oppression operating simultaneously, specifics of racialized belonging may vary. Differences overlaying the baseline of racial inequality that color experience means that pathways to desired futures may also fluctuate based on group affiliation.

The multiple arenas of social life in which race and "problem" status matter yielded by this ground-up investigation indicates the omnipresence and social weight of race. Bespeaking burdened belonging, messages issuing from multiple levels of an institution (institutional, community, and interactional), such as schools, produce *comfort* for White people who are centered, authenticated, and supported and *discomfort* for people of color who are decentered, invisibilized, dismissed, and derogated. In addition to the burden of discomfort in predominately White institutional spaces, racialized bodies are bogged down by the burdens of settler-colonial intergenerational trauma and racial stress. Bodies are marked by racial status—not just "externally" as in physical characteristics but also "internally" as in health, well-being, and sense of safety. Lack of health and wellness, as in intergenerational trauma and (anticipatory) racial stress, are symptoms and reminders of inequality. Given the numerous systems of oppression that bear on those navigating multiple marginalities, burdens can accumulate and compound. These health-related burdens of belonging shouldered by people of color issue from the headwaters of White supremacy.

Yet belonging can be fostered. As a counterweight to peripheral status, respondents of color advocated for eradicating barriers to visibility and widening opportunity and representation as well as redistributing power. All arenas of social life are relevant: media, politics, education, occupations, friendships, family, culture, rhetoric, and more. A reallocation of power that opens possibilities for confident and unquestioned belonging first requires unseating Whiteness from its central position in the nation, both in institutions and a widely held (if contested) cultural core. This redistribution means not only amplifying the voices of those on the periphery (who see and critique power imbalances that harm them) but also enjoining White people to cede power in the interest of recognizing and investing in the humanity of all people. A caveat is that inclusion is not the goal for all. Native American respondents prioritized autonomy over inclusion; sovereignty preserves Indigenous history and culture whereas inclusion threatens to quash Native people and lifeways. Some non-Native people of color were also wary of inclusion, worrying that inclusion would demand conformity and stamp out their distinctive cultures and perspectives. Considering concerns over freedom and cultural vitality, creatively devising belonging that can honor and embrace the varied people who comprise the nation would be an admirable goal.

Belonging weighed down by marginality is not doomed to continue in perpetuity. While exclusionary mechanisms churn, people can engage in protest and other collective action efforts to influence their futures. As shown, people who wish for greater belonging do not lie idle but act to advance their desires. Aspirations for belonging and decolonization steer action, manifesting as individual and collective goals (chapter 6). Political engagement can also be a response to negative messaging about a group that can mobilize affected portions of the electorate.[3] Further, when several groups are marginalized simultaneously, oppressions crisscross groupings, which creates multiple marginalities as well as opportunities for intersectional and cross-movement coalitions.[4] All burdens of belonging traced in this book derive from White supremacist ideology and practice. But people can respond.

People freedom-dream. Especially those racialized as subordinate, people are invested in seeding futures that embrace them and address their needs. People of color did this by articulating affirming counter-narratives and creating concentric circles of belonging, and putting effort toward remedying trouble spots they faced and smoothing the path for others. People from all racial groups can destabilize White supremacy by questioning, creating alliances, and working to include or decolonize rather than defend centuries-old systems that privilege only a segment of the nation's inhabitants. People of color can use insights and emotions from racialized experiences to transform unjust social systems. Racialized life experience (or "racial biography") and accompanying racialized feelings shape goals for respondents of color who use their race-based hurdles as guideposts for routes to social change. For White respondents, overcoming racial "transparency" or non-recognition of White people as part of a racial system, and having racial identities and racial privilege,[5] was necessary to see and work against racial injustice, though not all did so. Whatever one's social location, there is work to be done to build on-ramps to belonging.

The Value of Experiential Knowledge and Emotions

A through-line argument of this book is that experiential knowledge, structured by race and other axes of difference, is indispensable for perceiving, navigating, and contesting hierarchies that organize society. Experiential knowledge, shaped by a person's varying levels of privilege or oppression, materializes in racialized emotions, behaviors, and aspirations. Agency—how people choose to act and react—can express experiential knowledge. Free will, or agency, can be used to craft counternarratives, engage in anti-racist and decolonial thought and action, and seed dreams. Resisting inequality can not only change power dynamics but it also offers emotional dividends. As Eduardo Bonilla-Silva reminds, "Resistance to domination . . . produces emotional well-being among the racially oppressed and is central for their efforts to improve their circumstances."[6]

Emotions are a conduit that express both racial status and reaction to that status. As an interviewer, I am privy to an array of racialized emotions that are verbalized in words, those that spill out in tears, sniffles, agitated tones, exasperated sighs, hand gestures, and fidgeting bodies, as well as those that are held back by strained voices and deep breaths. In the social world, emotions are "stratified" (they come from different structural locations, are given unequal consideration, and are endowed with different meanings depending on who they come from). But in an interview, my goal is to honor, listen, and hear what emotions and words convey. The mutual gratitude that characterizes the closure of most interviews illustrates the value of listening with care. People want to be heard. They want their sentiments and perspectives to be taken seriously. An affirming subject-centered interview space gives a clue about how to invest in justice. A liberatory pathway requires willingness to learn from and become galvanized by subordinated people's truths.

Listening and learning that moves into caring and crosscuts groups has the capacity to alleviate burdens. Knowledge-sharing and receptivity to learning from others can precipitate change in individual-level ways, such as how people think about and talk to others, as well as inspire collective action. Shifts in understanding can transform emotions and subsequently generate a positive emotional charge for others. Sociologist Victor Rios speaks to the ripple effect of supportive interactions: "Interactions are one kind of resource. How authority figures label and engage with young people often determines the kind of *emotional energy* created for their decision-making and thought processes."[7] Attention to how institutions, communities, and individuals treat people—the emotional energy that policies and interpersonal exchanges engender—is a crucial step in moving toward a more equitable racial future. This book is replete with emotions and yet one that is missing is the ultimate, implicit goal: a "feeling of equality . . . the positive emotions we feel when we believe we enjoy equal status in relation to others."[8] Honoring experiential knowledge and emotions—and seeing them as reflecting histories and hierarchies—can open lines of communication and move the dial on racial justice efforts and build a feeling of equality.

Final Thoughts from This "Knowledge Project"

This book began from a premise articulated by critical race scholar Derrick Bell: "We simply cannot prepare realistically for our future without assessing honestly our past."[9] Historical forces shape the present and, as a "knowledge project"[10] this book has delved into the experiences, opinions, and (counter)narratives of respondents from an array of racial backgrounds who are reacting to the racial inheritances bequeathed to them by the nation. Respondents of color must wrangle with burdensome racialization that truncates their social worth and hampers their freedom and belonging. In contrast, White respondents inhabit privilege in their ability to assert belonging in the United States, feel institutionally supported comfort and safety, and be at liberty to make unbridled choices when crafting goals and futures.

Given the light *Burdens of Belonging* has shed on issues circumscribing belonging, what do we do with what we now know? Because the "system of racial rule" operates "through macro-level, large-scale activities" as well as "through micro-level, small-scale practices,"[11] racial justice overhauls are required at every level. Racial inequality is a multilevel problem and thus requires remedies at multiple levels. Dismantling racial domination is a system-wide anti-racist project. Decoloniality, or "movement toward possibilities of other modes of being, thinking, knowing, sensing and living,"[12] as a partner project to anti-racist efforts, would break away from colonial power. Decolonial effort includes bucking "hegemonic depictions of North American Indigenous peoples as a racial or cultural group rather than as members of legitimate political entities," embracing a "land-inclusive framework" that unseats "human-centric settler frameworks as normative," and analyzing the gendered processes constructing heteropatriarchy and heteropaternalism.[13] With anti-racist and decolonizing work, reviving subordinated knowledge could breathe self-determining life into long-suppressed populations and cultures.

Federal, state, and institutional policies can be reimagined in anti-racist, decolonial, and inclusive manners. Comprehensive immigration reform that rolls out a welcome mat and acknowledges that many migrants, asylees, and refugees who come to the United States do so as the result of US presence in sending countries[14] would alleviate legal and emotional burdens for newcomers. The education system that structures knowledge production needs revision, from diversifying curricula to supporting the success of people of color. Recruitment, hiring, and enrollment of people of color should be done in a meaningfully inclusive way rather than in a "non-performative" fashion or "tick box approach" that "*does not produce* the effects that it names."[15] Deploying solutions that are informed by the critical insights of marginalized students and families in order to better serve them is key to more equal and holistic representation, teaching, and learning.

At the community level, a lesson gifted by interviewees is that fostering environments conducive to "concentric circles of belonging," in places like schools and workplaces, is crucial for marginalized groups to create supportive relationships. These smaller networks of belonging were usually curated to include people of color from one's racial category. In this way, structural diversity can offer entryways into belonging. Instituting mentorship and support programs, which many respondents of color identified as their "organic goals," is another route to support community-building and achievement simultaneously. Capitalizing on organic knowledge for the benefit of disadvantaged communities should not be the work of people of color alone. As education professor Bettina Love writes, "The fact that dark people are tasked with the work of dismantling these centuries-old oppressions is a continuation of racism."[16] This raises the question of how White people can be allies. One suggestion is to listen to and follow the lead of people of color. Cede space. Reject colorblindness; instead, see color. Upon learning racial facts, do not become wedded to an "epistemology of ignorance" that insists on colorblind logics to "foreclose or otherwise distort the outcomes of racially conscious learning."[17] Also insidious is "race-conscious racism," when people position themselves as racially progressive but enact racial injury, thus using race consciousness as an "alibi for racial harm."[18] Instead of falling into these traps, be open to emotional discomfort on the road to racial justice and do not guard contemporary power relations because the "*status quo* is replete with repressed violence."[19] Work to undo injustice.

Interaction-level recommendations include listening to people from different racial statuses who are speaking their truth from experience. Be mindful that marginality is a condition of belonging for many people of color. Someone speaking from a vantage point of critical colonial consciousness or (intersectional) double consciousness is articulating counternarratives based on the wisdom of their situated experience. Be willing to be educated by others without demanding that they educate you. Be open to empathy-building based on even the smallest of connections. Be sensitive to how a long and continuing history of settler colonialism and systemic racism saddles people from oppressed communities with racial baggage that is onerous to carry. Allow yourself to be reeducated by people in the know, for lived experience itself is a "criterion for credibility."[20] Because belonging centers membership in a collective, influence to and from the community, fulfillment of needs, and emotional bonds,[21] fostering belonging rests not only on bureaucratic means but also on interpersonal exchanges that generate a welcoming spirit. Concretely, this means giving fellow national community members space to articulate their experiences and needs and responding with a humble and generous spirit. Belonging is not zero-sum; it need not be apportioned selectively.

Appreciating the Black feminist tradition of bearing witness to violence for the sake of love and world-making,[22] this book is an invitation to readers to be witnesses. Burdens are eased through sharing. This book is a call for witnessing and active learning. It is my hope that readers will be moved to act with more empathy now that they are equipped with more understanding of the deep roots of contemporary stratification. In arguing against the "ahistorical fallacy" that "renders history impotent,"[23] I hope that this book unveils the collusion of multiple historical and contemporary forces that amount to disadvantage. I also hope that the arguments and narratives presented in this book serve as solace for marginalized people. Such readers may find comfort in the community of diverse voices represented here and discover that their racial and colonial pains are neither unique nor a result of individual failings. A goal for using narratives where people speak for themselves is for readers to behold the humanity of the speakers and learn from them. As a keystone of critical race pedagogy, "Narratives provide a language to bridge the gaps in imagination. . . . They reduce alienation for members of excluded groups, while offering opportunities for members of the majority to meet them halfway."[24] There is need for political will to tilt toward social justice, and what better forward motion than learning from people's stories, bearing witness, and acting with deeper knowledge and compassion?

A centerpiece of *Burdens of Belonging* is the subordinated knowledge (narratives principally from people of color representing multiple racial groups) upon which it rests. This subordinated knowledge "provides epistemic foundations for mindful resistance of standard ways of knowing and being that . . . reproduce racial and colonial violence."[25] My aim here is to contribute to a "knowledge ecology"[26] that destabilizes the "epistemic exclusion"[27] of communities of color whose wealth of knowledge and culture has gone unrecognized.[28] By reading history against the grain and attending to the voices of people of color, readers are equipped to be more attuned to the precarity of dominated groups, boost their empathy and caring, and transcend traditional borders of knowing that have embargoed the intelligence and earnest critiques of the oppressed.

A strength of this qualitative study is how it mines meaning from people's articulations of their racialized experiences. Limitations present openings for future research. For example, my sample skewed toward the higher educated and middle class, so a study on people with less education or lower-class status may uncover how race and class compound. Quantitative research that surveys larger numbers of people could test the findings and concepts presented here for generalizability among a larger population. Since this study was situated in Oregon, a study that pursues a related agenda in other contexts (such as racially heterogeneous or communities of color) would test the robustness and limits of findings. Nexus points of solidarity or sites of competition among groups deserve greater exploration. This book intentionally decenters Whiteness, bringing to the fore people of color and placing them in relationship to other groups of color as well as the White category. There is ample room for exploring intra-group variation, a way to push forward racial and ethnic studies and critical Whiteness studies. If "American race and racism remains . . . the problem of whites and whiteness,"[29] it is imperative to interrogate White people's enforcement of colorblindness and racism as well as attempts to divest themselves of White privilege.

Burdens of Belonging balances a dual focus on the power of racialized systems and individual agency, examines the historical underpinnings of the racial-colonial hierarchy, and interrogates the influence this interwoven hierarchy has on racialized life experience and pathways. Tracing the historical foundations and mechanisms of exclusion that construct non-White racial groups as Du Boisian "problems" is a counternarrative in that this effort excavates and validates subordinated knowledge and elevates it for learning purposes. This aim is liberatory in intent and is hopefully liberatory in outcome. "A-ha moments" in classes I teach often occur when students learn to see their lives positioned within larger social structures that deliver both opportunities and constraints. This book has been a similar undertaking in that I had the twin aims of highlighting both the power of social structure and the power of agency. Societal organization matters immensely and yet individual choices and actions have power as well. Burdens of belonging took time and energy to build, and so too will it take time and energy for change to occur. Illuminating the omnipresence and multiple forms of burdens of belonging is a prerequisite to revisioning a more just society. We all hold responsibility to work toward justice. To borrow Du Bois's words once again, he was referring to the race problem when he asserted, "in fact the burden belongs to the nation, and the hands of none of us are clean if we bend not our energies to righting these great wrongs."[30] As this book has endeavored to make clear, belonging in the United States is conditioned by racial and colonial status and branches out to affect a host of spheres of life. Understanding the causes and manifestations of burdens of belonging is a necessary starting point for advancing social change.

ACKNOWLEDGMENTS

This book benefited from the support of a sabbatical provided by the University of Oregon that was the first deep dive into analysis and write-up. Financial support from the University of Oregon was used for payment to subjects, transcription services, and indexing. With respect to transcription, gratitude for her interest and accuracy goes to Lettie Thomas, owner of Ad Astra. Tuck Swords, a former student who was a short-term research assistant, performed valuable literature review and recruitment work. I very much appreciate the enthusiasm that New York University Press Executive Editor, Ilene Kalish, brought to the project and the guidance she provided. Anonymous reviewers arranged by NYU Press also deserve credit for pushing me to deepen certain facets of the book which have improved it in multiple dimensions. Pierrette Hondagneu-Sotelo, whose work I first admired in graduate school and who is now a mentor, offered helpful advice on strengthening the manuscript. Michael Omi remains an unwavering and inspiring mentor and a beacon of race scholarship and human kindness I admire. I extend gratitude to Nilda Flores-González for her enthusiasm for the manuscript and input. Many thanks go to fellow race scholar, Christina Sue, who provided thoughtful feedback on a full draft of the manuscript (and then some). I value the insights and questions offered by Kelly Chong, who read a chapter of the manuscript. Thanks to Catherine (Katie) Bolzendahl for the opportunity to present on this research at Oregon State University. Friends and colleagues provided counsel, support, and invigorated me about the value of this project: Priscilla Yamin, Krystale Littlejohn, Christopher Wetzel, Jill Harrison, Christina Bejarano, Megha Ramaswamy, Kari Norgaard, Kristin Yarris, C. J. Pascoe, Aaron Gullickson, Jody Agius Vallejo, Ashley Woody, and Kathryn Norton-Smith. I appreciate multiple supportive collective writing spaces at the University of Oregon: a Sociology faculty writing group initiated by Claire Herbert, a Critical Race Writing group, Center on Diversity and Community (CoDaC) Writing Circles, and Michelle Jacob's "Auntie Way" Writing time. Steadfast friends who buoy me (and for whom I try to do the same) deserve a grateful shout-out: Kim Clarke Arce, Carrie Clough, Jason Foley, Kanika Saniford, and Linda Flory. This book would not be possible without the interviewees who opened up to me about their lives, including their recollections, opinions, hurts, and hopes. As a social scientist, it is my privilege and challenge to do justice to the narratives offered to me. On a personal note, love and appreciation go to my parents and brother (Dorothy, David, Jason, Earl), husband Derrick, stepdaughters Sam and Lauren, and daughter Juliana. Mom, you have been a cheerleader for me for as long as I can remember, thank you. Dad, of course I remember your stories—they are a piece of my racial biography that contributes to my organic goal of researching, teaching, and writing about race. Sam and Lauren, thank you for being generous of heart from the moment I entered your life. Derrick and Juliana, you are my precious lights, brightening and warming my world—I love you dearly.

APPENDIX

This interview-based book, with a sample of seventy interviewees, draws from residents of Oregon, a state with a population of 4.2 million people. According to Census 2020, Oregon is a majority-White state, with 86.7% of residents claiming White (and 75.1% claiming White and *not* Hispanic/Latino).[1] The Latino population of Oregon stands at 13.4%, followed by Asian at 4.9%, Black at 2.2%, American Indian at 1.8%, and Native Hawaiian/Pacific Islander at 0.5%. The multiracial category ("two or more races") describes 4.0% of the Oregon population. In comparison to the nation, Oregon is Whiter and less racially diverse. Nationwide, 76.3% of the population is White (and 60.1% non-Hispanic White), a full ten percentage points more racially heterogeneous than Oregon. This field site provides a lens into racial dynamics in a slowly changing predominately White space.

I recruited interview participants from two hubs: Eugene and Corvallis, homes to the two major land-grant institutions of the state, University of Oregon (UO) and Oregon State University (OSU), respectively. With a minimum of ten respondents per category (racial group classification done after respondents answered an open-ended question), my sample of seventy is composed of people who identify as the following: Twelve non-Hispanic White, fifteen Latino, eleven Black, eleven Indigenous (Native American and Pacific Islander), eleven "mixed race" and Middle Eastern combined, and ten Asian American. All respondent names are pseudonyms. Including multiple groups that fall under the "people of color" umbrella term avoids a binary and allows for investigation of intra-group and inter-group variation. Including multiple groups of color in a research study can shed light on "shared marginalization" or "shared racial status" as well as race-specific uniqueness.[2] By putting respondents from multiple communities of color and White people side by side, a more informed perspective of how coloniality and race facilitates, thwarts, and impinges upon national belonging emerges.

A faculty member at University of Oregon, I advertised in a few colleagues' summer classes and had a research assistant reach out to her networks. Desiring to expand beyond Eugene, I selected Corvallis for its geographic proximity as well as OSU being known for agriculture and engineering, a complement to UO's reputation for liberal arts. In both cities, I approached identity-based organizations for recruitment and advertised with flyers at public establishments like coffeeshops. I conducted snowball sampling, routinely asking respondents to help me advertise the study and handing them recruitment flyers at the conclusion of the interview. The seventy interviewees were signed up through the following sources: university-affiliated groups such as classes or centers (9), civic organizations (5), my professional networks (8), direct ask at a public establishment (5), advertisement through a list-serve, flyer, or research assistant's outreach (20), and snowball sampling (23). The referrals from snowball sampling come from fifteen different sources, a broad array of networks represented. I compensated each interviewee $30 as a thank you for their time.

To reach the seventy interviews with racial variation, I employed quota sampling, a non-probability sampling method, suitable for qualitative methods where comparison is desired. I did not set a native-born or citizenship status requirement to participate in the study. 81% of respondents (57 people) were US-born (including US territories) and 19% (thirteen people) were foreign-born. I included immigrants because they may choose to reside in the United States near-permanently or naturalize. Citizenship should not be the gold standard for belonging. I did not ask about documentation status.

In the sample, gender skews heavily toward women: Forty-four respondents identify as women, twenty-one as men, and five as non-binary or genderqueer. The sample overrepresents people with higher education: 30% have a doctoral, masters, law, or professional degree (21 respondents), 24% hold a college degree (17 respondents), 41% answered "some college" (29 respondents, the vast majority current students), and 4% completed all or some of high school (3 respondents). Socioeconomic status is a marker of who belongs and who does not, so an implication of the middle- and high-class skew to the sample is that I missed more dire stories from the class-disadvantaged. Lower-class standing can curb belonging in mainstream institutions such as education.[3] Middle-class status can be leveraged as a legitimator of mainstream inclusion,[4] yet racism continues to affect middle-class people of color.[5]

While the ill effects of racism are exacerbated by lower-class status, middle- and higher-class status does not correlate to unfettered belonging. Among Mexican Americans, for example, being a college graduate is associated with higher likelihood of identifying as American compared to lower levels of education.[6] However, education level, an indicator of class status, and self-identification as American does not necessarily correspond to equal treatment. These same more educated Mexican Americans report more stereotyping and discrimination than their less educated counterparts, which is partly due to their greater contact with White people who operate under the assumption that Mexican Americans are less educated and treat them prejudicially.[7] It is a paradox that people of color who experience socioeconomic mobility continue to encounter barriers to belonging (which was true for Du Bois).[8]

Semi-structured, in-depth interviews access a person's internal world and the process of meaning-making, feelings, and opinions required to answer the research question. Open to discovery in qualitative research, I have found that in response to interview protocol prompts, interviewees move to topics they care about that significantly affect their lives. I engage in a "subject-centered approach" where respondents, their lived experiences, the meanings they give to those experiences, attitudes, and actions are the focal point of analysis.[9] Subject-centered, inductive research unearths nuance and complexity and I heed themes that emerge within and across interviews.[10] My goal as an interviewer is to ask probing questions and listen for narratives that provide insights about complex social issues.

Interviews were conducted in English and lasted an hour and a half on average. I wrote field notes after every interview, capturing pertinent details like physical description and nonverbal behavior along with my first analytical impressions. Field notes constituted a preliminary step in conducting "issue-focused" coding[11] as I identified and summarized key emergent themes. Interviews were conducted during two time periods: the bulk was done in person in 2018 and a handful were completed in 2021 (conducted over the videoconferencing software program Zoom, in compliance with safety protocols in place during the COVID-19 pandemic). Most interviews were transcribed verbatim by a professional transcriptionist. For interviews conducted over Zoom, I used the auto-transcription feature embedded in the Zoom and then reviewed and cleaned transcripts for accuracy.

For data analysis, I conducted line-by-line coding of interview transcripts. In "initial coding,"[12] I returned to the transcripts to generate codes capturing repeated themes. Codes during initial coding were wide-ranging so I next moved into "focused coding," meant to "condense and sharpen" the analytic categories.[13] I combed through the data for patterns in the data. I looked for systematic variation: Were people with a certain racial background or other social identity cohering around similar themes? Which themes crosscut racial status? Capitalizing on a strength of qualitative data, analysis endeavors to show the range of forms and experiences of non-belonging and marginality. Developing themes, connected to the coherent framework of belonging, was the next step, which generated the organizing principles for the chapters.

NOTES

PREFACE

1 Feagin 2014, 4.
2 Du Bois 2005 [1903], 8.
3 Sullivan and Agiesta 2020.
4 Sadeghi 2021.
5 Masuoka and Junn 2013, 4.
6 Walton 2018; McMillan and Chavis 1986.

INTRODUCTION

1 A term with renewed popularity since the 1970s (after a hiatus from its original usage in the late-1700s to mid-1800s), "people of color" is an umbrella term for non-White people that has broadened over time to reflect demographic change (Starr 2023). With the term BIPOC (Black, Indigenous, and People of Color) on the rise and meant to highlight critical group distinctions, "people of color" has become questioned as "insufficiently specific" (Starr 2023, 2). Patricia Hill Collins and Sirma Bilge (2016, 185) also caution that "terms such as 'people of color' flatten the experiences of racial/ethnic groups into a homogenous 'color' category" and threaten to reduce "all racial others as equivalent and interchangeable." Their concern specifies that "*when imposed from above*," the conglomerate term "reinstall[s] a white frame of seeing the world as white" (2016, 185, emphasis added)—whereas, in contrast, my usage of the term is grounded in "bottom-up" data that break away from a White racial frame. I use the term people of color to refer to a non-White/White divide while *also* analyzing specific subgroup (e.g., race-/ethnicity-specific) phenomena. This dual attention to collective racialization (as people of color or non-White) and group-specific racialization (e.g., Black, Latino, etc.) is a way to identify processes pertaining to cross-racial and panethnic collectivities (larger groups) and more particular subpopulations, an analytic lens that counteracts homogenization.
2 Western 2006.
3 Native Women's Wilderness. 2024. "Murdered & Missing Indigenous Women." Accessed July 10, 2024. www.nativewomenswilderness.org/. Also Petrosky et al. 2021.
4 US Census Bureau. 2024. "QuickFacts: Oregon." Accessed March 1, 2024. www.census.gov.

5 Du Bois 2005 [1903].
6 King 2019, 10.
7 Love 2019, 40.
8 Cornell and Hartmann 1998, 20.
9 Hunter et al. 2016.
10 Collins 2009.
11 US Census Bureau. 2021. "QuickFacts: United States." Accessed September 20, 2021. www.census.gov.
12 Lopez, Passel, and Rohal 2015.
13 Yuen 2017, 5.
14 Grieco 2020.
15 Grieco 2020.
16 Leguizamo 2016.
17 Collins 2009.
18 Omi and Winant 1994.
19 Steinman 2022, 2.
20 McKay, Vinyeta, and Norgaard 2020.
21 Jacobs 2023, 58.
22 Meer 2018, 1167.
23 De Genova 2005.
24 Ngai 2004.
25 Espiritu 2023, 26.
26 Huntington 2004.
27 Schlesinger 1998.
28 Gómez 2007; Haney López 1996; Flores-González 2017.
29 Smith 2012.
30 Almaguer 1994; Ngai 2004; Tichenor 2002.
31 De Genova 2005, 218.
32 Gómez 2007, 4.
33 Lacayo 2017.
34 McDermott 2020.
35 Schildkraut 2014, 447.
36 Horowitz 2019.
37 Schildkraut 2014, 447.
38 Schildkraut 2014, 448.
39 Telles and Sue 2019, 37–38.
40 Masuoka and Junn 2013, 27.
41 Lipsitz 2007, 12.
42 Barajas and Ronnkvist 2007; Lipsitz 2007, 2011.
43 Neely and Samura 2011, 1936.
44 powell 2005.
45 Ray 2019; Brunsma et al. 2020.
46 Barajas and Ronnkvist 2007.

47 Hondagneu-Sotelo and Pastor 2021, 3.
48 Hondagneu-Sotelo and Pastor 2021, 12.
49 Bonilla-Silva 2013; Warren and Twine 1997; Lee and Bean 2010; Haney López 1996.
50 Alba 2009.
51 Jiménez, Fields, and Schachter 2015; Telles and Ortiz 2008; Vasquez 2011; Jiménez 2010.
52 Menjívar and Abrego 2012.
53 Flores-González 2017, 148.
54 Collins and Bilge 2016.
55 HoSang and Molina 2019.
56 Fusco 1988.
57 Anderson 1991.
58 Lanham 2020.
59 Tharps 2014.
60 National Association of Black Journalists. 2020. "NABJ Statement on Capitalizing Black and Other Racial Identifiers." Accessed March 13, 2023. www.nabjonline.org/.
61 Noe-Bustamante, Mora, and Lopez 2020.
62 Painter 2020.
63 Painter 2020.
64 Tajfel and Turner 1986.
65 Yuval-Davis 2006, 197.
66 Brasher, Alderman, and Inwood 2017, 293.
67 Dwanna 2019; Krakoff 2012; Steinman 2011.
68 See Steinman (2011) on why a race framework alone is inadequate to address Natives' dual citizenship status.
69 Feagin and Sikes 1994.
70 Haney López 1996, 64.
71 Haney López 1996, 64.
72 Fleming, Lamont, and Welburn 2012; Norgaard and Reed 2017; Vasquez-Tokos and Norton-Smith 2017.
73 Kim 2016.
74 Bonilla-Silva 2019, 2, italics in original.
75 Norgaard and Reed 2017, 464.
76 Itzigsohn and Brown 2020, 196–197.
77 Oliver and Shapiro 1995.
78 Collins 2015, 3.4.
79 Kim 2016.
80 Migration Policy Institute. "Immigration Population by State, 1990-Present." Accessed March 22, 2023. www.migrationpolicy.org/.
81 US Census Bureau. 2021, August 12. "2020 Census: Racial and Ethnic Diversity Index by State." www.census.gov.

82 Anderson 2021.
83 US Census Bureau. 2024. "QuickFacts: United States." Accessed March 1, 2024. www.census.gov/.
84 USA Facts. "Our Changing Population: Oregon." Accessed July 8, 2022. https://usafacts.org/.
85 USA Facts. "Our Changing Population: Oregon." Accessed July 8, 2022. https://usafacts.org/.
86 Vaidya 2019, 7.
87 Vaidya 2019, 2.
88 Vaidya 2019, 3.
89 The Institutional Review Board (IRB) granted this research an Exempt Determination (IRB Protocol Number: 03312017.032).
90 Vaidya 2019.
91 Budiman 2020.
92 Arredondo and Bustamante 2022.
93 Jetté 2015.
94 Jetté 2015.
95 Bussel and Tichenor 2017.
96 Carpenter 2020, 161.
97 Jetté 2015, 180, 214.
98 Robbins 2020.
99 Robbins 2020.
100 Smith 2014.
101 Robbins 2020.
102 Whaley 2010, 137.
103 Lewis 2018.
104 Lewis 2018.
105 Editorial from southwestern Oregon settler John Beeson to the *True Californian*, in *Oregon Superintendent: Letters Received, 1824–1881*, roll 609, frame 20. As quoted in Whaley (2010, 225, fn 273).
106 Lewis 2018.
107 Fixico 2018.
108 Smith 2012.
109 Fixico 2018.
110 Tuck and Yang 2012; Wolfe 2006.
111 Xing 2007; Loewen 2005.
112 Smith 2014.
113 Imarisha 2020.
114 Loewen 2005.
115 Smith 2014.
116 Smith 2014, 167.
117 Loewen 2005.
118 McLagan 2007.

119 Smith 2014, 167.
120 Smith 2014, 168–170.
121 Smith 2014.
122 Smith 2014, 168–170.
123 Pascoe 2007, 28.
124 Smith 2014, 171.
125 Almaguer 1994; Ngai 2004.
126 Bussel and Tichenor 2017.
127 Bussel and Tichenor 2017.
128 McGregor 2004b.
129 McGregor 2004a.
130 Department of Defense 2019.
131 Foss 2017.
132 Gusinow 2022.
133 Imarisha 2020.
134 Imarisha 2020.
135 Bruce 2019.
136 King 1986.
137 King 1986.
138 Woody 2023.
139 Du Bois 2005 [1903], 99.
140 Morris 2015, 134.
141 Collins 2009, 276.
142 Collins 2009, 281; Bhambra 2014.
143 Collins 2009, 281–282.
144 Fujii 2018.
145 Go 2020, 80.
146 Go 2020.
147 Go 2020, 91.
148 Go 2020, 91.
149 Itzigsohn and Brown 2020, 184.
150 Delgado and Stefancic 2001, 41.

CHAPTER 1. CONSTRUCTING A "PROBLEM"

1 The line "The only good Indian's a dead Indian" has been attributed to Philip Henry Sheridan, who was a career US Army officer and a Union general in the American Civil War.
2 Desmond and Emirbayer 2009.
3 Benjamin 2022, 52, emphasis in original.
4 Tuck and Yang 2012, 5.
5 Wolfe 2006, 388.
6 Dunbar-Ortiz 2021, 21.
7 Glenn 2015; Moreton-Robinson 2015.

8 Fenelon 2016.

9 Wolfe 2006, 388.

10 Steinmetz, Schaefer, and Henderson 2017, 68, 69.

11 Glenn 2015.

12 Glenn 2015, 55.

13 Du Bois 1920.

14 Monteiro 2007, 45.

15 Norgaard 2011, 27.

16 Lipsitz 1990.

17 Lipsitz 1990, 227.

18 Wolfe 2016, 37.

19 Steinman 2016.

20 Steinman 2022, 146.

21 Dunbar-Ortiz 2014, 6.

22 National Indian Council on Aging, Inc. 2021. "Census Shows Increase in Native Population." September 9. www.nicoa.org/.

23 Deem 2019.

24 Bonilla-Silva 2013; Mueller 2017.

25 Deloria 1998.

26 Dunbar-Ortiz 2014.

27 Arvin 2019.

28 Pulido 2018.

29 Castellanos 2017, 220; see also Zamora 2022.

30 Hondagneu-Sotelo 1997.

31 Chavez 2013.

32 De Genova 2005; De León 2015.

33 Anzaldúa 1987.

34 Pulido 2018.

35 Tuck and Yang 2012, 7.

36 Tuck and Yang 2012.

37 Glenn 2015.

38 Steinman 2022; Glenn 2015.

39 Dunbar-Ortiz 2014, 229.

40 Said [1978] 1994, 3.

41 Smith 2016, 68.

42 Smith 2016, 68.

43 Tuan 1998.

44 Espiritu 2014, 39.

45 Jiménez et al. 2021.

46 Padilla 2022, 5.

47 Itzigsohn and Brown 2015, 232.

48 Itzigsohn and Brown 2020, 29.

49 Du Bois 2005 [1903], 7.
50 Hughey 2012, 159.
51 Woody 2020, 2.
52 Nakano 2023.
53 Molina 2014, 7.
54 Qureshi 2013.
55 Freire 1970, 35.
56 Freire 1970, 36.
57 Freire 1970, 72.
58 Adams et al. 2018.
59 Freire 1970, 73.
60 Roth 2012.
61 Overbye 2018; Witze 2020.
62 Overbye 2018.
63 Norgaard 2019, 20.
64 Ramos, Garriga-López, and Rodríguez-Díaz 2022.
65 Roth 2012.
66 Valle 2019; Godreau and Bonilla 2021.
67 Dropp and Nyhan 2017.
68 Dropp and Nyhan 2017.
69 Fu 2022.
70 Sue and Telles 2007.
71 Sue and Telles 2007.
72 Sue 2023.
73 Confederated Tribes of Coos, Lower Umpqua and Siuslaw Indians. "A Brief History of the Coos, Lower Umpqua & Siuslaw Indians." Accessed July 10, 2024. www.ctclusi.org/.
74 Sabzalian 2019.
75 Ogbu 1994.
76 Wolfe 2016, 2.
77 Oregon Department of Education. 2021. "Tribal History/Shared History." www.oregon.gov.
78 Delgado and Stefancic 2001, 7.
79 Brayboy 2005, 429.
80 Fenelon 2016.
81 Delgado and Stefancic 2001.
82 Ray 2022, 86.
83 Steinman 2022.
84 Valenzuela 1999.
85 Sparks 2015.
86 Du Bois 2005 [1903]; Itzigsohn and Brown 2020.
87 Omi and Winant 2015.

CHAPTER 2. BEING A "PROBLEM"

1 McCann and Jones-Correa 2020.
2 Lipsitz 2011, 13.
3 Ocampo 2015; Okamoto and Mora 2014; Wimmer 2013.
4 Choo and Ferree 2010.
5 King 2019.
6 Garland-Thomson 2009.
7 Frankenberg 1993; McDermott 2020; Schildkraut 2014.
8 Hunter 2002.
9 Telles and Murguia 1990.
10 Murguia and Telles 1996.
11 Monk 2015.
12 Marrow et al. 2022; Ortiz and Telles 2012; Abascal and Garcia 2022.
13 Thompson and Keith 2001.
14 Sims, Pirtle, and Johnson-Arnold 2020.
15 Krogstad 2015.
16 Crawford 1992.
17 Crawford 1992, 255–6.
18 Jiménez 2010.
19 Devlin 2015.
20 Woody 2020.
21 Sue and Telles 2007; Sue 2023.
22 Pager 2007; Bertrand and Mullainathan 2004.
23 Norgaard, Reed, and Bacon 2017.
24 Shute 2022.
25 Tuck and Yang 2012.
26 Alba 2020, 68.
27 Alba 2020, 68.
28 Alba 2020.
29 Alba 2020; Rodríguez-Muñiz 2021.
30 Schlesinger 1998.
31 Huntington 2004; Lacayo 2017.
32 Lacayo 2017.
33 Vasquez 2010a.
34 Telles and Sue 2019.
35 US Census Bureau. "QuickFacts: Texas." Accessed October 7, 2021. www.census.gov.
36 Montejano 1987.
37 Chong 2020; Vasquez-Tokos 2017b.
38 Hartigan 1999; McDermott 2015.
39 Alba, Jiménez, and Marrow 2014; Telles and Sue 2019; Vasquez 2011.
40 Jiménez and Horowitz 2013; Vasquez 2014b.
41 Feagin 2010, 3, 14.

42 Go 2016.

43 Rodriguez 2023, 25.

44 Warikoo and Bloemraad 2018.

45 Fenelon 2016; Lomawaima 1995; Glenn 2015; Jacobs 2009.

46 Wolfe 2006.

47 Omi and Winant 1994, 106.

48 Du Bois 2005 [1903], 7.

49 Itzigsohn and Brown 2020, 37.

50 Collins and Bilge 2016, 25.

51 Hancock 2005.

52 Hine 1993.

53 Falcón 2008.

54 Martinez 2002; Falcón 2008.

55 Anzaldúa 1987, 77.

56 Anzaldúa 1987, 79.

57 Butler 2006, 88.

58 Martinez 2002, 158.

59 Lugones 1992; Scott 2023.

60 Lynne 2021, 264.

61 Anzaldúa 1987, 20.

62 Itzigsohn and Brown 2020, 17.

63 Wingfield 2007, 198.

64 Silvestrini 2020.

65 Han 2021; Silvestrini 2020.

66 Selod 2018.

67 Islam 2020.

68 Goffman [1959] 1973.

69 Zamora 2022.

70 Du Bois 1920, 17–18.

71 McDermott and Ferguson 2022, 258.

72 McDermott and Ferguson 2022, 258.

73 McDermott 2020, 12.

74 Hughey 2012, 80.

75 Saunders and Panchal 2023.

76 Bonilla-Silva 2013.

77 Bonilla-Silva 2013.

78 Vasquez-Tokos 2020a.

CHAPTER 3. ON BEING "AMERICAN"

1 Kahn et al. 2016.

2 McDermott 2020.

3 Alba 2020, 72.

4 Alba 2020, 75.

5 Frankenberg 1993.
6 McDermott 2020, 12.
7 Phinney 1997.
8 Merskin 2007; Vasquez 2010a.
9 See also Bloemraad 2013; Warikoo and Bloemraad 2018.
10 Roth 2012, 12.
11 Bloemraad 2013, 56.
12 Flores-González 2017, 148.
13 Telles and Sue 2019, 37.
14 Telles and Sue 2019.
15 Vision (the ability to see) is implied as important to apprehend race and racial meanings. However, a study on how blind and sighted people understand race finds that "social practices . . . produce our very ability to see race" (Obasogie 2014, 3).
16 Vasquez-Tokos 2020a.
17 Dawson 1994.
18 Barroso 2020.
19 Barroso 2020.
20 Yuval-Davis 2006.
21 Flores 2021.
22 Tajfel and Turner 1986.
23 Flores and Benmayor 1997.
24 Lipsitz 2011.
25 Lipsitz 2011.
26 LaFleur 2021.
27 Lipsitz 2011.
28 Anderson 1991.
29 HECC 2022.
30 HECC 2022.
31 Yosso et al. 2009, 644.
32 Hondagneu-Sotelo and Pastor 2021.
33 Mueller 2017, 220.
34 Abascal and Ganter 2022.
35 Jiménez, Fields, and Schachter 2015.
36 LaFleur 2021, 523.
37 Mueller 2017, 220.
38 McDermott 2020.
39 Bonilla-Silva, Goar, and Embrick 2006.
40 Theiss-Morse 2009, 83–84.
41 Composed by Lewis Allan and recorded by Billie Holiday in 1939, with lyrics drawn from a poem by Abel Meeropol (1937), "Strange Fruit" is a protest song decrying the lynching of Black Americans.
42 Alexander 2010.

43 Byrd 2011, xxiii.
44 Ngai 2004, 100, emphasis added.
45 Suárez-Orozco et al. 2011; Yoshikawa 2011.
46 Dreby 2015; Gonzales 2011.
47 Suárez-Orozco et al. 2011.
48 Enriquez 2015; Fernández 2021; Rodriguez 2023.
49 McCann and Jones-Correa 2020.
50 Enriquez 2020.
51 Canizales and Vallejo 2021; Newman, Merolla, and Shah 2021; Flores-González and Salgado 2022.
52 Theiss-Morse 2009.
53 Schachter, Flores, and Maghbouleh 2021.
54 Cornell and Hartmann 1998, 20.
55 Theiss-Morse 2009, 87.
56 Jiménez 2010.
57 Chavez 2013.
58 Anzaldúa 1987, 38.
59 Anzaldúa 1987, 39.
60 Vitali, Hunt, and Thorp V 2018.
61 Canizales and Vallejo 2021; Newman et al. 2021; Flores-González and Salgado 2022.
62 Horowitz, Brown, and Cox 2019.
63 Omi and Winant 1994, 55.
64 Kim 1999, 106.
65 Molina, HoSang, and Gutiérrez 2019.
66 Omi and Winant 1994, 56.
67 Jones 2022.
68 See also Pan and Reyes 2021.
69 Roth 2012; Bonilla-Silva 2004; Yancey 2003; Lee and Bean 2010.
70 Collins 1991, 2004.
71 Collins 1991; Dow 2016.
72 Collins 1991, 68.
73 Vasquez-Tokos and Norton-Smith 2017; Deckard et al. 2020.
74 Cheng 2013.
75 Zamora 2018; Molina 2014.
76 Omi and Winant 2015, 60.
77 See Rawls and Duck 2020.
78 Waters 1999.
79 Bonilla-Silva and Zuberi 2008, 7.
80 Delgado and Stefancic 2017, 81–82.
81 Collins 2009.
82 Molina 2014, 3.
83 Ignatiev 1995; Jacobson 1998; Roediger 1999.

84 Flores 2021, 6.

85 Alba and Nee 2003, 10.

86 Alba and Nee 2003.

87 Flores-González 2017; Warikoo and Bloemraad 2018.

88 Telles and Sue 2019, 23.

89 Telles and Sue 2019, 18, 184.

90 Vasquez-Tokos 2020b.

91 Vasquez-Tokos 2020a.

92 See also Bloemraad 2013; Flores-González 2017; Maldonado 2017; Warikoo and Bloemraad 2018.

93 Warikoo and Bloemraad 2018.

94 Daniel 1996.

95 Collins 2009.

96 Delgado and Stefancic 2017.

97 Tuck and Yang 2012; Glenn 2015.

98 Grollman 2018.

CHAPTER 4. WHITE COMFORT AND NON-WHITE DISCOMFORT

1 KVAL. 2016. "University of Oregon Strips Name of Former KKK Leader from Campus Building." September 8. https://kval.com.

2 Brown 2016.

3 Oregon State University. 2022. "Names Under Consideration." Accessed June 9, https://leadership.oregonstate.edu/; Bahde et al. 2017.

4 Brasher, Alderman, and Inwood 2017, 293.

5 Hauge 2019.

6 Ray 2019.

7 Ahmet 2021; Gadd 2023.

8 Leonardo and Porter 2010, 139.

9 Hauge 2019, 229.

10 Bonilla-Silva 2019, 2.

11 Leonardo 2004, 137.

12 Wolfe 2016, 271.

13 Ray 2019, 27.

14 Chung 2019, 16.

15 Reskin 2012.

16 Reskin 2012.

17 Leonardo 2004.

18 Flores 2021; Reyes 2018; Love 2019.

19 Brunsma et al. 2020, 2010.

20 Brunsma et al. 2020.

21 Joseph et al. 2020, 170.

22 Adams et al. 2018.

23 Du Bois 1920, 23, emphasis added.

24 Apple 1996, 22.

25 Collins and Bilge 2016, 159.

26 Sabzalian 2019, xiii.

27 This statement is not to override the progressive educational programs operative in the United States whose practices and goals resist inequality. However, most respondents who identified as a race other than White experienced multiple hardships in schools where they were treated as marginal, unimportant, and predestined for a limited future. An exception is respondents from Hawai'i who observed that subjugated knowledge relevant to the place and people was taught in school. This finding of race-conscious curriculum is place-specific, racial awareness of teachers and students shaped by region (Vasquez-Tokos 2020a). Overall, respondents testify that race-based knowledge outside of Whiteness is not embedded into curricula, perpetuating the exoticization, objectification, and "unknowability" of people of color.

28 Oh and Kim 2020.

29 Brunsma et al. 2020.

30 Castillo-Montoya and Reyes 2020.

31 Chapman-Hilliard and Beasley 2018.

32 Feagin 2014.

33 Motel and Patten 2012.

34 Ochoa 2013, 2.

35 Bourdieu and Passeron 1979; Ferguson 2000; Giroux 1981.

36 Shear et al. 2015.

37 Mueller 2017.

38 World Population Review. 2023. "Critical Race Theory Ban Status." Accessed March 3. https://worldpopulationreview.com/.

39 Florida Senate. 2022. "SB 148." Accessed March 3, 2023. www.flsenate.gov/.

40 Simonson 2022.

41 Brunsma et al. 2020.

42 Robertson 2015, 114.

43 Robertson 2015, 115.

44 Collins 2009.

45 Tuck and Yang 2012.

46 King and Springwood 2001, 7.

47 Davis-Delano, Galliher, and Gone 2023.

48 King and Springwood 2001, 2.

49 Rhodes 2017.

50 Anzaldúa 1987, 58.

51 Yosso 2005.

52 See ch. 6 of Vasquez 2011.

53 Reyes 2018, 10.

54 Lipsitz 2011, 12.

55 Anderson 2021; Combs 2022.

56 Flores-González 2017, 44.
57 Flores-González 2017.
58 HECC 2018.
59 University of Oregon Office of the Provost. 2022. "Data Dashboards: Undergraduate Student Dashboards." Accessed May 25. https://provost.uoregon.edu/.
60 Griffith, Hurd, and Hussain 2019, 116.
61 Garland-Thomson 2009, 46.
62 Garland-Thomson 2009, 39.
63 Garland-Thomson 2009, 17.
64 Anderson 2021; Combs 2022.
65 Fanon 1967.
66 Fanon 1967, 116.
67 Flores 2011; Collins 2009.
68 Tatum 1997.
69 DATA USA. 2022. "Computer Science." Accessed April 5. https://datausa.io/.
70 Brunsma et al. 2020, 2002.
71 Flores-González 2017, 33.
72 McDermott 2020.
73 Fry, Kennedy, and Funk 2021.
74 Feagin and Cobas 2008; Pyke 2010.
75 Smith, Hung, and Franklin 2011.
76 Garland-Thomson 2011.
77 Hochschild 1979.
78 Wingfield 2010.
79 Tatum 1997.
80 Mueller 2017.
81 Blumer 1969, 11.
82 Wolfe 2006; Glenn 2015.
83 French 2016, 41.
84 Anzaldúa and Keating 2015, 127.
85 Ahmed 2012, 113.
86 On how encountering Latino-authored literature affects Latino and non-Latino readers, see Vasquez (2005).
87 Rios 2017.
88 Rios 2017, 76.
89 Valenzuela 1999.
90 Ferguson 2000; Rios 2017.
91 Ray 2019, 27.
92 Spencer, Steele, and Quinn 1999; Steele and Aronson 1995.
93 Ochoa 2013.
94 Bruce 2004; Messner 1992; Vasquez-Tokos and Norton-Smith 2017.
95 Teaiwa 2014.
96 Leonardo and Porter 2010, 139.

97 Gibson et al. 2021.

98 Goyette and Lareau 2014; Hagerman 2018.

99 Bonilla-Silva 2013.

100 Ellison and Powers 1994; Jackman and Crane 1986; Perry 2002; Perry 2013.

101 Acuña 2011; Almaguer 1994; Dunbar-Ortiz 2014.

102 Apple 1996, 22.

103 Hondagneu-Sotelo and Pastor 2021.

104 Ahmed 2012; Mayorga-Gallo 2014; Smith and Mayorga-Gallo 2017; Woody 2020.

105 Moore 2017; Zambrana et al. 2015.

106 Vallejo 2012b.

107 Brooms 2020.

108 Pan 2017, 4.

109 Griffith, Hurd, and Hussain 2019.

CHAPTER 5. EMBODIED BURDENS

1 Ramos, Garriga-López, and Rodríguez-Díaz 2022, 305.

2 Omi and Winant 2015, 145, emphasis in original.

3 Phelan and Link 2015; Reskin 2012; Roberts and Rollins 2020.

4 Krieger 2012, 5.

5 Alvarez and Evans 2021; Littlejohn 2021; Sewell 2016; Williams and Sternthal 2010.

6 Gómez 2013, 4.

7 Karina, Jane, and Teresa 2002; Brave Heart et al. 2011.

8 Balogun 2012.

9 Phelan and Link 2015.

10 Smith, Hung, and Franklin 2011; Geronimus 1992; Phelan and Link 2015; Goosby et al. 2015.

11 Link and Phelan 1995, 80.

12 Helms and Mereish 2013, 146.

13 Helms and Mereish 2013, 146.

14 Asad and Clair 2018.

15 Link and Phelan 1995, 80.

16 Dreby 2015, 64.

17 Nemoto 2009.

18 Vasquez-Tokos and Yamin 2021; Stern 2005; Washington 2006; Lombardo 2011.

19 Brown 2003; Suinn 2001.

20 Lorde 1984, 129, emphasis in original.

21 Ocampo 2022.

22 Suinn 2001, 297.

23 Wingfield 2010.

24 Anderson 2021; Lipsitz 2011; Combs 2022.

25 Dow 2016; Vasquez 2010b.

26 Fernández 2021, 10.

27 Du Bois 2005 [1903], 173.

28 Dow 2019.
29 Sewell et al. 2020.
30 Zamora 2022.
31 Yosso et al. 2009.
32 Link and Phelan 1995.
33 Garland-Thomson 2011.
34 Garland-Thomson 2011, 42.
35 Garland-Thomson 2011, 42.
36 Bonilla-Silva 2019.
37 Brave Heart et al. 2011.
38 Krieger 2012.
39 O'Brien 2010.
40 O'Brien 2010.
41 Walters and Simoni 2002.
42 Dunbar-Ortiz 2014, 69.
43 Dunbar-Ortiz 2014.
44 Dunbar-Ortiz 2014, 41.
45 Child 2000; Fear-Segal 2016; Lomawaima 2006; Unger 1977; White 2016.
46 Chung 2019, 20.
47 Norgaard 2019.
48 Walters and Simoni 2002.
49 Norgaard 2019, 147.
50 Demir 2022.
51 Tuck and Yang 2012.
52 Walters and Simoni 2002.
53 National Center for Health Statistics. 2021. "Life Expectancy." Accessed June 2. www.cdc.gov/nchs.
54 Omi and Winant 2015, 146.
55 Omi and Winant 2015, 146.
56 Benjamin 2022.
57 Selod 2018.
58 Rios 2011; Gilbert and Ray 2015.
59 Selod 2018.
60 Maghbouleh 2017.
61 Selod 2018, 24.
62 Anderson 2021, 13.
63 Kim 2016, 472.
64 Louie and Viladrich 2021, 1.
65 Jones et al. 2021.
66 McCann and Jones-Correa 2020.
67 Du Bois 1935, 700.
68 Du Bois 1935, 700.
69 Gilbert and Ray 2015, S123.

70 Bell 2020.

71 Itzigsohn and Brown 2020, 188.

72 Cabrera 2014.

73 Woody 2020.

74 Gilmore 2007.

75 Kruk and Matsick 2021.

76 Blumer 1969.

77 See Selod (2018) on the racialization of Muslims.

78 Omi and Winant 2015.

79 Almaguer 1994.

80 Link and Phelan 1995.

CHAPTER 6. RACIAL BIOGRAPHY AND GOAL FORMATION

1 Gramsci 1992.

2 Mannheim 1936, 296.

3 Bonilla-Silva, Goar, and Embrick 2006.

4 Latham and Locke 2013.

5 Latham and Locke 2013, 6.

6 Eberly et al. 2013, 36.

7 Bonilla-Silva 2019, 2; Kim 2016.

8 Bonilla-Silva 2019, 2.

9 Bonilla-Silva 2019, 3.

10 Norgaard and Reed 2017, 467.

11 Bonilla-Silva 2019, 2.

12 Du Bois 2005 [1903], 48.

13 Du Bois 2005 [1903], 48.

14 Bonilla-Silva 2019, 2.

15 Lamont and Mizrachi 2012; Vasquez 2011.

16 Flores 2017, 66.

17 Vasquez 2011, 2014a.

18 Rios 2017.

19 Go 2018, 1–13.

20 hooks 2000.

21 Pan 2017, 4, emphasis added.

22 Go 2018, 1.

23 Gonzales 2011.

24 Menjívar and Abrego 2012.

25 Flores, Escudero, and Burciaga 2019, 13.

26 Mejía 2023.

27 Flores, Escudero, and Burciaga 2019, 13.

28 Enriquez 2020.

29 Menjivar 2006.

30 Enriquez 2020, 108.

31 Gonzales 2016; Zhou et al. 2008; Abrego 2014.

32 Louie 2012, 173.

33 Lee and Zhou 2015.

34 Espiritu 2023, 33.

35 Kibria 1999; Shiao and Tuan 2008.

36 Williams and Cooper 2019.

37 Vallejo 2012a.

38 Flores 2017, 65.

39 Vasquez-Tokos and Norton-Smith 2017.

40 Lewis 2004.

41 Bonilla-Silva, Goar, and Embrick 2006.

42 McDermott 2020, 12.

43 Mannheim 1936.

44 Multiracial respondents listed "White" most often as their "street race," followed by "no idea," "international," "ambiguous," and "Latina."

45 López et al. 2018.

46 Alba and Islam 2009.

47 Omi and Winant 2015.

48 See Roth 2016 on the multidimensionality of race.

49 Simpson and Willer 2015.

50 Mueller 2017.

CONCLUSION
1 powell 2005, 17, emphasis added.

2 Omi and Winant 2015.

3 Sanchez and Gomez-Aguinaga 2017; Sanchez, Fraga, and Ramírez 2020.

4 Zepeda-Millán and Wallace 2018.

5 Haney López 1996.

6 Bonilla-Silva 2019, 7.

7 Rios 2017, 157, emphasis added.

8 Kim 2016, 498.

9 Bell 1992.

10 Collins 2015, 3.4.

11 Omi and Winant 2015, 137.

12 Mignolo and Walsh 2018, 81.

13 Steinman 2022, 18, 24.

14 Sassen 1989; Espiritu 2023.

15 Ahmed 2012, 113, 117, emphasis in original.

16 Love 2019, 9.

17 Mueller 2017, 220.

18 Ray 2023, 4.

19 Matias 2016, 129, emphasis in original.

20 Collins 2009, 276.

21 McMillan and Chavis 1986.

22 Nash 2019.

23 Desmond and Emirbayer 2009, 343.

24 Delgado and Stefancic 2017, 52.

25 Adams et al. 2018, 342.

26 Adams et al. 2018, 347.

27 Go 2020.

28 Yosso 2005.

29 Torkelson and Hartmann 2021, 14.

30 Du Bois 2005 [1903], 60.

APPENDIX

1 US Census Bureau. 2021. "QuickFacts: Oregon." Accessed September 20. www.census.gov/.

2 Vasquez-Tokos 2017b; Jones 2022.

3 Ostrove and Long 2007; Valdez and Golash-Boza 2020.

4 Vasquez-Tokos 2020a.

5 Feagin and Sikes 1994; Vallejo and Vasquez-Tokos 2024.

6 Telles and Ortiz 2008, 275.

7 Ortiz and Telles 2012.

8 See also Feagin and Sikes 1994; Pattillo-McCoy 1999; Vallejo and Vasquez-Tokos 2024; Morris 2015.

9 Zhou et al. 2008.

10 On the dynamism between interviewer and interviewee, see Vasquez-Tokos (2017a).

11 Weiss 1994.

12 Charmaz 2014.

13 Charmaz 2014, 138.

BIBLIOGRAPHY

Abascal, Maria, and Flavien Ganter. 2022. "Know It When You See It? The Qualities of the Communities People Describe as 'Diverse' (or Not)." *City & Community* 21 (4):314–339.

Abascal, Maria, and Denia Garcia. 2022. "Pathways to Skin Color Stratification: The Role of Inherited (Dis)Advantage and Skin Color Discrimination in Labor Markets." *Sociological Science* 9:346–373.

Abrego, Leisy. 2014. *Sacrificing Families: Navigating Laws, Labor, and Love Across Borders*. Stanford, CA: Stanford University Press.

Acuña, Rodolfo. 2011. *Occupied America: A History of Chicanos*. 7th ed. New York: Longman.

Adams, Glenn, Phia S. Salter, Tuğçe Kurtiş, Pegah Naemi, and Sara Estrada-Villalta. 2018. "Subordinated Knowledge as a Tool for Creative Maladjustment and Resistance to Racial Oppression." *Journal of Social Issues* 74 (2):337–354.

Ahmed, Sara. 2012. *On Being Included: Racism and Diversity in Institutional Life*. Durham, NC: Duke University Press.

Ahmet, Akile. 2021. "Stop the Pain: Black and Minority Ethnic Scholars on Diversity Policy Obfuscation in Universities." *Equality, Diversity and Inclusion: An International Journal* 40 (2):152–164.

Alba, Richard. 2020. *The Great Demographic Illusion: Majority, Minority, and the Expanding American Mainstream*. Princeton, NJ: Princeton University Press.

Alba, Richard D. 2009. *Blurring the Color Line: The New Chance for a More Integrated America*. Cambridge, MA: Harvard University Press.

Alba, Richard D., and Victor Nee. 2003. *Remaking the American Mainstream: Assimilation and Contemporary Immigration*. Cambridge, MA: Harvard University Press.

Alba, Richard, and Tariqul Islam. 2009. "The Case of the Disappearing Mexican Americans: An Ethnic-Identity Mystery." *Population Research and Policy Review* 28 (2):109–121.

Alba, Richard, Tomás R. Jiménez, and Helen B. Marrow. 2014. "Mexican Americans as a Paradigm for Contemporary Intra-group Heterogeneity." *Ethnic and Racial Studies* 37 (3):446–466.

Alexander, Michelle. 2010. *The New Jim Crow: Mass Incarceration in the Age of Colorblindness*. New York: New Press.

Almaguer, Tomás. 1994. *Racial Fault Lines*. Berkeley: University of California Press.

Alvarez, Camila H., and Clare Rosenfeld Evans. 2021. "Intersectional Environmental Justice and Population Health Inequalities: A Novel Approach." *Social Science & Medicine* 269, 113559.

Anderson, Benedict R. 1991. *Imagined Communities: Reflections on the Origin and Spread of Nationalism*. 2nd ed. New York: Verso.

Anderson, Elijah. 2021. *Black in White Space: The Enduring Impact of Color in Everyday Life*. Chicago: University of Chicago Press.

Anzaldúa, Gloria. 1987. *Borderlands/La Frontera: The New Mestiza*. 1st ed. San Francisco: Spinsters / Aunt Lute.

Anzaldúa, Gloria, and AnaLouise Keating. 2015. *Light in the Dark = Luz en lo Oscuro: Rewriting Identity, Spirituality, Reality*. Durham, NC: Duke University Press Books.

Apple, Michael W. 1996. *Cultural Politics & Education*. New York: Teachers College Press.

Arredondo, Aaron, and Juan Jose Bustamante. 2022. "White Spaces in Brown(ing) Places: Toward the Spatialization of Critical Immigration Studies." *Ethnic and Racial Studies* 45 (13):2445–67.

Arvin, Maile Renee. 2019. *Possessing Polynesians: The Science of Settler Colonial Whiteness in Hawai'i and Oceania*. Durham, NC: Duke University Press.

Asad, Asad L., and Matthew Clair. 2018. "Racialized Legal Status as a Social Determinant of Health." *Social Science & Medicine* 199:19–28.

Bahde, Thomas, Stephen Dow Beckham, Marisa Chappell, Dwaine Plaza, and Stacey L. Smith. 2017. Historic Reports on OSU Building Names: Arnold Dining Center. Oregon State University.

Balogun, Oluwakemi M. 2012. "Cultural and Cosmopolitan: Idealized Femininity and Embodied Nationalism in Nigerian Beauty Pageants." *Gender & Society* 26 (3):357–381.

Barajas, Heidi Lasley, and Amy Ronnkvist. 2007. "Racialized Space: Framing Latino and Latina Experience in Public Schools." *Teachers College Record* 109 (6):1517–1538.

Barroso, Amanda. 2020. "Most Black Adults Say Race Is Central to Their Identity and Feel Connected to a Broader Black Community." Washington, DC: Pew Research Center.

Bell, Derrick. 1992. *Faces at the Bottom of the Well*. New York: Basic Books.

Bell, Marcus. 2020. "Becoming White Teachers: Symbolic Interactions and Racializing the Raceless Norm in Predominantly Black Schools." *Sociology of Race and Ethnicity* 6 (2):209–222.

Benjamin, Ruha. 2022. *Viral Justice: How We Grow the World We Want*. Princeton, NJ: Princeton University Press.

Bertrand, Marianne, and Sendhil Mullainathan. 2004. "Are Emily and Greg More Employable than Lakisha and Jamal? A Field Experiment on Labor Market Discrimination." *American Economic Review* 94 (4):991–1013.

Bhambra, Gurminder K. 2014. "A Sociological Dilemma: Race, Segregation and US Sociology." *Current Sociology Monograph* 62 (4):472–492.

Bloemraad, Irene. 2013. "Being American/Becoming American: Birthright Citizenship and Immigrants' Membership in the United States." *Studies in Law, Politics, and Society* 60 (60):55–84.

Blumer, Herbert. 1969. *Symbolic Interactionism: Perspective and Method*. Englewood Cliffs, NJ: Prentice-Hall.

Bonilla-Silva, Eduardo. 2004. "From Bi-racial to Tri-racial: Towards a New System of Racial Stratification in the USA." *Ethnic and Racial Studies* 27 (6):931–950.

Bonilla-Silva, Eduardo. 2013. *Racism Without Racists: Color-Blind Racism and the Persistence of Racial Inequality in the United States.* 4th ed. Lanham, MD: Rowman & Littlefield.

Bonilla-Silva, Eduardo. 2019. "Feeling Race: Theorizing the Racial Economy of Emotions." *American Sociological Review* 84 (1):1–25.

Bonilla-Silva, Eduardo, Carla Goar, and David G. Embrick. 2006. "When Whites Flock Together: The Social Psychology of White Habitus." *Critical Sociology* 32 (2–3):229–253.

Bonilla-Silva, Eduardo, and Tukufu Zuberi. 2008. "Toward a Definition of White Logic and White Methods." In *White Logic, White Methods: Racism and Methodology,* edited by Tukufu Zuberi and Eduardo Bonilla-Silva, 3–30. New York: Rowman & Littlefield.

Bourdieu, Pierre, and Jean-Claude Passeron. 1979. *The Inheritors.* Translated by Richard Nice. Chicago: University of Chicago Press.

Brasher, Jordan P., Derek H. Alderman, and Joshua F. J. Inwood. 2017. "Applying Critical Race and Memory Studies to University Place Naming Controversies: Toward a Responsible Landscape Policy." *Papers in Applied Geography* 3 (3–4):292–307.

Brave Heart, Maria Yellow Horse, Josephine Chase, Jennifer Elkins, and Deborah B. Altschul. 2011. "Historical Trauma Among Indigenous Peoples of the Americas: Concepts, Research, and Clinical Considerations." *Journal of Psychoactive Drugs* 43 (4):282–290.

Brayboy, Bryan McKinley Jones. 2005. "Toward a Tribal Critical Race Theory in Education." *Urban Review* 37 (5):425–446.

Brooms, Derrick R. 2020. "'It's the Person, but Then the Environment, Too': Black and Latino Males' Narratives about Their College Successes." *Sociology of Race and Ethnicity* 6 (2):195–208.

Brown, Doug. 2016. "A Black Teen Was Run Down in Gresham: His Killer Is in a Notorious Oregon White Supremacist Prison Gang." *Portland Mercury.* Portland, OR.

Brown, Tony N. 2003. "Critical Race Theory Speaks to the Sociology of Mental Health: Mental Health Problems Produced by Racial Stratification." *Journal of Health and Social Behavior* 44 (3):292–301.

Bruce, Ben. 2019. "The Rise and Fall of the Ku Klux Klan in Oregon During the 1920s." *Voces Novae* 11 (2):1–26.

Bruce, Toni. 2004. "Marking the Boundaries of 'Normal' in Televised Sports: The Play-by-Play of Race." *Media, Culture, and Society* 26 (6):861–879.

Brunsma, David L., Nathaniel G. Chapman, Joong Won Kim, Lellock J. Slade, Megan Underhill, Erik T. Withers, and Jennifer Padilla Wyse. 2020. "The Culture of White Space: On the Racialized Production of Meaning." *American Behavioral Scientist* 64 (14):2001–2015.

Budiman, Abby. 2020. "Americans Are More Positive About the Long-Term Rise in U.S. Racial and Ethnic Diversity Than in 2016." Washington, DC: Pew Research Center.

Bussel, R., and Daniel J. Tichenor. 2017. "Trouble in Paradise: A Historical Perspective on Immigration in Oregon." *Oregon Historical Quarterly* 118 (4):460–487.

Butler, Johnnella E. 2006. "Black Studies and Ethnic Studies: The Crucible of Knowledge and Social Action." In *A Companion to African-American Studies*, edited by Jane Anna Gordon and Lewis Gordon, 76–95. Oxford, UK: Blackwell.

Byrd, Jodi A. 2011. *The Transit of Empire: Indigenous Critiques of Colonialism*. Minneapolis: University of Minnesota Press.

Cabrera, Nolan León. 2014. "Exposing Whiteness in Higher Education: White Male College Students Minimizing Racism, Claiming Victimization, and Recreating White Supremacy." *Race Ethnicity and Education* 17 (1):30–55.

Canizales, Stephanie L., and Jody Agius Vallejo. 2021. "Latinos & Racism in the Trump Era." *Daedalus* 150:150–164.

Carpenter, Marc James. 2020. "Pioneer Problems: 'Wanton Murder,' Indian War Veterans, and Oregon's Violent History." *Oregon Historical Quarterly* 121 (2):156–185.

Castellanos, M. Bianet. 2017. "Rewriting the Mexican Immigrant Narrative: Situating Indigeneity in Maya Women's Stories." *Latino Studies* 15 (2):219–241.

Castillo-Montoya, Milagros, and Daisy Verduzco Reyes. 2020. "Learning Latinidad: The Role of a Latino Cultural Center Service-Learning Course in Latino Identity Inquiry and Sociopolitical Capacity." *Journal of Latinos and Education* 19 (2):132–147.

Chapman-Hilliard, Collette, and Samuel T. Beasley. 2018. "'It's Like Power to Move': Black Students' Psychosocial Experiences in Black Studies Courses at a Predominantly White Institution." *Journal of Multicultural Counseling and Development* 46 (2):129–151.

Charmaz, Kathy. 2014. *Constructing Grounded Theory: A Practical Guide through Qualitative Analysis*. 2nd ed. Thousand Oaks, CA: Sage.

Chavez, Leo R. 2013. *The Latino Threat: Constructing Immigrants, Citizens, and the Nation*. 2nd ed. Stanford, CA: Stanford University Press.

Cheng, Wendy. 2013. *The Changs Next Door to the Díazes: Remapping Race in Suburban California*. Minneapolis: University of Minnesota Press.

Child, Brenda J. 2000. *Boarding School Seasons: American Indian Families*. Lincoln: University of Nebraska Press.

Chong, Kelly H. 2020. *Love Across Borders: Asian Americans and the Politics of Intermarriage and Family-Making*. New York: Routledge.

Choo, Hae Yeon, and Myra Marx Ferree. 2010. "Practicing Intersectionality in Sociological Research: A Critical Analysis of Inclusions, Interactions, and Institutions in the Study of Inequalities." *Sociological Theory* 28 (2):129–149.

Chung, Sae Hoon Stan. 2019. "The Courage to Be Altered: Indigenist Decolonization for Teachers." *New Directions for Teaching & Learning* 2019 (157):13–25.

Collins, Patricia Hill. 1991. *Black Feminist Thought*. New York: Routledge.

Collins, Patricia Hill. 2004. *Black Sexual Politics: African Americans, Gender, and the New Racism*. New York: Routledge.

Collins, Patricia Hill. 2009. *Black Feminist Thought*. 2nd ed. New York: Routledge.

Collins, Patricia Hill. 2015. "Intersectionality's Definitional Dilemmas." *Annual Review of Sociology* 41:3.1–3.20.

Collins, Patricia Hill, and Sirma Bilge. 2016. *Intersectionality*. Malden, MA: Polity.

Combs, Barbara Harris. 2022. *Bodies Out of Place: Theorizing Anti-blackness in U.S. Society*. Atlanta: University of Georgia Press.

Cornell, Stephen E., and Douglass Hartmann. 1998. *Ethnicity and Race: Making Identities in a Changing World*. Thousand Oaks, CA: Pine Forge Press.

Crawford, James. 1992. *Hold Your Tongue: Bilingualism and the Politics of English Only*. New York: Addison-Wesley.

Daniel, G. Reginald. 1996. "Black and White Identity in the New Millennium: Unsevering the Ties that Bind." In *The Multiracial Experience: Racial Borders as the New Frontier*, edited by Maria P. P. Root, 121–139. Thousand Oaks, CA: Sage.

Davis-Delano, Laurel R., Renee V. Galliher, and Joseph P. Gone. 2023. "Native Appropriation in Sport: Cultivating Bias Toward American Indians." *Race and Social Problems* 15:395–407.

Dawson, Michael C. 1994. *Behind the Mule: Race and Class in African-American Politics*. Princeton, NJ: Princeton University Press.

De Genova, Nicholas. 2005. *Working the Boundaries: Race, Space, and "Illegality" in Mexican Chicago*. Raleigh, NC: Duke University Press.

De León, Jason. 2015. *The Land of Open Graves: Living and Dying on the Migrant Trail*. Berkeley: University of California Press.

Deckard, Natalie Delia, Irene Browne, Cassaundra Rodriguez, Marisela Martinez-Cola, and Sofia Gonzalez Leal. 2020. "Controlling Images of Immigrants in the Mainstream and Black Press: The Discursive Power of the 'Illegal Latino.'" *Latino Studies* 18 (4):581–602.

Deem, Alexandra. 2019. "Mediated Intersections of Environmental and Decolonial Politics in the No Dakota Access Pipeline Movement." *Theory, Culture & Society* 36 (5):113–131.

Delgado, Richard, and Jean Stefancic. 2001. *Critical Race Theory: An Introduction*. New York: New York University Press.

Delgado, Richard, and Jean Stefancic. 2017. *Critical Race Theory: An Introduction*. 3rd ed. New York: New York University Press.

Deloria, Philip Joseph. 1998. *Playing Indian*. New Haven, CT: Yale University Press.

Demir, Ipek. 2022. "How and Why Should We Decolonize Global Health Education and Research?" *Annals of Global Health* 88 (30):1–3.

Department of Defense. 2019. Indo-Pacific Strategy Report: Preparedness, Partnerships, and Promoting a Networked Region. Washington, DC.

Desmond, Matthew, and Mustafa Emirbayer. 2009. "What Is Racial Domination?" *Du Bois Review* 6 (2):335–355.

Devlin, Kat. 2015. "Learning a Foreign Language a 'Must' in Europe, Not So in America." Washington, DC: Pew Research Center.

Dow, Dawn Marie. 2016. "The Deadly Challenges of Raising African American Boys: Navigating the Controlling Image of the 'Thug.'" *Gender & Society* 30 (2):161–188.

Dow, Dawn Marie. 2019. *Mothering While Black: Boundaries and Burdens of Middle-Class Parenthood*. Berkeley: University of California Press.

Dreby, Joanna. 2015. *Everyday Illegal: When Policies Undermine Immigrant Families*. Oakland: University of California Press.

Dropp, Kyle, and Brendan Nyhan. 2017. "Nearly Half of Americans Don't Know Puerto Ricans Are Fellow Citizens." *New York Times*, September 26.

Du Bois, W.E.B. 1920. *Darkwater: Voices from within the Veil*. New York: Harcourt, Brace and Howe.

Du Bois, W.E.B. 1935. *Black Reconstruction: An Essay Toward a History of the Part Which Black Folk Played in the Attempt to Reconstruct Democracy in America, 1860–1880*. 1st ed. New York: Harcourt, Brace and Company.

Du Bois, W.E.B. 2005 [1903]. *The Souls of Black Folk*. New York: Simon & Schuster.

Dunbar-Ortiz, Roxanne. 2014. *An Indigenous Peoples' History of the United States*. Boston: Beacon Press.

Dunbar-Ortiz, Roxanne. 2021. *Not "A Nation of Immigrants": Settler Colonialism, White Supremacy, and a History of Erasure and Exclusion*. Boston: Beacon Press.

Dwanna, L. McKay. 2019. "Masking Legitimized Racism: Indigeneity, Colorblindness, and the Sociology of Race." In *Seeing Race Again*, edited by Kimberlé Williams Crenshaw, Luke Charles Harris, Daniel Martinez HoSang, and George Lipsitz, 85–104. Berkeley: University of California Press.

Eberly, Marion B., Dong Liu, Terence R. Mitchell, and Thomas W. Lee. 2013. "Attributions and Emotions as Mediators and/or Moderators in the Goal-Striving Process." In *New Developments in Goal Setting and Task Performance*, edited by Edwin A. Locke and Gary P. Latham, 35–50. New York: Routledge.

Ellison, Christopher C., and Daniel A. Powers. 1994. "The Contact Hypothesis and Racial Attitudes among Black Americans." *Social Science Quarterly* 75 (2):385–400.

Enriquez, Laura E. 2015. "Multigenerational Punishment: Shared Experience of Undocumented Immigration Status within Mixed-Status Families." *Journal of Marriage and Family* 77 (4):939–953.

Enriquez, Laura E. 2020. *Of Love and Papers: How Immigration Policy Affects Romance and Family*. Berkeley: University of California Press.

Espiritu, Yen Le. 2014. *Body Counts: The Vietnam War and Militarized Refuge(es)*. Berkeley: University of California Press.

Espiritu, Yen Le. 2023. "Critical Immigration and Refugee Studies: An Interdisciplinary Approach." In *Disciplinary Futures: Sociology in Conversation with American, Ethnic, and Indigenous Studies*, edited by Nadia Y. Kim and Pawan Dhingra, 21–41. New York: New York University Press.

Falcón, Sylvanna M. 2008. "Mestiza Double Consciousness: The Voices of Afro-Peruvian Women on Gendered Racism." *Gender & Society* 22 (5):660–680.

Fanon, Frantz. 1967. *Black Skin, White Masks*. New York: Grove Press.

Feagin, Joe R. 2010. *The White Racial Frame: Centuries of Racial Framing and Counter-Framing*. New York: Routledge.

Feagin, Joe R. 2014. *Racist America: Roots, Current Realities, and Future Reparations.* 3rd ed. New York: Routledge.

Feagin, Joe R., and Jose Cobas. 2008. "Latinos/as and the White Racial Frame: The Procrustean Bed of Assimilation." *Sociological Inquiry* 78 (1):39–53.

Feagin, Joe R., and Melvin P. Sikes. 1994. *Living with Racism: The Black Middle-Class Experience.* Boston: Beacon Press.

Fear-Segal, Jacqueline, ed. 2016. *Carlisle Indian Industrial School: Indigenous Histories, Memories, and Reclamations.* Lincoln: University of Nebraska Press.

Fenelon, James V. 2016. "Critique of Glenn on Settler Colonialism and Bonilla-Silva on Critical Race Analysis from Indigenous Perspectives." *Sociology of Race and Ethnicity* 2 (2):237–242.

Ferguson, Ann Arnett. 2000. *Bad Boys: Public Schools in the Making of Black Masculinity.* Ann Arbor: University of Michigan Press.

Fernández, Jesica Siham. 2021. *Growing Up Latinx: Coming of Age in a Time of Contested Citizenship.* New York: New York University Press.

Fixico, D. 2018. Termination and Restoration in Oregon. *The Oregon Encyclopedia*: Oregon Historical Society.

Fleming, Crystal M., Michèle Lamont, and Jessica S. Welburn. 2012. "African Americans Respond to Stigmatization: The Meanings and Salience of Confronting, Deflecting Conflict, Educating the Ignorant and 'Managing the Self.'" *Ethnic and Racial Studies* 35 (3):400–417.

Flores-González, Nilda. 2017. *Citizens but Not Americans: Race and Belonging among Latino Millennials.* New York: New York University Press.

Flores-González, Nilda, and Casandra D. Salgado. 2022. "Shifting Racial Schemas: From Post-racial to New 'Old-fashioned' Racism." *Sociological Inquiry* 92 (2):341–363.

Flores, Andrea. 2021. *The Succeeders: How Immigrant Youth Are Transforming What It Means to Belong in America.* Berkeley: University of California Press.

Flores, Andrea, Kevin Escudero, and Edelina Burciaga. 2019. "Legal–Spatial Consciousness: A Legal Geography Framework for Examining Migrant Illegality." *Law & Policy* 41 (1):12–33.

Flores, Glenda M. 2017. *Latina Teachers: Creating Careers and Guarding Culture.* New York: New York University Press.

Flores, Glenda Marisol. 2011. "Racialized Tokens: Latina Teachers Negotiating, Surviving and Thriving in a White Woman's Profession." *Qualitative Sociology* 34 (2):313–335.

Flores, William Vincent, and Rina Benmayor. 1997. *Latino Cultural Citizenship: Claiming Identity, Space, and Rights.* Boston: Beacon Press.

Foss, Christopher. 2017. "'I Wanted Oregon to Have Something': Governor Victor G. Atiyeh and Oregon-Japan Relations." *Oregon Historical Quarterly* 118 (3):338–365.

Frankenberg, Ruth. 1993. *White Women, Race Matters: The Social Construction of Whiteness.* Minneapolis: University of Minnesota Press.

Freire, Paolo. 1970. *Pedagogy of the Oppressed*. Translated by Myra Bergman Ramos. New York: Continuum Publishing.

French, Laurence. 2016. *Policing American Indians: A Unique Chapter in American Jurisprudence*. Boca Raton, FL: Taylor & Francis Group.

Fry, Richard, Brian Kennedy, and Cary Funk. 2021. "STEM Jobs See Uneven Progress in Increasing Gender, Racial and Ethnic Diversity." Washington, DC: Pew Research Center.

Fu, Albert S. 2022. "Can Buildings Be Racist? A Critical Sociology of Architecture and the Built Environment." *Sociological Inquiry* 92 (2):442–65.

Fujii, Lee Ann. 2018. *Interviewing in Social Science Research: A Relational Approach*. New York: Routledge.

Fusco, Coco. 1988. "Fantasies of Oppositionality." *Afterimage* 16 (5):6–9.

Gadd, Rebecca. 2023. "'You Can Say That They Were Being Racist': Confronting White Comfort in Anti-Racist Teacher Education." *Whiteness and Education* 8 (2):159–176.

Garland-Thomson, Rosemarie. 2009. *Staring: How We Look*. New York: Oxford University Press.

Garland-Thomson, Rosemarie. 2011. "Misfits: A Feminist Materialist Disability Concept." *Hypatia* 26 (3):591–609.

Geronimus, A. T. 1992. "The Weathering Hypothesis and the Health of African-American Women and Infants: Evidence and Speculations." *Ethnicity & Disease* 2 (3):207.

Gibson, Karen, Darrell Millner, Carmen P. Thompson, and Adrienne Nelson. 2021. "White Supremacy in Oregon History: Mark O. Hatfield Lecture Series Post-Lecture Discussion." *Oregon Historical Quarterly* 122 (1):60–77.

Gilbert, Keon L., and Rashawn Ray. 2015. "Why Police Kill Black Males with Impunity: Applying Public Health Critical Race Praxis (PHCRP) to Address the Determinants of Policing Behaviors and 'Justifiable' Homicides in the USA." *Journal of Urban Health* 93 (S1):122–140.

Gilmore, Ruth Wilson. 2007. *Golden Gulag: Prisons, Surplus, Crisis, and Opposition in Globalizing California*. Berkeley: University of California Press.

Giroux, Henry A. 1981. *Ideology, Culture & the Process of Schooling*. Philadelphia: Temple University Press.

Glenn, Evelyn Nakano. 2015. "Settler Colonialism as Structure: A Framework for Comparative Studies of U.S. Race and Gender Formation." *Sociology of Race and Ethnicity* 1 (1):52–72.

Go, Julian. 2016. "Globalizing Sociology, Turning South. Perspectival Realism and the Southern Standpoint." *Sociologica* 10 (2):1–42.

Go, Julian. 2018. "Postcolonial Possibilities for the Sociology of Race." *Sociology of Race and Ethnicity* 4 (4):439–451.

Go, Julian. 2020. "Race, Empire, and Epistemic Exclusion: Or the Structures of Sociological Thought." *Sociological Theory* 38 (2):79–100.

Godreau, Isar, and Yarimar Bonilla. 2021. "Nonsovereign Racecraft: How Colonialism, Debt, and Disaster Are Transforming Puerto Rican Racial Subjectivities." *American Anthropologist* 123 (3):509–525.

Goffman, Erving. [1959] 1973. *The Presentation of Self in Everyday Life*. Woodstock, NY: Overlook Press.

Gómez, Laura E. 2007. *Manifest Destinies: The Making of the Mexican American Race*. New York: New York University Press.

Gómez, Laura E. 2013. "Introduction." In *Mapping "Race": Critical Approaches to Health Disparities Research*, edited by Laura E. Gómez and Nancy Lopez, 1–22. New Brunswick, NJ: Rutgers University Press.

Gonzales, Roberto G. 2011. "Learning to Be Illegal: Undocumented Youth and Shifting Legal Contexts in the Transition to Adulthood." *American Sociological Review* 76 (4):602–619.

Gonzales, Roberto G. 2016. *Lives in Limbo: Undocumented and Coming of Age in America*. Berkeley: University of California Press.

Goosby, Bridget J., Sarah Malone, Elizabeth A. Richardson, Jacob E. Cheadle, and Deadric T. Williams. 2015. "Perceived Discrimination and Markers of Cardiovascular Risk Among Low-Income African American Youth." *American Journal of Human Biology* 27 (4):546–552.

Goyette, Kimberly A., and Annette Lareau. 2014. *Choosing Homes, Choosing Schools*. New York: Russell Sage Foundation.

Gramsci, Antonio. 1992. *Prison Notebooks*. New York: Columbia University Press.

Grieco, Elizabeth. 2020. "10 Charts About America's Newsrooms." Washington, DC: Pew Research Center.

Griffith, Aisha N., Noelle M. Hurd, and Saida B. Hussain. 2019. " 'I Didn't Come to School for This': A Qualitative Examination of Experiences with Race-Related Stressors and Coping Responses Among Black Students Attending a Predominantly White Institution." *Journal of Adolescent Research* 34 (2):115–139.

Grollman, Eric Anthony. 2018. "Sexual Orientation Differences in Whites' Racial Attitudes." *Sociological Forum* 33 (1):186–210.

Gusinow, Sander. 2022. "Oregon-China Trade Grows, But Leaders Fear 'Decoupling.'" Oregon Business, April 19.

Hagerman, Margaret A. 2018. *White Kids: Growing Up with Privilege in a Racially Divided America*. New York: New York University Press.

Han, C. Winter. 2021. *Racial Erotics: Gay Men of Color, Sexual Racism, and the Politics of Desire*. Seattle: University of Washington Press.

Hancock, Ange-Marie. 2005. "W.E.B. Du Bois: Intellectual Forefather of Intersectionality?" *Souls* 7 (3–4):74–84.

Haney López, Ian. 1996. *White by Law: The Legal Construction of Race*. New York: New York University Press.

Hartigan Jr., John. 1999. *Racial Situations: Class Predicaments of Whiteness in Detroit*. Princeton, NJ: Princeton University Press.

Hauge, Daniel. 2019. "The Power of a Comfortable White Body: Race and Habitual Emotion." *Religious Education* 114 (3):227–238.

HECC. 2018. University Evaluation: University of Oregon. Higher Education Coordinating Commission, Salem.

HECC. 2022. Oregon Public University Student Head Count by Race/Ethnicity. Salem, OR: Higher Education Coordinating Commission (HECC) Office of Research and Data.

Helms, Janet E., and Ethan H. Mereish. 2013. "How Racial-Group Comparisons Create Misinformation in Depression Research: Using Racial Identity Theory to Conceptualize Health Disparities." In *Mapping "Race": Critical Approaches to Health Disparities Research*, edited by Laura E. Gómez and Nancy López, 146–162. New Brunswick, NJ: Rutgers University Press.

Hine, Darlene Clark. 1993. "'In the Kingdom of Culture': Black Women and the Intersection of Race, Gender, and Class." In *Lure and Loathing: Essays on Race, Identity, and the Ambivalence of Assimilation*, edited by Gerald Ed Early, 337–351. New York: Penguin Books.

Hochschild, Arlie Russell. 1979. "Emotion Work, Feeling Rules, and Social Structure." *American Journal of Sociology* 85 (3):551–575.

Hondagneu-Sotelo, Pierrette. 1997. "The History of Mexican Undocumented Settlement in the United States." In *Challenging Fronteras: Structuring Latina and Latino Lives in the U.S.*, edited by Mary Romero, Vilma Ortiz, and Pierrette Hondagneu-Sotelo, 115–134. New York: Taylor & Francis.

Hondagneu-Sotelo, Pierrette, and Manuel Pastor. 2021. *South Central Dreams: Finding Home and Building Community in South L.A.* New York: New York University Press.

hooks, bell. 2000. *Feminist Theory: From Margin to Center*. 2nd ed. New York: South End Press.

Horowitz, Juliana Menasce. 2019. "Americans See Advantages and Challenges in Country's Growing Racial and Ethnic Diversity." Washington, DC: Pew Research Center.

Horowitz, Juliana Menasce, Anna Brown, and Kiana Cox. 2019. "Race in America 2019." Washington, DC: Pew Research Center.

HoSang, Daniel Martinez, and Natalia Molina. 2019. "Introduction: Toward a Relational Consciousness of Race." In *Relational Formations of Race: Theory, Method, and Practice*, edited by Natalia Molina, Daniel Martinez HoSang, and Ramón A. Gutiérrez, 1–18. Oakland: University of California Press.

Hughey, Matthew W. 2012. *White Bound: Nationalists, Antiracists, and the Shared Meanings of Race*. Stanford, CA: Stanford University Press.

Hunter, Marcus Anthony, Mary Pattillo, Zandria F. Robinson, and Keeanga-Yamahtta Taylor. 2016. "Black Placemaking: Celebration, Play, and Poetry." *Theory, Culture & Society* 33 (7–8):31–56.

Hunter, Margaret. 2002. "'If You're Light You're Alright': Light Skin Color as Social Capital for Women of Color." *Gender & Society* 16 (2):175–193.

Huntington, Samuel P. 2004. *Who Are We?* New York: Simon & Schuster.

Ignatiev, Noel. 1995. *How the Irish Became White*. New York: Routledge.

Imarisha, Walidah. 2020, March. "How Oregon's Racist History Can Sharpen Our Sense of Justice Right Now." *Portland Monthly*, online.

Islam, Inaash. 2020. "Muslim American Double Consciousness." *Du Bois Review* 17 (2):429–448.

Itzigsohn, José, and Karida Brown. 2015. "Sociology and the Theory of Double Consciousness." *Du Bois Review* 12 (02):231–248.

Itzigsohn, José, and Karida L. Brown. 2020. *The Sociology of W. E. B. Du Bois: Racialized Modernity and the Global Color Line*. New York: New York University Press.

Jackman, Mary R., and Marie Crane. 1986. "'Some of My Best Friends Are Black . . .': Interracial Friendship and Whites' Racial Attitudes." *Public Opinion Quarterly* 50 (4):459–486.

Jacobs, Margaret D. 2009. *White Mother to a Dark Race: Settler Colonialism, Maternalism, and the Removal of Indigenous Children in the American West and Australia, 1880–1940*. Lincoln: University of Nebraska Press.

Jacobs, Michelle R. 2023. *Indigenous Memory, Urban Reality: Stories of American Indian Relocation and Reclamation*. New York: New York University Press.

Jacobson, Matthew Frye 1998. *Whiteness of a Different Color: European Immigrants and the Alchemy of Race*. Boston: Harvard University Press.

Jetté, Melinda Marie. 2015. *At the Hearth of the Crossed Races: A French-Indian Community in Nineteenth-Century Oregon, 1812–1859*. Corvallis: Oregon State University Press.

Jiménez, Tomás R. 2010. *Replenished Ethnicity: Mexican Americans, Immigration, and Identity*. Berkeley: University of California Press.

Jiménez, Tomás R., Corey D. Fields, and Ariela Schachter. 2015. "How Ethnoraciality Matters: Looking inside Ethnoracial 'Groups.'" *Social Currents* 2 (2):107–115.

Jiménez, Tomás R., and Adam L. Horowitz. 2013. "When White Is Just Alright: How Immigrants Redefine Achievement and Reconfigure the Ethnoracial Hierarchy." *American Sociological Review* 78 (5):849–871.

Jiménez, Tomás, Deborah J. Schildkraut, Yuen J. Huo, and John F. Dovidio. 2021. *States of Belonging: Immigration Policies, Attitudes, and Inclusion*. New York: Russell Sage Foundation.

Jones, Bradford S., Jeffrey W. Sherman, Natalie E. Rojas, Adrienne Hosek, David L. Vannette, Rene R. Rocha, Omar García-Ponce, Maria Pantoja, and Jesus Manuel García-Amador. 2021. "Trump-Induced Anxiety Among Latina/os." *Group Processes & Intergroup Relations* 24 (1):68–87.

Jones, Jennifer A. 2022. "'They Are There with Us': Theorizing Racial Status and Intergroup Relations." *American Journal of Sociology* 128 (2):411–461.

Joseph, Ameil J., Julia Janes, Harjeet Badwall, and Shana Almeida. 2020. "Preserving White Comfort and Safety: The Politics of Race Erasure in Academe." *Social Identities* 26 (2):166–185.

Kahn, Kimberly Barsamian, Phillip Atiba Goff, J. Katherine Lee, and Diane Motamed. 2016. "Protecting Whiteness: White Phenotypic Racial Stereotypicality Reduces Police Use of Force." *Social Psychological & Personality Science* 7 (5):403–411.

Karina, L. Walters, M. Simoni Jane, and Evans-Campbell Teresa. 2002. "Substance Use Among American Indians and Alaska Natives: Incorporating Culture in an 'Indigenist' Stress-Coping Paradigm." *Public Health Reports (1974)* 117 (Suppl 1):S104–S117.

Kibria, Nazli. 1999. "College and Notions of 'Asian American.'" *Amerasian Journal* 25 (1):29–51.

Kim, Claire. 1999. "The Racial Triangulation of Asian Americans." *Politics & Society* 27 (1):105–138.

Kim, Janine Young. 2016. "Racial Emotions and the Feeling of Equality." *University of Colorado Law Review* 87:437–500.

King, C. Richard, and Charles Fruehling Springwood, eds. 2001. *Team Spirits: The Native American Mascots Controversy*. Lincoln: University of Nebraska Press.

King, Katrina Quisumbing. 2019. "Recentering U.S. Empire: A Structural Perspective on the Color Line." *Sociology of Race and Ethnicity* 5 (1):11–25.

King, Wayne. 1986. "Neo-Nazis' Dream of a Racist Territory in Pacific Northwest Refuses to Die." *New York Times*, July 5, p. 10.

Krakoff, Sarah. 2012. "Inextricably Political: Race, Membership, and Tribal Sovereignty." *Washington Law Review* 87 (4):1041.

Krieger, Nancy. 2012. "Methods for the Scientific Study of Discrimination and Health: An Ecosocial Approach." *American Journal of Public Health* 102 (5):936–944.

Krogstad, Jens Manuel. 2015. "Hawaii Is Home to the Nation's Largest Share of Multiracial Americans." Washington, DC: Pew Research Center.

Kruk, Mary, and Jes L. Matsick. 2021. "A Taxonomy of Identity Safety Cues Based on Gender and Race: From a Promising Past to an Intersectional and Translational Future." *Translational Issues in Psychological Science* 7 (4):487–510.

Lacayo, Celia Olivia. 2017. "Perpetual Inferiority: Whites' Racial Ideology toward Latinos." *Sociology of Race and Ethnicity* 3 (4):566–579.

LaFleur, Jennifer. 2021. "The Race That Space Makes: The Power of Place in the Colonial Formation of Social Categorizations." *Sociology of Race & Ethnicity* 7 (4):512–526.

Lamont, Michèle, and Nissim Mizrachi. 2012. "Ordinary People Doing Extraordinary Things: Responses to Stigmatization in Comparative Perspective." *Ethnic and Racial Studies* 35 (3):365–381.

Lanham, David. 2020. "A Public Letter to the Associated Press: Listen to the Nation and Capitalize Black." Brookings Institution.

Latham, Gary P., and Edwin A. Locke. 2013. "Goal Setting Theory, 1990." In *New Developments in Goal Setting and Task Performance*, edited by Edwin A. Locke and Gary P. Latham, 3–15. New York: Routledge.

Lee, Jennifer, and Frank D. Bean. 2010. *The Diversity Paradox: Immigration and the Color Line in Twenty-First Century America*. New York: Russell Sage Foundation.

Lee, Jennifer, and Min Zhou. 2015. *The Asian American Achievement Paradox*. New York: Russell Sage Foundation.

Leguizamo, John. 2016. "Too Bad You're Latin." *New York Times*, October 21, Op-Ed.

Leonardo, Zeus. 2004. "The Color of Supremacy: Beyond the Discourse of 'White Privilege.'" *Educational Philosophy and Theory* 36 (2):137–152.

Leonardo, Zeus, and Ronald K. Porter. 2010. "Pedagogy of Fear: Toward a Fanonian Theory of 'Safety' in Race Dialogue." *Race, Ethnicity and Education* 13 (2):139–157.

Lewis, Amanda E. 2004. "'What Group?' Studying Whites and Whiteness in the Era of 'Color-Blindness.'" *Sociological Theory* 22 (4):623–646.

Lewis, D. 2018. "Coast Indian Reservation." *The Oregon Encyclopedia*: Oregon Historical Society.

Link, Bruce G., and Jo Phelan. 1995. "Social Conditions As Fundamental Causes of
Disease." *Journal of Health and Social Behavior* 35:80–94.

Lipsitz, George. 1990. *Time Passages: Collective Memory and American Popular Culture,
American Culture*. Minneapolis: University of Minnesota Press.

Lipsitz, George. 2007. "The Racialization of Space and the Spatialization of Race: Theorizing the Hidden Architecture of Landscape." *Landscape Journal* 26 (1):10–23.

Lipsitz, George. 2011. *How Racism Takes Place*. Philadelphia: Temple University Press.

Littlejohn, Krystale E. 2021. *Just Get On the Pill*. Berkeley: University of California Press.

Loewen, James W. 2005. *Sundown Towns: A Hidden Dimension of American Racism*.
New York: New Press.

Lomawaima, K. Tsianina. 1995. *They Called It Prairie Light: The Story of Chilocco
Indian School*. Lincoln: University of Nebraska Press.

Lomawaima, K. Tsianina. 2006. *To Remain an Indian: Lessons in Democracy from a
Century of Native American Education*. New York: Teachers College Press.

Lombardo, Paul A., ed. 2011. *A Century of Eugenics in America: From the Indiana Experiment to the Human Genome Era*. Bloomington: Indiana University Press.

Lopez, Mark Hugo, Jeffrey Passel, and Molly Rohal. 2015. "Modern Immigration Wave
Brings 59 Million to U.S., Driving Population Growth and Change through 2065:
Views of Immigration's Impact on U.S. Society Mixed." Washington, DC: Pew
Research Center.

López, Nancy, Edward Vargas, Melina Juarez, Lisa Cacari-Stone, and Sonia Bettez.
2018. "What's Your 'Street Race'? Leveraging Multidimensional Measures of Race
and Intersectionality for Examining Physical and Mental Health Status among
Latinxs." *Sociology of Race and Ethnicity* 4 (1):49–66.

Lorde, Audre. 1984. *Sister Outsider*. Trumansburg, NY: Crossing Press.

Louie, Vivian S. 2012. *Keeping the Immigrant Bargain: The Costs and Rewards of Success
in America*. New York: Russell Sage Foundation.

Louie, Vivian, and Anahí Viladrich. 2021. "'Divide, Divert, & Conquer': Deconstruct-
ing the Presidential Framing of White Supremacy in the COVID-19 Era." *Social
Sciences* 10 (8):280.

Love, Bettina L. 2019. *We Want to Do More than Survive: Abolitionist Teaching and the
Pursuit of Educational Freedom*. Boston: Beacon Press.

Lugones, Maria. 1992. "On Borderlands/La Frontera: An Interpretive Essay." *Hypatia* 7
(4):31–37.

Lynne, Alyssa. 2021. "Paired Double Consciousness: A Du Boisian Approach to Gender
and Transnational Double Consciousness in Thai Kathoey Self-Formation." *Social
Problems* 68 (2):250.

Maghbouleh, Neda. 2017. *The Limits of Whiteness: Iranian Americans and the Everyday
Politics of Race*. Stanford, CA: Stanford University Press.

Maldonado, Marta Maria. 2017. "Not Just Laborers: Latina/o Claims of Belonging in
the U.S. Heartland." In *The Latina/o Midwest Reader*, edited by Omar Valerio-

Jimenez and Santiago Vaquera-Vasquez, 102–119. Champaign: University of Illinois Press.

Mannheim, Karl. 1936. *Ideology and Utopia: An Introduction to the Sociology of Knowledge*. Translated by Louis Wirth and Edward Shils. New York: Harcourt Brace Jovanovich.

Marrow, Helen B., Dina G. Okamoto, Melissa J. García, Muna Adem, and Linda R. Tropp. 2022. "Skin Tone and Mexicans' Perceptions of Discrimination in New Immigrant Destinations." *Social Psychology Quarterly* 85 (4):374–385.

Martinez, Theresa A. 2002. "The Double-Consciousness of Du Bois & The 'Mestiza Consciousness' of Anzaldúa." *Race, Gender & Class* 9 (4):158–176.

Masuoka, Natalie, and Jane Junn. 2013. *The Politics of Belonging: Race, Public Opinion, and Immigration*. Chicago: University of Chicago Press.

Matias, Cheryl E. 2016. *Feeling White: Whiteness, Emotionality, and Education*. Boston: Sense Publishers.

Mayorga-Gallo, Sarah. 2014. *Behind the White Picket Fence: Power and Privilege in a Multiethnic Neighborhood*. Durham: University of North Carolina Press.

McCann, James A., and Michael Jones-Correa. 2020. *Holding Fast: Resilience and Civic Engagement Among Latino Immigrants*. New York: Russell Sage Foundation.

McDermott, Monica. 2015. "Color-Blind and Color-Visible Identity Among American Whites." *American Behavioral Scientist* 59 (11):1452–1473.

McDermott, Monica. 2020. *Whiteness in America*. Medford, MA: Polity Press.

McDermott, Monica, and Annie Ferguson. 2022. "Sociology of Whiteness." *Annual Review of Sociology* 48 (1):257–276.

McGregor, Davianna Pomaika'i. 2004a. "Engaging Hawaiians in the Expansion of the U.S. Empire." *Journal of Asian American Studies* 7 (3):209–222, 289.

McGregor, Davianna Pomaika'i. 2004b. "Weaving Together Strands of Pacific Islander, Asian, and American Interactions." *Journal of Asian American Studies* 7 (3):vii–xii.

McKay, Dwanna L., Kirsten Vinyeta, and Kari Marie Norgaard. 2020. "Theorizing Race and Settler Colonialism Within U.S. Sociology." *Sociology Compass* 14 (9):1–17.

McLagan, Elizabeth. 2007. "A Very Prejudiced State: Discrimination in Oregon from 1900–1940." In *Seeing Color: Indigenous Peoples and Racialized Ethnic Minorities in Oregon*, edited by Jun Xing, 78–92. Lanham, MD: University Press of America.

McMillan, David W., and David M. Chavis. 1986. "Sense of Community: A Definition and Theory." *Journal of Community Psychology* 14 (1):6–23.

Meer, Nasar. 2018. "'Race' and 'Post-Colonialism': Should One Come Before the Other?" *Ethnic and Racial Studies* 41 (6):1163–1181.

Mejía, Yoshira D. Macías. 2023. "Beyond Racial Linked Fate: Inter-Minority Political Solidarity and Political Participation." *Political Behavior* 9 (February):1–23.

Menjívar, Cecilia. 2006. "Liminal Legality: Salvadoran and Guatemalan Immigrants' Lives in the United States." *American Journal of Sociology* 111 (4):999–1037.

Menjívar, Cecilia, and Leisy J. Abrego. 2012. "Legal Violence: Immigration Law and the Lives of Central American Immigrants." *American Journal of Sociology* 117 (5):1380–1421.

Merskin, Debra. 2007. "Three Faces of Eva: Perpetuation of the Hot-Latina Stereotype in Desperate Housewives." *Howard Journal of Communications* 18 (2):133–151.

Messner, Michael A. 1992. *Power at Play: Sports and the Problem of Masculinity*. Boston: Beacon Press.

Mignolo, Walter, and Catherine E. Walsh. 2018. *On Decoloniality: Concepts, Analytics, Praxis*. Durham, NC: Duke University Press.

Molina, Natalia. 2014. *How Race Is Made in America: Immigration, Citizenship, and the Historical Power of Racial Scripts*. Berkeley: University of California Press.

Molina, Natalia, Daniel Martinez HoSang, and Ramón A. Gutiérrez, eds. 2019. *Relational Formations of Race: Theory, Method, and Practice*. Berkeley: University of California Press.

Monk, Ellis P. 2015. "The Cost of Color: Skin Color, Discrimination, and Health among African-Americans." *American Journal of Sociology* 121 (2):396–444.

Monteiro, Anthony. 2007. "Race and Empire: W.E.B. Du Bois and the US State." *Black Scholar* 37 (2):35–52.

Montejano, David. 1987. *Anglos and Mexicans in the Making of Texas, 1836–1986*. Austin: University of Texas Press.

Moore, Mignon R. 2017. "Women of Color in the Academy: Navigating Multiple Intersections and Multiple Hierarchies." *Social Problems* 64 (2):200–205.

Moreton-Robinson, Aileen. 2015. *The White Possessive: Property, Power, and Indigenous Sovereignty*. Minnesota: University of Minnesota Press.

Morris, Aldon D. 2015. *The Scholar Denied: W.E.B. Du Bois and the Birth of Modern Sociology*. Berkeley: University of California Press.

Morrison, Toni. 2017. *The Origin of Others*. Cambridge, MA: Harvard University Press.

Motel, Seth, and Eileen Patten. 2012. "The 10 Largest Hispanic Origin Groups: Characteristics, Rankings, Top Counties." Washington, DC: Pew Research Center.

Mueller, Jennifer C. 2017. "Producing Colorblindness: Everyday Mechanisms of White Ignorance." *Social Problems* 64 (2):219–238.

Murguia, Edward, and Edward Telles. 1996. "Phenotype and Schooling among Mexican Americans." *Sociology of Education* 69 (October):276–289.

Nakano, Dana Y. 2023. *Japanese Americans and the Racial Uniform*. New York: New York University Press.

Nash, Jennifer C. 2019. *Black Feminism Reimagined: After Intersectionality*. Durham, NC: Duke University Press.

Neely, Brooke, and Michelle Samura. 2011. "Social Geographies of Race: Connecting Race and Space." *Ethnic and Racial Studies* 34 (11):1933–1952.

Nemoto, Kumiko. 2009. *Racing Romance: Love, Power, and Desire Among Asian American/White Couples*. New Brunswick, NJ: Rutgers University Press.

Newman, Benjamin, Jennifer Merolla, and Sono Shah. 2021. "The Trump Effect: An Experimental Investigation of the Emboldening Effect of Racially Inflammatory Elite Communication." *British Journal of Political Science* 51 (3):1138–1159.

Ngai, Mae M. 2004. *Impossible Subjects: Illegal Aliens and the Making of Modern America*. Princeton, NJ: Princeton University Press.

Noe-Bustamante, Luis, Lauren Mora, and Mark Hugo Lopez. 2020. "About One-in-Four U.S. Hispanics Have Heard of Latinx, but Just 3% Use It." Washington, DC: Pew Research Center.

Norgaard, Kari Marie. 2011. *Living in Denial: Climate Change, Emotions, and Everyday Life*. Cambridge, MA: MIT Press.

Norgaard, Kari Marie. 2019. *Salmon & Acorns Feed Our People: Colonialism, Nature & Social Action*. New Brunswick, NJ: Rutgers University Press.

Norgaard, Kari Marie, and Ron Reed. 2017. "Emotional Impacts of Environmental Decline: What Can Native Cosmologies Teach Sociology About Emotions and Environmental Justice?" *Theory and Society* 46 (6):463–495.

Norgaard, Kari Marie, Ron Reed, and J. M. Bacon. 2017. "How Environmental Decline Restructures Indigenous Gender Practices: What Happens to Karuk Masculinity When There Are No Fish?" *Sociology of Race and Ethnicity* 4 (1):98–113.

Obasogie, Osagie. 2014. *Blinded by Sight: Seeing Race Through the Eyes of the Blind*. Stanford, CA: Stanford University Press.

O'Brien, Jean M. 2010. *Firsting and Lasting: Writing Indians Out of Existence in New England*. Minneapolis: University of Minnesota Press.

Ocampo, Anthony Christian. 2015. *The Latinos of Asia: How Filipinos Break the Rules of Race*. Stanford, CA: Stanford University Press.

Ocampo, Anthony Christian. 2022. *Brown and Gay in LA: The Lives of Immigrant Sons*. New York: New York University Press.

Ochoa, Gilda L. 2013. *Academic Profiling: Latinos, Asian Americans, and the Achievement Gap*. Minneapolis: University of Minnesota Press.

Ogbu, John U. 1994. "From Cultural Differences to Differences in Cultural Frame of Reference." In *Cross-Cultural Roots of Minority Child Development*, edited by Patricia and Rodney Cocking Greenfield. Hillsdale, NJ: Lawrence Erlbaum Associates.

Oh, Byeongdon, and ChangHwan Kim. 2020. "Broken Promise of College? New Educational Sorting Mechanisms for Intergenerational Association in the 21st Century." *Social Science Research* 86:102375.

Okamoto, Dina G., and G. Cristina Mora. 2014. "Panethnicity." *Annual Review of Sociology* 40 (1):219–239.

Oliver, Melvin L., and Thomas M. Shapiro. 1995. *Black Wealth/White Wealth: A New Perspective on Racial Inequality*. New York: Routledge.

Omi, Michael, and Howard Winant. 1994. *Racial Formation in the United States: From the 1960s to the 1990s*. 2nd ed. New York: Routledge.

Omi, Michael, and Howard Winant. 2015. *Racial Formation in the United States: From the 1960s to the 1990s*. 3rd ed. New York: Routledge.

Ortiz, Vilma, and Edward Telles. 2012. "Racial Identity and Racial Treatment of Mexican Americans." *Race and Social Problems* 4 (1):41–56.

Ostrove, Joan M., and Susan M. Long. 2007. "Social Class and Belonging: Implications for College Adjustment." *Review of Higher Education* 30 (4):363–389.

Overbye, Dennis. 2018. "Hawaiian Supreme Court Approves Giant Telescope on Mauna Kea." *New York Times*, October 30.

Padilla, Yajaira M. 2022. *From Threatening Guerrillas to Forever Illegals: US Central Americans and the Cultural Politics of Non-Belonging*. Austin: University of Texas Press.

Pager, Devah. 2007. *Marked: Race, Crime, and Finding Work in an Era of Mass Incarceration*. Chicago: University of Chicago Press.

Painter, Nell Irvin. 2020. "Why 'White' Should Be Capitalized, Too." *Washington Post*, July 22.

Pan, Yung-Yi Diana. 2017. *Incidental Racialization: Performative Assimilation in Law School*. Philadelphia: Temple University Press.

Pan, Yung-Yi Diana, and Daisy Verduzco Reyes. 2021. "The Norm among the Exceptional? Experiences of Latino Students in Elite Institutions." *Sociological Inquiry* 91 (1):207–230.

Pascoe, Peggy. 2007. "'A Mistake to Simmer the Question Down to Black and White': The History of Oregon's Miscegenation Law." In *Seeing Color: Indigenous Peoples and Racialized Ethnic Minorities in Oregon*, edited by Jun Xing, 27–43. Lanham, MD: University Press of America.

Pattillo-McCoy, Mary. 1999. *Black Picket Fences: Privilege and Peril among the Black Middle Class*. Chicago: University of Chicago Press.

Perry, Pamela. 2002. *Shades of White: White Kids and Racial Identities in High School*. Durham, NC: Duke University Press.

Perry, Samuel L. 2013. "Racial Composition of Social Settings, Interracial Friendship, and Whites' Attitudes Toward Interracial Marriage." *Social Science Journal* 50 (1):13–22.

Petrosky, Emiko, Laura M. Mercer Kollar, Megan C. Kearns, Sharon G. Smith, Carter J. Betz, Katherine A. Fowler, and Delight E. Satter. 2021. "Homicides of American Indians/Alaska Natives—National Violent Death Reporting System, United States, 2003–2018." Vol. 70. *Surveillance Summaries*. Atlanta, GA: Center for Disease Control.

Phelan, Jo C., and Bruce G. Link. 2015. "Is Racism a Fundamental Cause of Inequalities in Health?" *Annual Review of Sociology* 41 (1):311–330.

Phinney, Jean S. 1997. "Ethnic and American Identity as Predictors of Self-Esteem among African American, Latino, and White Adolescents." *Journal of Youth and Adolescence* 26 (2):165–185.

powell, john a. 2005. "Dreaming of a Self Beyond Whiteness and Isolation." *Washington University Journal of Law & Policy* 18:13–35.

Pulido, Laura. 2018. "Geographies of Race and Ethnicity III." *Progress in Human Geography* 42 (2):309–318.

Pyke, Karen D. 2010. "What Is Internalized Racial Oppression and Why Don't We Study It? Acknowledging Racism's Hidden Injuries." *Sociological Perspectives* 53 (4):551–572.

Qureshi, Bilal. 2013. From Wrong to Right: A U.S. Apology for Japanese Internment. In *Codeswitch*, edited by Bilal Qureshi: NPR.

Ramos, José G. Perez, Adriana Garriga-López, and Carlos E. Rodríguez-Díaz. 2022. "How Is Colonialism a Sociostructural Determinant of Health in Puerto Rico?" *AMA Journal of Ethics* 24 (4):E305–312.

Rawls, Anne Warfield, and Waverly Duck. 2020. *Tacit Racism*. Chicago: University of Chicago Press.

Ray, Ranita. 2023. "Race-Conscious Racism: Alibis for Racial Harm in the Classroom." *Social Problems* 70 (3):682–697.

Ray, Victor. 2019. "A Theory of Racialized Organizations." *American Sociological Review* 84 (1):26–53.

Ray, Victor. 2022. *On Critical Race Theory: Why It Matters & Why You Should Care*. New York: Random House.

Reskin, Barbara. 2012. "The Race Discrimination System." *Annual Review of Sociology* 38 (1):17–35.

Reyes, Daisy Verduzco. 2018. *Learning to Be Latino: How Colleges Shape Identity Politics*. New Brunswick, NJ: Rutgers University Press.

Rhodes, Dean. 2017. "Board of Education Oks Grand Ronde-Molalla River Mascot Agreement." May 31. Smoke Signals. www.smokesignals.org.

Rios, Victor M. 2011. *Punished: Policing the Lives of Black and Latino Boys*. New York: New York University Press.

Rios, Victor M. 2017. *Human Targets: Schools, Police, and the Criminalization of Latino Youth*. Chicago: University of Chicago Press.

Robbins, William G. 2020. "Oregon Donation Land Act." *The Oregon Encyclopedia*: Oregon Historical Society.

Roberts, Dorothy E., and Oliver Rollins. 2020. "Why Sociology Matters to Race and Biosocial Science." *Annual Review of Sociology* 46 (1):195–214.

Robertson, Dwanna L. 2015. "Invisibility in the Color-Blind Era." *American Indian Quarterly* 39 (2):113–153.

Rodríguez-Muñiz, Michael. 2021. *Figures of the Future: Latino Civil Rights and the Politics of Demographic Change*. Princeton, NJ: Princeton University Press.

Rodriguez, Cassaundra. 2023. *Contested Americans: Mixed-Status Families in Anti-Immigrant Times*. New York: New York University Press.

Roediger, David R. 1999. *The Wages of Whiteness: Race and the Making of the American Working Class*. New York: Verso.

Roth, Wendy D. 2012. *Race Migrations: Latinos and the Cultural Transformation of Race*. Stanford, CA: Stanford University Press.

Roth, Wendy D. 2016. "The Multiple Dimensions of Race." *Ethnic and Racial Studies* 39:1310–1338.

Sabzalian, Leilani. 2019. *Indigenous Children's Survivance in Public Schools*. New York: Routledge.

Sadeghi, McKenzie. 2021. "Fact Check: Viral Images Compare Handling of Black Lives Matter Protests and Capitol Riot." *USA TODAY*, January 7.

Said, Edward W. [1978] 1994. *Orientalism*. 25th anniversary edition. New York: Vintage.

Sanchez, Gabriel R., Luis Ricardo Fraga, and Ricardo Ramírez, eds. 2020. *Latinos and the 2016 Election: Latino Resistance and the Election of Donald Trump*. East Lansing: Michigan State University Press.

Sanchez, Gabriel R., and Barbara Gomez-Aguinaga. 2017. "Latino Rejection of the Trump Campaign: How Trump's Racialized Rhetoric Mobilized the Latino Electorate as Never Before." *Aztlán* 42 (2):165–181.

Sassen, Saskia. 1989. "America's Immigration 'Problem.'" *World Policy Journal* 6 (4):811–832.

Saunders, Heather, and Nirmita Panchal. August 4, 2023. "A Look at the Latest Suicide Data and Change over the Last Decade." San Francisco: KFF. www.kff.org.

Schachter, Ariela, René D. Flores, and Neda Maghbouleh. 2021. "Ancestry, Color, or Culture? How Whites Racially Classify Others in the U.S." *American Journal of Sociology* 126 (5):1220–1263.

Schildkraut, Deborah J. 2014. "Boundaries of American Identity: Evolving Understandings of 'Us.'" *Annual Review of Political Science* 17 (1):441–460.

Schlesinger, Arthur M., Jr. 1998. *The Disuniting of America*. Revised ed. New York: Norton.

Scott, Jennifer. 2023. "La Lucha: Framing the Struggle for Survival, Double Consciousness and the Economy of Identity for Undocumented Latina/os." *Journal of Ethnic and Migration Studies* 49 (13):3492–3510.

Selod, Saher. 2018. *Forever Suspect: Racialized Surveillance of Muslim Americans in the War on Terror*. New Brunswick, NJ: Rutgers University Press.

Sewell, Abigail A. 2016. "The Racism-Race Reification Process: A Mesolevel Political Economic Framework for Understanding Racial Health Disparities." *Sociology of Race and Ethnicity* 2 (4):402–432.

Sewell, Alyasah Ali, Justin M. Feldman, Rashawn Ray, Keon L. Gilbert, Kevin A. Jefferson, and Hedwig Lee. 2020. "Illness Spillovers of Lethal Police Violence: The Significance of Gendered Marginalization." *Ethnic and Racial Studies* 44 (7):1089–1114.

Shear, Sarah B., Ryan T. Knowles, Gregory J. Soden, and Antonio J. Castro. 2015. "Manifesting Destiny: Re/presentations of Indigenous Peoples in K–12 U.S. History Standards." *Theory & Research in Social Education* 43 (1):68–101.

Shiao, Jiannbin Lee, and Mia H. Tuan. 2008. "Korean Adoptees and the Social Context of Ethnic Exploration." *American Journal of Sociology* 113 (4):1023–1066.

Shute, Megan. 2022. "The History of This Sacred Hawaiian Valley Is Terribly Heartbreaking." www.onlyinyourstate.com.

Silvestrini, Molly. 2020. " 'It's not something I can shake': The Effect of Racial Stereotypes, Beauty Standards, and Sexual Racism on Interracial Attraction." *Sexuality & Culture* 24 (1):305–325.

Simonson, Amy. 2022. "Florida Bill to Shield People from Feeling 'Discomfort' over Historic Actions by Their Race, Nationality or Gender Approved by Senate Committee." CNN, January 20.

Simpson, Brent, and Robb Willer. 2015. "Beyond Altruism: Sociological Foundations of Cooperation and Prosocial Behavior." *Annual Review of Sociology* 41 (1):43–63.

Sims, Jennifer Patrice, Whitney Laster Pirtle, and Iris Johnson-Arnold. 2020. "Doing Hair, Doing Race: The Influence of Hairstyle on Racial Perception Across the US." *Ethnic and Racial Studies* 43 (12):2099–2119.

Smith, Andrea. 2016. "Heteropatriarchy and the Three Pillars of White Supremacy: Rethinking Women of Color Organizing." In *Color of Violence*. Chapel Hill, NC: Duke University Press.

Smith, Candis Watts, and Sarah Mayorga-Gallo. 2017. "The New Principle-Policy Gap: How Diversity Ideology Subverts Diversity Initiatives." *Sociological Perspectives* 60 (5):889–911.

Smith, Linda Tuhiwai. 2012. *Decolonizing Methodologies: Research and Indigenous Peoples*. 2nd ed. New York: Zed Books.

Smith, Stacey L. 2014. "Oregon's Civil War: The Troubled Legacy of Emancipation in the Pacific Northwest." *Oregon Historical Quarterly* 115 (2):154–173.

Smith, William, Man Hung, and Jeremy Franklin. 2011. "Racial Battle Fatigue and the MisEducation of Black Men: Racial Microaggressions, Societal Problems, and Environmental Stress." *Journal of Negro Education* 80 (1):63–82.

Sparks, Lillian. 2015. "Preserving Native Languages: No Time to Waste." Administration for Native Americans. www.acf.hhs.gov.

Spencer, Steven J., Claude M. Steele, and Diane M. Quinn. 1999. "Stereotype Threat and Women's Math Performance." *Journal of Experimental Social Psychology* 35 (1):4–28.

Starr, Paul. 2023. "The Re-Emergence of 'People of Color.'" *Du Bois Review* 20 (1):1–20.

Steele, Claude M., and Joshua Aronson. 1995. "Stereotype Threat and the Intellectual Test Performance of African Americans." *Journal of Personality and Social Psychology* 69 (5):797–811.

Steinman, Erich. 2011. "Sovereigns and Citizens? The Contested Status of American Indian Tribal Nations and Their Members." *Citizenship Studies* 15 (1):57–74.

Steinman, Erich W. 2016. "Decolonization Not Inclusion." *Sociology of Race and Ethnicity* 2 (2):219–236.

Steinman, Erich W. 2022. "Settler Colonialism and Sociological Knowledge: Insights and Directions Forward." *Theory and Society* 51 (1):145–176.

Steinmetz, Kevin F., Brian P. Schaefer, and Howard Henderson. 2017. "Wicked Overseers: American Policing and Colonialism." *Sociology of Race and Ethnicity* 3 (1):68–81.

Stern, Alexandra Minna. 2005. *Eugenic Nation: Faults and Frontiers on Better Breeding in Modern America*. Berkeley: University of California Press.

Suárez-Orozco, Carola, Hirokazu Yoshikawa, Robert T. Teranishi, and Marcelo Suárez-Orozco. 2011. "Growing Up in the Shadows: The Developmental Implications of Unauthorized Status." *Harvard Educational Review* 81 (3):438–472.

Sue, Christina A. 2023. "Intensive Naming: Concerted Cultivation and Flexible Ethnicity among U.S. Middle-Class Mexican-Origin Parents." *Social Problems* (iFirst):1–15.

Sue, Christina, and Edward Telles. 2007. "Assimilation and Gender in Naming." *American Journal of Sociology* 112 (5):1383–1415.

Suinn, Richard M. 2001. "The Terrible Twos—Anger and Anxiety: Hazardous to Your Health." *American Psychologist* 56 (1):27–36.

Sullivan, Kate, and Jennifer Agiesta. 2020. "Biden's Popular Vote Margin over Trump Tops 7 Million." CNN, December 4.

Tajfel, Henri, and J. C. Turner. 1986. "The Social Identity Theory of Intergroup Behaviour." In *Psychology of Intergroup Relations*, edited by S. Worchel and W. G. Austin, 7–24. Chicago: Nelson-Hall.

Tatum, Beverly Daniel. 1997. *"Why Are All the Black Kids Sitting Together in the Cafeteria?": A Psychologist Explains the Development of Racial Identity*. New York: Basic Books.

Teaiwa, Katerina Martina. 2014. "Reframing Oceania: Lessons from Pacific Studies." In *Framing the Global: Entry Points for Research*, edited by Hilary E. Kahn. Bloomington: Indiana University Press.

Telles, Edward E., and Edward Murguia. 1990. "Phenotypic Discrimination and Income Differences among Mexican Americans." *Social Science Quarterly* 71 (4):682–708.

Telles, Edward, and Vilma Ortiz. 2008. *Generations of Exclusion: Mexican Americans, Assimilation, and Race*. New York: Russell Sage Foundation.

Telles, Edward, and Christina A. Sue. 2019. *Durable Ethnicity: Mexican Americans and the Ethnic Core*. New York: Oxford University Press.

Tharps, Lori L. 2014. "The Case for Black With a Capital B." *New York Times*, November 18, Opinion.

Theiss-Morse, Elizabeth. 2009. *Who Counts As An American?: The Boundaries of National Identity*. New York: Cambridge University Press.

Thompson, Maxine S., and Verna M. Keith. 2001. "The Blacker the Berry: Gender, Skin Tone, Self-Esteem, and Self-Efficacy." *Gender & Society* 15 (3):336–357.

Tichenor, Daniel J. 2002. *Dividing Lines: The Politics of Immigration Control in America*. Princeton, NJ: Princeton University Press.

Torkelson, Jason, and Douglas Hartmann. 2021. "The Heart of Whiteness: On the Study of Whiteness and White Americans." *Sociology Compass* 15 (11):1–19.

Tuan, Mia. 1998. *Forever Foreigners or Honorary Whites?: The Asian Ethnic Experience Today*. New Brunswick, NJ: Rutgers University Press.

Tuck, Eve, and K. Wayne Yang. 2012. "Decolonization Is Not a Metaphor." *Decolonization: Indigeneity, Education & Society* 1 (1):1–40.

Unger, Steven, ed. 1977. *The Destruction of American Indian Families*. New York: Association on American Indian Affairs.

Vaidya, Kanhaiya L. 2019. "Oregon's Demographic Trends." Office of Economic Analysis, Department of Administrative Services: State of Oregon.

Valdez, Zulema, and Tanya Golash-Boza. 2020. "Master Status or Intersectional Identity?: Undocumented Students' Sense of Belonging on a College Campus." *Identities* 27 (4):481–499.

Valenzuela, Angela. 1999. *Subtractive Schooling: U.S.-Mexican Youth and the Politics of Caring*. Albany: State University of New York Press.

Valle, Ariana J. 2019. "Race and the Empire-State: Puerto Ricans' Unequal U.S. Citizenship." *Sociology of Race and Ethnicity* 5 (1):26–40.

Vallejo, Jody Agius. 2012a. *Barrios to Burbs: The Making of the Mexican American Middle Class*. Stanford, CA: Stanford University Press.

Vallejo, Jody Agius. 2012b. "Socially Mobile Mexican Americans and the Minority Culture of Mobility." *American Behavioral Scientist* 56 (5):666–681.

Vallejo, Jody Agius, and Jessica Vasquez-Tokos. 2024. "The Latino Middle Class." *Annual Review of Sociology* 50: 521–546.

Vasquez-Tokos, Jessica. 2017a. "'If I Can Offer You Some Advice': Rapport and Data Collection in Interviews Between Adults of Different Ages." *Symbolic Interaction* 40 (4):1–20.

Vasquez-Tokos, Jessica. 2017b. *Marriage Vows and Racial Choices*. New York: Russell Sage Foundation.

Vasquez-Tokos, Jessica. 2020a. "Do Latinos Consider Themselves Mainstream?: The Influence of Region." *Sociological Perspectives* 63 (4):571–588.

Vasquez-Tokos, Jessica. 2020b. "The 'Ethnic Core' as an Unsung Reference Group." *Ethnic and Racial Studies* 43 (13):2396–2403.

Vasquez-Tokos, Jessica, and Kathryn Norton-Smith. 2017. "Talking Back to Controlling Images: Latinos' Changing Responses to Racism over the Life Course." *Ethnic and Racial Studies* 40 (6):912–930.

Vasquez-Tokos, Jessica, and Priscilla Yamin. 2021. "The Racialization of Privacy: Racial Formation as a Family Affair." *Theory & Society* 50 (5):717–740.

Vasquez, Jessica M. 2005. "Ethnic Identity and Chicano Literature: How Ethnicity Affects Reading and Reading Affects Ethnic Consciousness." *Ethnic and Racial Studies* 28 (5):903–924.

Vasquez, Jessica M. 2010a. "Blurred Borders for Some but not 'Others': Racialization, 'Flexible Ethnicity,' Gender, and Third Generation Mexican American Identity." *Sociological Perspectives* 53 (1):45–71.

Vasquez, Jessica M. 2010b. "Chicana Mothering in the Twenty-First Century: Challenging Stereotypes and Transmitting Culture." In *Twenty-First-Century Motherhood: Experience, Identity, Policy, Agency*, edited by Andrea O'Reilly, 23–39. New York: Columbia University Press.

Vasquez, Jessica M. 2011. *Mexican Americans Across Generations: Immigrant Families, Racial Realities*. New York: New York University Press.

Vasquez, Jessica M. 2014a. "Gender Across Family Generations: Change in Mexican American Masculinities and Femininities." *Identities* 21 (5):532–550.

Vasquez, Jessica M. 2014b. "The Whitening Hypothesis Challenged: Biculturalism in Latino and Non-Hispanic White Intermarriage." *Sociological Forum* 29 (2):386–407.

Vitali, Ali, Kasie Hunt, and Frank Thorp V. 2018. "Trump Referred to Haiti and African Nations as 'Shithole' Countries." NBC News, January 11.

Walters, Karina L., and Jane M. Simoni. 2002. "Reconceptualizing Native Women's Health: An 'Indigenist' Stress-Coping Model." *American Journal of Public Health (1971)* 92 (4):520–524.

Walton, Emily C. 2018. "Asian Americans in Small-Town America." *Contexts* 17 (4):18–23.

Warikoo, Natasha, and Irene Bloemraad. 2018. "Economic Americanness and Defensive Inclusion: Social Location and Young Citizens' Conceptions of National Identity." *Journal of Ethnic and Migration Studies* 44 (5):736–753.

Warren, Jonathan W., and France Winddance Twine. 1997. "White Americans, the New Minority?: Non-Blacks and the Ever-Expanding Boundaries of Whiteness." *Journal of Black Studies* 28 (2):200–218.

Washington, Harriet A. 2006. *Medical Apartheid: The Dark History of Medical Experimentation on Black Americans from Colonial Times to the Present.* New York: Doubleday.

Waters, Mary C. 1999. *Black Identities: West Indian Immigrant Dreams and American Realities.* New York: Russell Sage Foundation.

Weiss, Robert. 1994. *Learning from Strangers.* New York: Free Press.

Western, Bruce. 2006. *Punishment and Inequality in America.* New York: Russell Sage Foundation.

Whaley, Gray H. 2010. *Oregon and the Collapse of Illahee: U.S. Empire and the Transformation of an Indigenous World, 1792–1859.* Chapel Hill: University of North Carolina Press.

White, Louellyn. 2016. "White Power and the Performance of Assimilation: Lincoln Institute and Carlisle Indian School." In *Carlisle Indian Industrial School: Indigenous Histories, Memories, and Reclamations,* edited by Jacqueline Fear-Segal and Susan D. Rose, 106–123. Lincoln: University of Nebraska Press.

Williams, David R., and Lisa A. Cooper. 2019. "Reducing Racial Inequities in Health: Using What We Already Know to Take Action." *International Journal of Environmental Research and Public Health* 16 (4):606.

Williams, David R., and Michelle Sternthal. 2010. "Understanding Racial-ethnic Disparities in Health: Sociological Contributions." *Journal of Health and Social Behavior* 51 (S):S15-S27.

Wimmer, Andreas. 2013. *Ethnic Boundary Making: Institutions, Power, Networks.* New York: Oxford University Press.

Wingfield, Adia Harvey. 2007. "The Modern Mammy and the Angry Black Man: African American Professionals' Experiences with Gendered Racism in the Workplace." *Race, Gender & Class* 14 (1/2):196–212.

Wingfield, Adia Harvey. 2010. "Are Some Emotions Marked 'Whites Only'? Racialized Feeling Rules in Professional Workplaces." *Social Problems* 57 (2):251–268.

Witze, Alexandra. 2020. "How the Fight Over a Hawaii Mega-Telescope Could Change Astronomy: Thirty Meter Telescope Controversy Is Forcing Scientists to Grapple with How Their Research Affects Indigenous Peoples." *Nature,* January 14.

Wolfe, Patrick. 2006. "Settler Colonialism and the Elimination of the Native." *Journal of Genocide Research* 8 (4):387–409.

Wolfe, Patrick. 2016. *Traces of History: Elementary Structures of Race.* Brooklyn, NY: Verso.

Woody, Ashley. 2020. " 'They Want the Spanish but They Don't Want the Mexicans': Whiteness and Consumptive Contact in an Oregon Spanish Immersion School." *Sociology of Race and Ethnicity* 6 (1):92–106.

Woody, Ashley. 2023. "Emotions and Ambient Racism in America's Whitest Big City." *Social Problems* 70 (4):981–998.

Xing, Jun. 2007. "Introduction." In *Seeing Color: Indigenous Peoples and Racialized Ethnic Minorities in Oregon*, edited by Jun Xing, 1–16. Lanham, MD: University Press of America.

Yancey, George A. 2003. *Who Is White?: Latinos, Asians, and the New Black/Nonblack Divide*. Boulder, CO: Lynne Rienner.

Yoshikawa, Hirokazu. 2011. *Immigrants Raising Citizens: Undocumented Parents and Their Young Children*. New York: Russell Sage Foundation.

Yosso, Tara J. 2005. "Whose Culture Has Capital? A Critical Race Theory Discussion of Community Cultural Wealth." *Race, Ethnicity and Education* 8 (1):69–91.

Yosso, Tara J., William A. Smith, Miguel Ceja, and Daniel G. Solorzano. 2009. "Critical Race Theory, Racial Microaggressions, and Campus Racial Climate for Latina/o Undergraduates." *Harvard Educational Review* 79 (4):659–690.

Yuen, Nancy Wang. 2017. *Reel Inequality: Hollywood Actors and Racism*. New Brunswick, NJ: Rutgers University Press.

Yuval-Davis, Nira. 2006. "Belonging and the Politics of Belonging." *Patterns of Prejudice* 40 (3):197–214.

Zambrana, Ruth Enid, Rashawn Ray, Michelle M. Espino, Corinne Castro, Beth Douthirt Cohen, and Jennifer Eliason. 2015. "'Don't Leave Us Behind': The Importance of Mentoring for Underrepresented Minority Faculty." *American Educational Research Journal* 52 (1):40–72.

Zamora, Sylvia. 2018. "Mexican Illegality, Black Citizenship, and White Power: Immigrant Perceptions of the U.S. Socioracial Hierarchy." *Journal of Ethnic and Migration Studies* 44 (11):1897–1914.

Zamora, Sylvia. 2022. *Racial Baggage: Mexican Immigrants and Race Across the Border*. Stanford, CA: Stanford University Press.

Zepeda-Millán, Chris, and Sophia J. Wallace. 2018. "Mobilizing for Immigrant and Latino Rights under Trump." In *The Resistance: The Dawn of the Anti-Trump Opposition Movement*, edited by David S. Meyer and Sidney Tarrow, 90–108. New York: Oxford University Press.

Zhou, Min, Jennifer Lee, Jody Agius Vallejo, Rosaura Tafoya-Estrada, and Yang Sao Xiong. 2008. "Success Attained, Deterred, and Denied: Divergent Pathways to Social Mobility in Los Angeles's New Second Generation." *Annals of the American Academy of Political and Social Science* 620 (1):37–61.

INDEX

absorption, 7, 75

"abstract stress," 76

abuse, 170, 182, 205–6

acquired goals, 26, 200–203, 223–28, 231, 233

action: collective, 219–21; emotion and, 202; social, 13

actors, people of color, 4–5

addiction, 169, 171–72, 182, 204–6

African Americans: Africans and, 121–22; anti-Black racism and, 107–9; with Black exclusion laws in Oregon, 17, 108, 135; depression in, 168; double consciousness and, 58, 77; with driving, 189–90, 192; education and, 2–4, 139–40, 147–48; erasure of, 4; group-based stereotypes and, 118; land and, 16; lynchings of, 107, 262n41; populations, 4, 15, 249; queer and transgender, 78–79, 98, 108–9, 172–73, 187–88; racial hierarchy and, 3, 13; with racial identity, 98–99; racism and, viii, 2; respondents, 2–4, 63–64, 73, 76, 78–79, 98–101, 104–5, 107–9, 115, 121–22, 130–32, 139–40, 147–48, 172–75, 187–88, 236; settler colonialism and, 38–39; slavery and, 3, 32, 38–39, 100–101, 107–9, 131–32, 139–40, 187; voting rights, 17–18

Africans, 121–22

agency, 3, 5, 11–13, 125, 214, 239, 244–45

Alaska Natives, 4, 102

alcohol, 169, 182, 185, 205–6

Alien Land Law (1923), Oregon, 18, 19

"ambient racism," 20

American: belonging and decentering, 130–33; diversifying, 127–30; fact-of-the-matter, 93, 96–99, 133; "ideal," 24, 93–101, 128, 133, 235; identity, 7, 24, 95, 97, 99–100, 110, 114, 127, 166; respondents of color as, 92–93, 97, 99–101, 108–9, 111, 128, 166; with White as "ideal" image, 93–101; White people as undisputed, 92–93, 95–96, 166; White respondents on being, 92

American Indians, 4, 18, 32, 110, 144, 249. *See also* Native Americans

Americanness, 1, 6, 65, 74, 111, 114; people of color and, 97–98, 115, 134; Whiteness and, 7, 92–96, 99–107, 115, 133

American Samoa, 47, 208

Anderson, Elijah, 189

anger, 172–73, 175, 183, 190–91, 222

anti-Black, 17, 38, 133, 135, 140, 187, 216; racism, 39, 93, 100–101, 107–9, 121, 236; stereotypes, 147, 157, 158

anti-Mexican discourse, 73–74, 191, 221, 229

anti-Muslim sentiment, 80–81

anti-Semitism, 196

Anzaldúa, Gloria, 77–78, 115, 145

appearance, bodily presence and, 62, 63–65, 90

Army, US, 68–69, 184

Aryan Nations (the Order), 20

Asian Americans: depression in, 168; erasure of, 2; hate crimes against, 1; mixed-race, 64–66, 94, 98, 103–6, 122, 152–53, 176–79, 216; with model minority stereotype, 42, 75, 214–15; populations, 15, 249; respondents, 38, 41–45, 64–66, 75, 80, 94–95, 97–98, 103–6, 118,

ABOUT THE AUTHOR

JESSICA VASQUEZ-TOKOS is Professor of Sociology at the University of Oregon. She is the author of *Mexican Americans Across Generations: Immigrant Families, Racial Realities* and *Marriage Vows and Racial Choices.*

www.ingramcontent.com/pod-product-compliance
Lightning Source LLC
Chambersburg PA
CBHW031140020426
42333CB00013B/455

* 9 7 8 1 4 7 9 8 2 2 3 2 4 *